Franz Kafka Today

Franz Kafka Today

Edited by ANGEL FLORES

and HOMER SWANDER

The University of Wisconsin Press

MADISON, 1958

Published by The University of Wisconsin Press,
430 Sterling Court, Madison 6, Wisconsin.

Copyright © 1958 by the Regents of the
University of Wisconsin.

Copyright, Canada, 1958. Distributed in
Canada by Burns and MacEachern, Toronto.

Printed in the United States of America by
Vail-Ballou Press, Inc., Binghamton, New York.

Library of Congress Catalog Card No. 57–9818.

Acknowledgments

The editors wish to thank Professors Harold Lenz, Herman Salinger, and Dr. Ernst J. Schlochawer for invaluable assistance in translating and editing. And for permission to reprint the works indicated, they thank the following publishers and periodical publications:

Quarterly Review of Literature for "The Judgment" by Kate Flores

Modern Language Review for "The Metamorphosis" by F. D. Luke

Modern Language Quarterly for "A Report to An Academy" by William C. Rubinstein

Accent and Rinehart and Company, Inc., publishers of *The Art of Modern Fiction,* for "A Hunger-Artist" by R. W. Stallman

Scott, Foresman and Company, publishers of *Reading Modern Short Stories,* for "The Married Couple" by Jarvis Thurston

Etudes Germaniques for *"The Trial:* Its Meaning" by René Dauvin

The Northern Review for "Kafka's Divine Comedy" by Donald Pearce

Critique and Librairie Gallimard for "The Diaries: The Exigency of the Work of Art" by Maurice Blanchot (all rights reserved)

The Germanic Review for "Letter to His Father" by Heinz Politzer

Contents

Part Three. *Diaries and Letters*

Part Four. *Bibliographies and Index*

Introduction

"Had one to name the author who comes nearest to bearing the same kind of relation to our age as Dante, Shakespeare and Goethe bore to theirs, Kafka is the first one would think of."—W. H. Auden

"Besides Racine, who is for me the greatest writer, there is one other—Franz Kafka—before whom I doff my hat."—Paul Claudel

IF today the greatness of Racine is obvious, and the figures of Dante, Shakespeare, and Goethe stand out clearly both above their age and as representatives of it, they do so largely because of the light imparted to them by the passage of time, by the decades of their removal. And if Kafka, on the other hand, speaking out of our own baffling times, often frustrates and even repels us, if we cannot place him, and do not always understand him, it may be largely that the light of time is even more relentlessly necessary. For he was, as he described himself despairingly in his diary, "a man with too great a shadow." And as yet we are, in a sense, still living within that shadow.

We are, however, making progress. It is now nearly a third of a century since his death, and this much may be said with certainty: those who were closest to him knew him least, misunderstood him most. His friends, despite glimpses here and there of intimacy, failed to see the individual under their noses—the slippery creature, so charming, so human, yet so complex, so ferociously intelligent and infrared—failed especially to see that part of him which informs the writings. In every case, they contributed a personal image which, how-

1

ever accurate, told us little about the works and did almost nothing to define their significance.

The critics, too—as one begins to see more clearly—have too often been grinding their own axes. They have, depending upon their own points of view, described a schizophrenic Kafka or a God-intoxicated Kafka, an Expressionist Kafka or a Talmudic Kafka, a family-loving Kafka or an Existentialist Kafka—forever endeavoring to fit his work into some preconceived pattern or other.

The present critical symposium has been prepared with the purpose of bringing together some of those essays which, on the contrary, let the work of art speak forcibly for itself. Each essay concentrates on one of Kafka's outstanding works (and here we count the diaries and letters), looking closely into the genesis, structure, or meaning of the text. Such meticulous explication sheds more light, we feel, than those rambling essays of the past which, within the narrow compass of a few pages, endeavored to take in all about Kafka's form and content— his style, his psychology, his metaphysics, his total outlook.

We have not been primarily interested, then, in the critic's "point of view." What mattered was how fruitfully he addressed himself to the work of art. And we have made no attempt either to develop controversy or to present an harmonious front, although occasionally (as in the two essays on *Amerika*) controversy appears, and occasionally (as in "K.'s Village" and the discussion of the diaries) two essays written independently reinforce one another.

Six of the eighteen contributions were written especially for this collection; of the remaining twelve, five have been revised, in varying degrees, for publication here, and six are now printed in this country for the first time. It is our hope that each contributes in its own way to the growing understanding of Kafka's greatness.

Part One

THE SHORT STORIES

Claude-Edmonde Magny, on the basis of a literal reading of the story.[2] According to Mr. Tauber, "The father . . . changes from a man in need of nursing into a God of Justice. . . . The father is . . . an aspect of God." One advantage of this hypothesis is that it permits the father's rather baffling remarks to be ascribed to divine inscrutability; however, it renders the story absurd. ". . . the sudden coming to life of God as a complete annulment of the might of man is absurd," Mr. Tauber admits. "But the man who just lives a life without principles cannot evade this madness of God when it suddenly becomes actual." Mr. Tauber finds religious meaning in the mere word "above," and even in the charwoman's exclamation "Jesus!" The death of the mother signifies, he suggests, "the decline of the church, of the synagogue, of religion as such."

Claude-Edmonde Magny, on the other hand, writes that "we ought not to do what Kafka himself always refrained from doing: provide dialectical constructions for the unfolding of events which should be taken as a *real* account. Otherwise Kafka is quickly converted into a kind of frustrated philosopher who needs to be explained to himself and to others for lack of sufficient power of analysis and abstraction." Basing herself thus on a literal reading of the story, Mme. Magny accepts the father's irrational remarks as such, i.e., he is irrational: "The question ['Do you really have this friend in St. Petersburg?'] does astonish us, but we think the old man is falling into second childhood. And this impression seems confirmed by the exceedingly painful and irrational scene which follows . . . . the end of his speech, when he solemnly condemns his son to death by drowning . . . only astounds us proportionately, as one proof more of the old man's insanity." Mme. Magny's entire analysis of "The Judgment" proceeds on the assumption that the father is insane, the story representing, she declares, "a discovery of the profound significance of insanity (as a paramount manifestation of the fundamental irreducibility of all points of view) . . . ." However, one wonders how the story can illustrate the fundamental irreducibility of all points of view when the viewpoints of the two protagonists meet. The father's arraignment has no sooner begun than Georg sees his friend "lost in the vastness of Russia." His answers to his father's charges turn into "deadly earnest" in "his very mouth." Finally he confesses: "So you spied on me!" and like "a starved man seizing food" executes his father's sentence. If the father in this story is insane, the son must be quite as insane. And since these are the only two characters in "The Judgment," to consider the father irrational is to reduce it entirely to an irrational level.

I suggest it is an evasion of the point of this story to dismiss the father's charges as insanity, human or divine. This miserable old man, Kafka intimates, lives in the past, a past which Georg can never know: the newspaper he is reading with failing vision as Georg enters his room—which, unlike his own sunny room overlooking the river and green hills beyond, faces a blank wall—is "an old paper, with a name quite unknown to Georg." This paper "somehow" gets carried along to bed too; but the father flings it in his face. The incident of the watch-chain (which Mme. Magny interprets as "insanity making its appearance under a physical and objective—almost medical—aspect, about which there can be no doubt") conveys a similar significance: we have the old man's desperate hold upon this symbol of the present and time's inexorable advance giving Georg "a terrible feeling" and making it difficult for him to put his burden down.

Except for his remarks on one subject—Georg's friend in St. Petersburg—the father's harangue is well within the borders of sanity. Indeed, the point would seem to be that his words are too intolerably sane. He charges Georg with wanting to cover him up, using the word "cover" in a figurative sense, of course, the entire passage preceding his tirade being a play on the word "cover," the son using it literally and the father figuratively. Now the story provides certain evidence that from the father's rather morbid point of view this charge may not be altogether baseless. Georg has scarcely given a thought to what is to become of the old man after his marriage, has had no plan other than to leave him living alone. In their office, the only place where the two men associate to any extent, the father is something of a hindrance, Georg feels. Now because of Georg's very unawareness of his indifferent if not negative attitude in these matters, it has probably been implicit in his manner. The father, therefore, in brooding on his son and his business—the only things left to him, apparently—has no alternative but to feel that as far as his son is concerned he is rather superfluous on both these scores. Doubtless he has had no occasion to raise these issues; but upon discussing with Georg a matter about which he (Georg) is evidently very sensitive, he succeeds, by probing his conscientious son in a way calculated to deflect attention upon himself, in making the son aware of a whole series of guilt feelings regarding his filial deficiencies; to these Georg gives expression, more in an effort to hide his uneasiness on the original subject than anything else. "Do you know what I think?" he asks, evading the question whether he has a friend in St. Petersburg and abruptly changing the subject to one which till this moment has given him no perceptible concern. "You don't take good care of yourself." In his rather excessive solicitude for his father's health—in which the old man neurotically detects evidence of an ulterior motive—Georg's guilty conscience is quite obvious. Thereupon the father, seizing this opportunity to vent his grievances, with cruel cunning decides to hold up Georg's insistence upon putting him to bed as an example of the attitude he resents—an attitude of indifference and worse: a tacit desire to have him out of the way. With a good deal of the dramatic sense he seems to possess, he suddenly feigns docility, allows himself to be undressed and put to bed, covers himself "particularly high over the shoulders." Treacherously he looks up at Georg "with a not un-friendly eye," urges Georg to cover him practically from head to toe, and then when assured his son thinks him well covered ("Just be quiet, you are well covered"), he flings back the covers and they stand upright on the bed. The moment it becomes apparent that he is using the word "cover" in its figurative sense, that he is charging this devoted son who is so tenderly urging him to rest with wanting to see him buried, he begins to seem insane. But in the figurative sense, hideous as it may be, may lie the profounder truth.

There is nothing insane about the rest of the father's statements, apart from his allusions to the friend. His attitude toward Georg's engagement is remarkable less for its singularity than for his sensa-tional expression of it; it is, of course, that of an embittered old man, whose young son cannot live his life without seeming to him to be "strutting through the world, tumbling head over heels with pleasure." Because he lives in the past, from his point of view Georg's engagement is a desecration of his mother's memory. His coolness toward Georg's business success is understandable: smug Georg Bendemann, who is so pleased with his prosperity, has doubtless allowed his father no illusions as to who is responsible. This is another of the father's justified resentments, hitherto unexpressed, perhaps, but harbored nonetheless.

Most old people have something deceitful, something perfidious, in their dealings with people younger than themselves; you live at peace with them, imagine you are on the best of terms with them, know their ruling prejudices, receive constant assurances of amity, take the whole thing for granted; but then when something decisive happens and those peaceful relations, so long nurtured, are put to the test, suddenly these old people rise before you like strangers, reveal that they have deeper and stronger convictions, and now for the first time literally unfurl their banner, and with terror you read upon it the new decree. The reason for this terror lies chiefly in the fact that what the old say now is really far more just and sensible than what they have said before; it is as if even the self-evident had degrees of validity, and their words now were more self-evident than ever. But the final deceit that lies in their words consists in this, that underneath they have always been saying what they say now.

Save that there is nothing just and sensible, and nothing in the least self-evident, in old Bendemann's words about Georg's friend in Russia, this passage by Kafka from "The Giant Mole" seems a fit commentary upon the interview between old Bendemann and his terrified son in "The Judgment"; and certainly the issue of this story seems to lie in Georg's recognition that his father's words are just and sensible and, in their self-evidentness, unbearable. However, the old man's allusions to the friend in Russia are not only unjust but absurd.

"Do you really have this friend in St. Petersburg?" he asks. "You have no friend in St. Petersburg." But then he reverses himself— "Well do I know your friend"—and proves that he knows him: "three years ago he was yellow," which is just what Georg had been thinking. "He would be a son after my own heart," he declares; though nothing in the story would explain this predilection; indeed, according to Georg his father had not cared for his friend. "That's why you have deceived him all these years," his father says. "Why else?" But the story gives no evidence of deception on Georg's part; nor of any deliberate malice toward his father, who first accuses Georg of betraying his friend by becoming engaged and then announces, "Still your friend hasn't been betrayed after all! I've been representing him here on the spot. . . . I've established a grand alliance with your friend and I have your customers here in my pocket!" It is Georg, it would seem, who has been betrayed by the friend. "He knows everything, foolish boy, he knows everything! I've been writing him because you forgot to take away my writing things." Apparently he has been betrayed by his father as well. "He crumples your letters unopened in his left hand while holding out my letters before him to read with his right."

Ludicrous as the father's references to the friend may seem, Georg explicitly accepts them, visualizing his friend "lost in the vastness of Russia," and asking himself, enigmatically, "Why did he have to go so far away?"

The friend in Russia is the only strange element in "The Judgment," the one aspect which transforms it from a simple naturalistic story into a truly Kafkan riddle. Taken literally, this friend renders the story anomalous, a tale from which no conclusion can logically be drawn. But he bears close inspection. Nearly three pages—about a third of the text of the story—are devoted to Georg's soliloquy about him. He seems to be a figure of major importance to the hero (despite the latter's seemingly casual and even patronizing attitude), who is presented almost exclusively with reference to his friend. Now this friend is no ordinary businessman, as might seem at first glance. He is a "difficult person," Georg tells his father; "he has his peculiarities," he says at another point. Georg corresponds with him on "odd terms," he informs his fiancée. That years ago this eccentric fellow fled from home stamps him as something of a romantic. Moreover, he seems to be rather antisocial: his visits home are becoming increasingly rare, yet in his self-imposed exile he has "little connection with either his com-patriots or the native inhabitants"; and he seems destined to become "a permanent bachelor." On this subject of marriage he is inordinately sensitive, as he is on all matters pertaining to his "lonely way of life," as Georg describes it to his father. A peculiar sort, who would be "embittered" and "estranged" if an old childhood friend were to urge him to come home. Georg can think of no tactful way of making such a suggestion; "the more one tried to spare him the more he would be insulted." And assuming he were, on this "painful advice," to re-turn, he would feel "humiliated," Georg reflects, "gaped at by every-one." His sensibilities are such that Georg hesitates to ask him to his wedding ("He would feel constrained and injured"), and even to inform him of his business successes. For this queer chap has a business in St. Petersburg. It cannot be a very remunerative one, judging by the "minute" figures with which he thought to entice Georg to Russia; and now it has been "stagnating for a long time." But does this matter? Not in the least. For more than three years he has allowed himself not the briefest absence from his business; and even though, to Georg's mind, he is "wearing himself out to no purpose," he refuses to give it up, to acknowledge his failure, even to countenance the thought of it.

This misanthropic idealist would seem to be the antithesis of Georg,

Georg who stayed at home, sensible, well-adjusted Georg, the success-ful businessman, who spends his evenings "with friends, or, as at the present time, with his fiancée," who, as he mentions twice, comes of a well-to-do family. There is inevitably a note of condescension in the attitude of this middle-class hero toward the misfit in Russia: "What can one write to a man like that," he muses, after a faintly ironical recital of the other's problems, "who had obviously got himself in a corner, whom one could pity but could not help." Georg's practicality as contrasted with his friend's impracticality, the normality of his out-look as opposed to his friend's rather aberrant one, is apparent in his very manner of discussing his friend's predicament. The friend's busi-ness is not prospering, wherefore Georg decides he is "wearing him-self out to no purpose," the conclusion of any good businessman. So far as the friend is concerned, resuming his old friendships would be difficult; but Georg, the extrovert, can see "no obstacle to it." It was impossible, if the correspondence were to be kept up at all, to give him any "real news such as could be told frankly to the most distant acquaintance," Georg meditates; unlike his painfully self-conscious friend, Georg seems uninhibited socially. The friend adduces Russian political uncertainty as his reason for not paying him a visit, but Georg has no patience with such timorousness: why, "thousands of Russians calmly travel abroad." Georg goes about his business, "like everything else, with great determination," neither requiring nor want-ing his father's advice. And his letter to his friend is so easy and suave, one feels that if the exile is rather quixotic, Georg is a rock of common sense.

It soon becomes evident, of course, that this impression of Georg is false or at least incomplete. Indeed, one of the reasons for the am-biguity of this story is the complete transformation in the character of Georg. For whether or not he has seemed vulnerable to his father's wild charges, certainly he has seemed impervious to their hysterical tone. But Georg, whom one thought level-headed and bold, suddenly becomes absent-minded, hesitates on the way to his father's bed, stands in a corner as far away as possible. Georg, who seemed self-possessed, suddenly forgets everything. He can scarcely speak; when he does he at once regrets it, bites his tongue till his knees give way. Georg, who has just appeared solicitous of his father's health, sud-denly hisses: "What if he topples and smashes himself!" Georg, who seemed capable of only reasoned judgment, seizes upon his father's reference to a pocket in his shirt as if that proved him "impossible to all the world." Finally he begins to agree with his father, at last confessing: "So you spied on me!" And when in the end he leaps into the river, one is forced to conclude that one's initial impression of Georg was mistaken, having been based on an outer picture of the man.

Now this outer picture of Georg Bendemann, the Georg of his reverie and the beginning of his interview with his father, corresponds rather closely with the outer Kafka, the Kafka whom his friends and associates knew: a normal enough young man, affable and debonair, suave, self-contained, decisive, the favored son of a well-to-do merchant. Thus Max Brod says:

I have experienced over and over again that admirers of Kafka who know him only from his books have a completely false picture of him. They think he must have made a sad, even desperate impression in company too. The opposite is the case. . . . The fact that from his books, and above all from his diary, such a totally different, much more depressing, picture may be drawn than when it is corrected and supplemented by the impressions one can add from having lived with him day by day—that is one of the reasons that persuaded me to write these memoirs. The portrait-from-life of Kafka that remains in the memory of our circle stands alongside his writings, and demands to be taken into account in any final judgment of him.[3]

If now the outer Georg Bendemann is to be identified with the outer Kafka, Georg's friend in Russia, it might be noted, bears a striking resemblance to the inner Kafka, the Kafka of his works and particularly of his diary. "I am . . . a reserved, silent, unsocial, dissatisfied person . . . . I live in my family . . . more strange than a stranger." Thus reads a passage from Kafka's diary (August 21, 1913) which happens to be part of a letter drafted in his diary but never posted. "At one time of my life I was employed in a little railroad station in the heart of Russia," begins one of Kafka's early stories. "The more I was encompassed by solitude, the more I was content." "Ever since I can remember, a deep anxiety to preserve my mental existence has made me indifferent to everything else" ("Letter to His Father"). "Outwardly, I fulfil my duties satisfactorily in the office, not my inner duties, however, and every unfulfilled inner duty becomes a misfortune that never leaves" (*Diaries*, March 28, 1911).

As Georg Bendemann sits at his private writing table that Sunday morning "in the very height of spring," gazing pensively at the river and the hills on the "farther bank with their tender green," might it not be that the letter he seals in "slow and dreamy fashion" is but a letter to his other self, to K., as he calls this entity in his diary, where he discusses K.'s behavior with all the detachment of another individual continually being amazed by it?

The dilemma which Georg ponders in such seemingly pointless detail is whether or not to advise his friend to return from his lonely exile and take up his old friendships again.

"Two opposite tendencies fought for supremacy in Kafka," states Max Brod, "the longing for loneliness, and the will to be sociable. But . . . it was life in the social community and significant work that meant the highest goal and ideal for him . . . . It is true that Kafka needed loneliness for his literary work, he needed a high degree of self-absorption, such as could sometimes be disturbed by a conversation . . . such as even communicating it to a friend could endanger." [4]

The literary work Brod is referring to here is Kafka's writing, of course, which, though it had seemed promising as early as 1903, had been stagnating for some time when he wrote "The Judgment" in 1912.[5] Could it be, then, that the friend's business, which had flourished at first but has been stagnating now, is Kafka's writing?

Just as Georg's friend remains anonymous, his business remains unspecified, but on close scrutiny one can piece together a fairly good picture of this business. Like the friend, it is not ordinary; it too has its peculiarities. Georg speaks of his friend's business activities as "attempts," and wonders whether to advise him to "desist from" them —rather curious terms to use in connection with a business. But just as the friend's personality seems incompatible with the designation "businessman," the nature of his business seems hardly to coincide with the customary notion of a money-making enterprise. As we have noted, it is not a lucrative business in any case, apparently, and at that it has not thrived for quite some time; that the friend is nonetheless keenly devoted to it suggests he is not motivated by economic considerations —which would really be none too surprising in view of his lonely way of life. Here is another peculiarity of this business: it permits its owner to lead a well-nigh isolated existence. It is a little hard to conceive of a business abroad which calls for no association with one's compatriots and practically none with the natives, but such it is. Indeed, isolation seems the *sine qua non* of this business; giving it up, or rather "desisting from" one's "attempts," appears to be tantamount to abandoning one's isolation: in pondering his friend's dilemma Georg considers only two courses of action for him: to stay abroad, in isolation, there to pursue his business, or to desist from his attempts, come back home, and rely on the help of his friends. In weighing the latter alternative he does not entertain the possibility of transferring the business and conducting it at home, which would seem to be the natural thing to do; returning home seems to involve solely the question whether he could be happy doing "what his successful, stay-at-home friends prescribed." If the business, then, is one which is concomitant with being abroad, if, as it seems, it cannot be conducted at home, small wonder Georg hesitates to suggest that his friend return, for evidently it is the business which concerns Georg most: in seeing his friend lost in the vastness of Russia, his dismay is at the collapse of the business—the friend himself is still intact—at the thought of the "empty, plundered shop . . . the ruins of his shelves, the tattered merchandise, the falling gas fixtures."

And here is a glimpse of the appurtenances of this business: gas fixtures, tattered merchandise. We know that Kafka wrote by gaslight; that he accumulated his manuscripts till they were "yellow enough to be tossed away," as Georg's father says rather quaintly of the friend; and that he often tore them up. To be sure, he never regarded them as "merchandise"; despite the pleas of his friends he rarely consented to publish his scribblings, as he called them; for when Kafka mentioned his writings at all he always, self-defensively, derided them.

The device of portraying two aspects of one's personality as separate characters, and even as friends, is familiar almost to the point of triteness. But the irony of disguising one's other self in a business suit, and the reticence implicit in this irony, are quintessentially Kafka. It is a double-edged irony, at once self-disparaging and self-defensive, an irony arising out of the discrepancy between his own and his environment's conception of the term, of which discrepancy he was a victim.

The question whether to "desist from" his "attempts" and "once and for all" give up his writing—which not only had been stagnating for a long time, but was threatening him with some latent illness, keeping him from his friends, and promising to keep him a "permanent bachelor"—had reached a crucial stage the night Kafka wrote "The Judgment." Six weeks before, on August 13, 1912, he had met Fräulein Felice Bauer, the young woman from Berlin to whom he was twice engaged. He was thus in the throes of his first agony of indecision whether or not to marry. Kafka's ledger-like tabulations of the pros and cons of marriage (which, as Brod observes, are "more likely to make a decision much harder than to prepare the way for one") suggest that of all divided personalities Kafka was most hopelessly divided:

July 21, 1913

1. Inability to bear life alone . . . . The connection with F. will give my existence more strength to resist.

2. . . . Yesterday my sister said, "All the married people (that we know) are happy, I don't understand it," this remark too gave me pause, I became afraid again.

3. I must be alone a great deal. What I accomplished was only the result of being alone.

4. . . . Conversations take the importance, the seriousness, the truth out of everything I think.

5. The fear of the connection, of passing into the other. Then I'll never be alone again.

6. In the past, especially, the person I am in the company of my sisters has been entirely different from the person I am in the company of other people. Fearless, powerful, surprising, moved as I otherwise am only when I write. If through the intermediation of my wife I could be like that in the presence of everyone! But then would it not be at the expense of my writing? Not that, not that!

August 20, 1916 [6]

To remain chaste.	To get married.
Bachelor.	Married man.
I remain chaste.	Chaste?
I preserve all my powers in coherence.	You [his other self] will remain without your coherence; you will become an idiot, will follow every wind, but will never get any forwarder. I draw from the blood circulation of human life all the power that is available for me.
Responsible only for myself.	The more infatuated with yourself. (Grillparzer, Flaubert.)
No worries, concentration on work.	As I grow in strength I shall stand more. But there is a certain kernel of truth in this.

Thus at the time Kafka wrote "The Judgment" the problem which hitherto had been relatively simple—Kafka the writer vs. Kafka the man—had been complicated by the appearance of the young woman from Berlin. And Kafka, as these diary entries indicate, feared that marriage—the "common route," as Flaubert called it—might entail a sacrifice of his writing.

"The Judgment" is the product of Kafka's quandary on first meeting Fräulein Bauer, a literary demonstration, for his own benefit, of the utter impossibility of marrying her.

The triangular conflict man vs. writer vs. marriage might, for most writers, be complication enough. But not for Kafka. Assuming, for the purposes of his demonstration, that he has become engaged, he begins his story at the point when Georg, having finally decided to inform his friend of his engagement, tucks this fateful announcement in his pocket and enters his father's room.

Georg Bendemann's soliloquy is Kafka's soliloquy, an objectification of his inner debate. It is an analogy, and a remarkably apt analogy: his inner self, his writing self, is a friend who for years has been in exile where, and only where, he can pursue his business. However, his outer self, Georg, now wishes to marry; indeed, the friend had begun to notice that his last few letters all dealt with this subject (e.g., "Preparations for a Country Wedding," 1909); and Georg is concerned lest his marriage alienate his peculiar friend and cost him his friendship. To be sure, there are certain incongruences in this analogy, for example the fiancée's remark, "So he won't come to our wedding, and still I have a right to know all your friends . . . . If you have such friends, Georg, you should never have got engaged at all," which, while quite applicable to the inner meaning, is nonsense outwardly. But on the whole the analogy—a private analogy, and perhaps all Kafka's stories are infinitely subtle private analogies—is incredibly perfect. The entire soliloquy has an inner meaning, a secret logic which it is one of the secrets of Kafka's art to conceal, and the friend an inner correspondence which, like Kafka's later, more universal and thus much more powerful symbols, is a close-guarded mystery.

Kafka guarded the symbolism of the friend not only in his story but even in his diary notes explaining "The Judgment," where he says (February 11, 1913): "The friend is the link between father and son, he is their strongest common bond. . . . In the course of the story the father, with the strengthened position that the other, lesser things they share in common give him—love, devotion to the mother, loyalty to her memory, the clientele that he (the father) had been the first to acquire for the business—uses the common bond of the friend to set himself up as Georg's antagonist." The friend, then, according to Kafka, is an element of greater importance to Georg than even his love for his father, the memory of his mother, or their business; the friend, moreover, is so important to Georg that even the fiancée, Kafka states, "lives in the story only in relation to the friend." But what this element is, Kafka does not say; it remains X. "The essence of a secret code," as his Investigating Dog remarks, "is that it remain a mystery."

Let us investigate further this secret code which Kafka evidently wished to remain a mystery, introducing the friend with disarming matter-of-factness and discussing him in a manner calculated to make him seem "ordinary to the point of banality," as Mme. Magny characterizes the whole of Kafka's work. For if Georg Bendemann's long and seemingly banal soliloquy assumes significance in every detail when the friend is regarded as Kafka's symbol for his writing, Georg's interview with his father in terms of this symbolism is something of a revelation.

"You once asked me why I am afraid of you," Kafka's "Letter to His Father" begins. ". . . I did not know what to answer, partly because of this very fear which you strike in me, partly because the reasons for this fear involve so many details that I cannot keep track of them even halfway while talking."

The opening scene between Georg Bendemann and his father might be considered an attempt to keep track of the details involved in the reasons for Kafka's fear of his father. As such it gives a truer picture, perhaps, of some of those details than Kafka's lengthy letter explaining them; for that letter was, after all, a real letter, a letter by the outer Georg Bendemann, as it were, while the meeting between old Bendemann and his son in "The Judgment" is a letter by Kafka the writer, a letter, that is, about his inner self, about K.

Kafka called his inner self "K." in his diary. And K., Kafka's secret self, his banished self, his suppressed but nonetheless idealized self, is the prototype of K. of *The Castle*, Joseph K. of *The Trial*, Karl Rossmann of *Amerika*, and the Georg Bendemann who faces his father in "The Judgment." "Everything," as Kafka wrote in his diary while working on *The Trial*, "has been subordinated to my desire to portray my own inner life."

In portraying his own inner life in *The Trial*—as he did, no doubt, in all his writing, even in little fables like "The Vulture"—Kafka did so from the point of view, from the vantage point, of his outer self. The implacable objectivity of his style may be attributed to this duality of personality. For his outer self was a detached, aloof, imperturbable, rather amused, even masochistic observer. This characteristic sentence from his "Autobiographical Sketch" seems an excellent description of his manner of transmuting his experience: "It was like receiving a tap with a brush . . . and one's reaction was to separate the bristles, insert their points one by one into one's body, and prick and scrape one's entrails according to one's own design, while the other hand still calmly held the handle of the brush."

The Georg Bendemann who in his soliloquy calmly contemplates his hapless friend in Russia undergoes, as we have seen, a remarkable transformation in the presence of his father whereby he assumes for the first time the aspect of the typical Kafka hero. For once Kafka's story begins, it is a story about his inner self told by his outer self. Thus the opening scene between Georg Bendemann and his father might be carefully examined. It shows the gradual disintegration of Georg's outer self, the father's uncanny way of destroying his reserve and exposing the man within.

"It's intolerably dark here," Georg says upon entering the old man's room.

"It's dark all right." This simple exchange typifies the entire dialogue between father and son, the father at once endowing Georg's apparently innocent remark with a deeper implication.

Georg makes no comment on his father's uneaten breakfast, though he is quite aware of it, just as he is aware of the old man's failing sight and the mementos of his mother surrounding him. But he seeks, by adhering to his normal attitude of indifference and nonchalance, to maintain the detachment of his outer self.

"I just wanted to tell you that I have announced my engagement to St. Petersburg after all . . . . My friend . . . ."

"Oh, yes. To your friend." Again the father's repetition, "with peculiar emphasis," implies the added significance he attaches to it.

"Let us forget about my friends." Georg rises in embarrassment. "You are indispensable to me at the office, that you know very well . . . ."

Now in his soliloquy Georg had told himself his father hindered him in the office. But that, it will be remembered, was the expression of the outer Georg Bendemann, the normal, sensible, more masculine Georg Bendemann. That Georg Bendemann had scarcely given a thought to what was to become of his father after his marriage, had tacitly expected him to stay on alone in the house. But now Georg Bendemann decides "abruptly and positively" that his father must share his bridal home. That Georg Bendemann had evinced no interest in his father's melancholy state as he sat brooding alone in his darkened room. But now Georg Bendemann expresses elaborate concern for his father's health and happiness. And that Georg Bendemann now strives to withstand the overpowering effect of his father's physical presence.

From the moment he enters his father's room—remarking, perhaps a trifle gratuitously, that he has had no need to enter it in some time, and somehow implying that his relationship with his father is quite casual and even cold—Georg Bendemann's attention is riveted to his father's person. "My father is still a giant of a man," he tells himself, noting how his father's dressing-gown opens, "the skirts of it fluttering round him," and, as he talks, "following the old man's movements." "At the office he is quite different," he thinks; "how he spreads himself here, crossing his arms upon his breast." Later Georg observes that as his father raises his clothing the scar on his upper thigh is visible. And now as Georg Bendemann is suddenly—and a bit surprisingly—possessed with the notion of putting his father to bed, suggesting even that he rest in his own bed ("that would be the most sensible thing"), one really cannot ignore, as he begs to be allowed to undress his father, his intense interest in his father's body. The sudden tenderness which Georg Bendemann displays for his father as he removes his clothing and tremulously carries him to bed is the quite genuine expression of his hidden and suppressed because rather aberrant and feminine self. This self adores his father.

The inner world of Kafka's heroes is always as unknown to the rest of his characters as the outer world is unfathomable to his heroes. Indeed, the obliviousness of an insensible world to the private world of his man of sensibility is one of Kafka's fundamental issues, of course; and the irony of this obliviousness is one of his major ironies.

In "A Hunger-Artist," for example, all the characters are oblivious of the hunger-artist's anguish at finding himself in a world which cannot understand his passion for his art, an art universally regarded as a commercial affair; no one can conceive of him as other than a performer. In that story—Kafka's finest statement, perhaps, of the irony of obliviousness—the characters who mean to be kindest are those who are cruelest: his guards, for example, when they good-naturedly give him chances to eat surreptitiously (though of course no food is anywhere in sight). Kafka's irony is, as usual, doubly distilled because of its double removal, that is, because he writes from the oblivious point of view of those inflicting the cruelty: "'I have always wanted you to admire my fasting,' said the hunger-artist. 'And so we do,' said the manager kindly . . . ." Where in all literature is there a crueler word than that word "kindly"?

In "The Judgment" Georg Bendemann's gesture of putting his father to bed—a gesture described as impassively as is the torture machine, let us say, in "In the Penal Colony" (which, for the objectivity of its description, might be a late-model motor car)—this gesture of supreme love the father mistakes for a gesture of supreme hate, for he is oblivious of his son's inner world, knowing only the outer self, only the normal man without and the mask of indifference and hatred and loathing beneath which the son strives to conceal, even from himself, the excessive love of his hidden, suppressed self: "You wanted to cover me up, that I know, my young sprig, but I'm far from being covered up yet . . . ."

But the ghastly irony of old Bendemann's obliviousness is not enough. In "A Hunger-Artist" the irony of the manager's obliviousness redounds upon the hero, who in his self-torturing scrupulousness cannot admit that the world *is* oblivious: "'But you oughtn't to admire it,' said the hunger-artist. 'Very well, then we won't admire it,' replied the obliging manager, 'but why shouldn't we admire it?' 'Because I can't help fasting, I have to,' said the hunger-artist." And in "The Judgment," too, Kafka's irony is the irony of irony. For the love of Georg Bendemann for his father, which his father mistakes for the longing for his death, *is* the longing for his death: it is the love of death.

"'What did Kafka need his father for?'" Max Brod asks himself in his biography:

Or, better put, "Why was he not able to break away from him, although he adopted a critical attitude towards him . . . why didn't he seek refuge in that distance which so many children feel obliged to put between themselves and their parents; or rather, since he did manage to put that distance between himself and his father, and in later years hardly spoke to him, why did he suffer so from this distance and coldness? Must he not have said to himself that between two such entirely different characters as his and his father's an intimate union was just impossible?" . . . In how many talks did I not try and make clear to my friend . . . how he overestimated his father . . . . It was all useless, the torrent of arguments that Kafka produced (when he didn't prefer, as he frequently did, to keep quiet) could really shatter and repel me for a moment. . . . The odd thing is that even as he was growing older he still wished above all for his father's approval, which *could* never be granted.[7]

Brod's observation that "The Judgment" seems at first glance to be easily explicable by psychoanalysis suggests that he may have seen a psychoanalytical answer to the problem of Georg Bendemann, though he saw none, apparently, to these questions about Kafka.

The sense of guilt common to all mankind, according to Freud, has its source in the Oedipus complex, inversions of which are by no means as rare as one might suppose; indeed, Freud avers that all children are fixated upon both parents at one time or another, more feminine boys having more difficulty outgrowing their father fixation, and more masculine girls their mother fixation. May not the "nerve-destroying fear and sense of guilt" (Kafka's own description) which haunted Kafka all his life be traceable, then, to his father fixation? Kafka's hatred of his father has often been considered the cause of his sense of guilt; but of course a hatred as violent as Kafka's for his father is hardly to be distinguished from a love as violent. And hatred as a reaction to unattainability is not confined to abnormal cases of love; neither is the desire for the death of the beloved. Normally, however, these impulses are conscious, because socially acceptable, and may even be overtly expressed; whereas abnormally they are repressed to the point of being largely if not entirely unconscious, particularly when the love is unconscious, as it often is in the case of an Oedipus complex, the sufferer being aware chiefly of an intangible sense of guilt.

May not this be the guilt Kafka dramatized in his writing, the agony, the self-contempt, the despair? From one point of view Kafka's life and work may be a long study in certain consequences upon the suppression of abnormal love: the ambivalent attitude of love and hate, the externalization of the inner struggle, the self-torturing conscientiousness and moral scrupulousness, the paralysis of the will, the dread of responsibility, the interminable rationalization tending to confuse issues in order to avoid decision, the fear, the hopelessness, the self-abasement, the masochism and sadism, the yearning for normalcy, the obsessive sense of guilt, and above all the delusions of persecution. "I hate him because he persecutes me!" is the frequent cry of this sufferer, who longs unconsciously not only for the torture and death of his persecutor, but for torture and death at the hands of his beloved.

The judgment—old Bendemann's diatribe—is not what Kafka's father might have said if Kafka were to become engaged. It is what Kafka, the guilty self-torturer, wished his father would say lest he become engaged. In this dreadful self-castigation, this unravelable emotional knot of hatred, love, guilt, despair over the state of his writing and his father's distaste for his writing, the father appears as the externalization of Kafka's unconscious, addressing him with his father's crudeness, incoherence, and melodramatic flourish. Thus the father's disdain for his son's "perfidious notes to Russia" is Kafka's own contempt for his "scribbling," the father's disgust with Georg's susceptibility to his fiancée's attractions is Kafka's own disgust with his susceptibility, and the father's inconsistent attitude toward Georg's engagement (he seems at first to resent it bitterly only to object to Georg's delay in becoming engaged) is Kafka's own vacillation in the face of marriage; for he felt guilty on both scores, guilty for wishing to marry and guilty for not being able to marry.

The father accuses Georg of betraying his friend by becoming engaged; then, "emphasizing the point with stabs of his forefinger," proclaims the betrayal could not be consummated because of himself: "Still your friend hasn't been betrayed after all! I've been representing him here on the spot . . . . I've established a grand alliance with your friend . . . . He knows everything, stupid boy." Georg's facetious reply to this turns into deadly earnest "in his very mouth," for old Bendemann's claim to a grand alliance with Georg's friend is but Kafka's recognition of his father's triumphant role in his struggle to write.

Until "The Judgment" Kafka had sought to escape from his father in his writing, only to find him, to his despair, dominating all his work. "He crumples your letters unopened in his left hand," old Bendemann exults, "while holding out my letters before him to read with his right." It was only upon accepting this shattering truth that, out of the ruins of his exiled shop, his fallen gas fixtures, his tattered merchandise, Kafka's "business" began to flourish. "The Metamorphosis," *Amerika,* "In the Penal Colony," *The Trial,* "The Giant Mole," *The Castle*—directly or indirectly the dread adored image of Kafka's father pervades them all.

"My writing was about you; in it I merely poured out the sorrow I could not sigh at your breast" ("Letter to His Father").

Kafka wrote not only of his father, but for his father. What more acceptable way of presenting his "friend" to his Philistine father than as a businessman, dealing in merchandise? He wrote as a propitiatory gesture, the one gesture he really could make and could not help making, "not that I hope thereby to conciliate my father," he said, in dedicating to him *A Country Doctor,* "but I must do something." He wrote as an expiation, that his father might know of his nameless guilt and his passion for judgment; and without the slightest hope of his father caring or understanding.

"Writing as a form of prayer," Kafka wrote. And his father as a kind of God. Kafka deified his father, his supreme authority and goal. In "The Judgment" as in *The Castle,* Kafka's father is the Father-God, at once terrible and desirable, ineludible and unattainable, incomprehensible and uncomprehending.

Kafka's quest for understanding before his father—a quest for love and guidance, for law and certainty, begins in "The Judgment," when Georg, as he says, "My friend, of course," tries to meet his father's eyes. Is the gesture a sign of innocence, or merely a show of it? And is his embarrassment at his father's question the embarrassment of a man suddenly faced with his father's feeble-mindedness, or is it the embarrassment of a guilty conscience?

In "The Judgment" Kafka is judged; but he does not allow himself that comfort again. For the ecstasy of attaining his ultimate self-justification before his father by executing his sentence—an ecstasy refined to the nth degree in "The Metamorphosis," after which he never sees his father's face or hears his voice ("Where was the Judge whom he had never seen? Where was the High Court, to which he had never penetrated?")—is not to be compared to the ecstasy of the hopeless, the preposterous, but unendable quest.

NOTES

1. Max Brod, *Franz Kafka: A Biography,* tr. by G. Humphreys Roberts (New York, 1947), pp. 128–30. Quotations from Brod's biography, Herbert

Tauber's *Franz Kafka,* and Kafka's *Diaries* are here given in the standard English translations, none of which were available when this essay, in slightly different form, was originally published in *Quarterly Review of Literature,* III (1947), 382–405.

2. Herbert Tauber, *Franz Kafka: An Interpretation of his Works,* tr. by G. Humphreys Roberts and Roger Senhouse (New Haven, 1948), pp. 12–17. Claude-Edmonde Magny, "The Objective Depiction of Absurdity," *The Kafka Problem,* ed. Angel Flores (New York, 1946), pp. 75–96.

3. Brod, pp. 39–40.

4. *Ibid.,* pp. 95–96.

5. *Ibid.,* p. 126.

6. *Ibid.,* p. 151. Kafka's entry for this day is quoted by Brod, but (oddly enough) it does not appear in the published *Diaries.*

7. *Ibid.,* pp. 22–23, 30.

F. D. Luke

The Metamorphosis

"THE METAMORPHOSIS" is one of a small number of Kafka's works that he finished, published, and at the end of his life thought worth leaving undestroyed. One of his notes addressed to Max Brod as his literary executor excepts from the general condemnation "The Judgment," "The Metamorphosis," the *Country Doctor* stories, the *Hunger-Artist* stories, and the first episode of the American novel, which had appeared separately as "The Stoker." The three incomplete novels and various other fragments that Brod nevertheless reconstructed from Kafka's scattered manuscripts are of profound artistic and documentary interest, but if they had never been published Kafka would have equal title to a place among the greatest of German writers. The published stories represent him at his highest artistic incandescence, and display together all the qualities for which he is most admired: his classical, subtle, sober prose with its ophidian but lucid syntax, his technique of infinitesimal analysis, his intense fusion of naturalism with fantasy and of tragedy with humor. All these combine in an especially satisfying equilibrium in "The Metamorphosis," the longest of the stories, a *Novelle*—exceptional in Kafka's work for its architectural completeness—divided into three chapters through which, as through three acts, the narrative moves in a smooth dramatic curve.

To focus correctly the artistic qualities of a story such as "The Metamorphosis" is for some readers made difficult at first by the peculiarly macabre nature of the subject-matter. "The Metamorphosis" (first published in book form by Kurt Wolff, Leipzig, in November, 1915) is one

25

of three stories that more or less thoroughly elaborate one of Kafka's central themes: namely, the punishment-fantasy associated with an extremely primitive father-image. Of the three, "The Judgment" (1912, published in 1913), in which the son drowns himself at the father's bidding, deals most directly and least objectively with the material; while "In the Penal Colony" (published in 1919) is the most mature, in that the father is here less an individual (the "old commandant") than a social and religious institution, and above all in that the parable envisages and tentatively incorporates an emotional advance, a revision of the fantasy (the "new commandant") in the light of rational self-criticism (the "traveller who had come to investigate"). Special affinities connect "The Metamorphosis" and "The Judgment," both of which are *Familienkatastrophen,* in both of which the manifest protagonist is a young man doing well in business, and in both of which Kafka deliberately indicates himself as the latent protagonist by means of a nomenclatural code: in "The Judgment" the first five letters of the name "Bendemann" are intended, as Kafka himself states in a diary entry,[1] to represent the five letters of "Kafka" ($e = a$), while "Georg" ($=$ Franz)'s fiancée "Frieda Brandenfeld" represents Kafka's fiancée Felice B.; and in "The Metamorphosis," as Charles Neider points out, the verbal parallelism between "Samsa" and "Kafka" ($s = k$) is even closer.

Kafka's relationship with his energetic father was neurotic enough for him to be capable at the age of thirty-six, as is well known, of writing to Hermann Kafka an elaborately self-justifying and self-condemning letter over 15,000 words long and sending it to his mother for transmission; this was in 1919. His vacillating relationship with Fräulein B., which prolonged itself from 1912 till 1917, and another short-lived engagement in 1919 seem only to have exacerbated his father-problem and reactivated its most primitive elements. In the three stories written during these years, "The Judgment," "The Metamorphosis," and "In the Penal Colony," the son-figures are all guilty of original sin, the unforgivable offense of self-assertion: Georg Bendemann and Gregor Samsa have replaced the father as practical head and breadwinner of the family (in both stories Kafka stresses the decline of the father and his dramatic recovery which causes or follows the self-effacement of the son), and the condemned man on the prison-island has rebelled against military (paternal, divine) authority. The manifest content of "The Judgment" mainly emphasizes the son's offense and the father's anger, and the punishment follows swiftly and automatically at the end; in that of the other two stories the offense becomes peripheral—in "The Metamorphosis" it is not even openly referred to as an offense, and the "metamorphosis" is not manifestly connected with any idea of punishment or self-punishment, but merely stated without explanation at the beginning; it is now on the punishment itself that Kafka dwells at length. To this is due the special ghastliness of this story, in which the protagonist changes into a verminous insect[2] the size of a human being and gradually starves to death, and of "In the Penal Colony," which describes in prurient detail a mechanical method of killing a man slowly in twelve hours by engraving a sentence into his flesh with a complicated system of vibrating needles. The obviously morbid masochism of Kafka's personality and the obviously compulsive character of his writings have, however, no immediate relevance to an evaluation of his stories as literature and cannot justify an abstraction of this clinical material from its artistic context. The transmuted final product has been raised by Kafka's genius, taste, and humor to a plane far above that of horrific pornography or exhibitionistic self-documentation.

In the mental world embodied in a work of literature, it is possible to distinguish two levels on which a descriptive or analytic approach to it may be made: its more primitive or infantile level (the level, psychologically speaking, of the id and of primary process) and its more developed or adult level (that of the ego and secondary process) at which aesthetic and moral judgments and not merely clinical correlations are appropriate; and, at least in the case of Kafka and similar writers, it is important to make this distinction. The critic's description or analysis should concern itself, in some degree at least, with both these levels and not merely with one. To confine attention to the latter only is superficial, and to confine it to the former only is in principle irrelevant: the diagram of a sound-wave is not an analysis of the music. A just combination of the two types of approach has been achieved in Hellmuth Kaiser's exemplary monograph,[3] which deals mainly with "In the Penal Colony" but also, by way of introduction, with "The Metamorphosis" and the last of the *Country Doctor* stories, "A Report to an Academy" (the autobiographical report of an ape which has turned into a human being). This study, the most detailed and illuminating work on Kafka that has yet appeared, begins with a close analysis of the id-material used in these stories, but proceeds then to discuss them in the light of Kafka's adult intelligence and personality, examining also some of the elements (such as the implications of "A Report to an Academy" about the nature of art and those of "In the Penal Colony" about the nature of religious and moral experience) that turn Kafka's personal parables into parables of wide and profound general significance. The present article is throughout deeply indebted to Dr. Kaiser's work, and attempts merely to augment it in certain directions with special reference to "The Metamorphosis," and more particularly to this story's more-than-personal (artistic) functions, since Dr. Kaiser's account of its personal (self-expressive, self-therapeutic) functions need not be repeated.

I describe Kafka's stories as parables assuming the following provisional distinctions: a symbol = an image with latent meaning; a myth (or *Märchen*) = a narrative complex with latent meaning as a whole; an allegory = a myth consciously systematized to correspond at all points to a "key" and to have didactic implications; a parable = something between a myth and an allegory, in which the degree of conscious systematization and didactic intention is uncertain. The parabolic significance of "The Metamorphosis" can best be appreciated after examination of the literary techniques that it employs, the details of the narrative, and the effects (notably the comic and humorous effects) derived from these. The story as a whole is developed in naturalistic terms from a single fantastic initial premise: namely, as already stated, the supernatural metamorphosis of a commercial traveller, Gregor Samsa, who on waking at home one morning finds that he has become a gigantic cockroach or bedbug.[4] It is important to notice that as far as the story's manifest content is concerned, this metamorphosis is intended to be taken literally, as a real (objective) event, and *not merely* as a symbol of physical or mental illness, or as a dream or other hallucination on the part of Gregor or of any other character. The function of the metamorphosis *within* the story is to be distinguished from the fantasy in Kafka's mind underlying its invention, and from the possible total implication of the story whereby the "change" may be thought of as a psychotic breakdown or other serious mental regression. Kafka's irony here is peculiarly subtle: within the story it is *the metamorphosis* (literally an impossible event) that represents objective reality for Gregor and his family—represents, that is, something monstrous, inacceptable, but nevertheless actual, unshakable, demanding adaptation; whereas it is *their behavior* that is strange, dreamlike, incongruous, inappropriate, and for this very reason lifelike—the ordinary behavior of humanity confronted with the ugliness of fact. Psychological superrealism here, as always, transcends and undercuts the usual categories. The characters in the story behave as if the metamorphosis were a natural event, one capable of correlation to the rest of their experience, while Gregor at first, as the person most closely affected, behaves as if it had not happened at all: it is through these reactions to it, at least as much as through the event itself, that Kafka conveys an impression of nightmare horror, nightmare comedy, and even more disturbingly, of nightmare truth.

After the metamorphosis Gregor remains almost continuously behind locked doors: in the two or three months till his death he leaves his room only three times, and from these three "outbreaks" are developed the three main episodes of the story, which thus achieves a diversified unity in the classical manner. The three chapters correspond to a dramatic pattern of exposition, conflict, and denouement. The first exploits the typical Kafkan tension between the horrible and the comic: Gregor, having by habit locked himself into his bedroom the previous evening, wakes up transformed, manoeuvres himself out of bed and to the door, unlocks it with his jaws, shows himself to the family, tries to speak but is not understood and is driven by his father back into his room, where he hides under a sofa; the room is now locked from the outside. In the second chapter this atmosphere is sustained and violent action develops. Gregor's food is now brought to him by his sister. He takes to crawling all over the walls and ceiling of his room, the family remove his furniture, he places himself over a picture on the wall to prevent its removal, his mother faints, he follows his sister into the living room, crawls all over it, and is attacked by his father (the central conflict) who wounds him by throwing an apple which lodges in his back, and who is apparently only prevented from killing him by the entreaties of the mother. In the third chapter, though comic elements persist, the main effect developed is one of pathos: the family, as a concession, leave Gregor's door open in the evenings, but neglect him more and more; [5] they take in three lodgers who eat succulent meals in the living room; Gregor's sister one evening plays the violin to them after dinner, and Gregor, strangely attracted by the music and longing to regain his sister's attention, slowly crawls out once more, weak with starvation and covered with dirt; the lodgers give notice, Gregor's sister becomes hysterical and declares that

Gregor must be got rid of, Gregor crawls back into his room and dies; with him out of the way, the family's economic position seems to improve overnight and his parents decide, significantly, that it is time to find a husband for his sister.

We may distinguish the humorous aspect of this story from its comic aspect by calling the former the expression (mainly by means of a technique of understatement) of a certain kind of tragically humorous attitude in the author (latent protagonist), and the latter an accumulation of comic (while at the same time tragic and horrific) effects derived from the behavior of Gregor and the other characters. These comic effects, which we shall consider first, may for convenience be separated into two main categories.

The first category includes all the effects derived more directly from the physical metamorphosis itself and from its physical corollaries. Comparisons between Gregor as an insect and Gregor as a human being are stated or implied. In his new shape, Gregor finds it difficult or impossible to do certain things that were previously easy, and capable of other feats previously beyond him; correspondingly, he suddenly or gradually loses desires and tastes that were normal to him before, and develops others that were not.

At the beginning of the story, for example, he finds himself no longer able to perform the simple operation of turning over in bed, and comedy here arises from an automatically suggested comparison between the small quantity of effort needed by a human being lying supine to turn on one side, and the large quantity often apparently used unavailingly for the same purpose by a beetle.[6] Similarly, Gregor now finds getting out of bed a difficult feat for which he has to learn a technique by trial and error. He is at the disadvantage of being (like infants and young animals) unacquainted with his own anatomy; he is instinctively anxious not to hurt his head in falling on the floor, but does so despite the utmost care. His further efforts to develop mobility are equally complicated, but he succeeds in dragging himself upright, leaning on the back of a chair, pushing it to the door, and turning the key with his jaws although "he hadn't really any teeth." Having opened the door, and still upright, he forgets in his excitement that he cannot now walk forward like a human being, and by suddenly falling to his feet, again produces comic effect of a simple type. Ludicrous difficulties, described in detail, arise when he is forced to retreat, both now and on the second occasion on which he is pursued by his father;

and to drape a sheet over the sofa under which he hides takes him four hours.

Comic effect is further derived from Gregor's loss of the human faculty of speech,[7] which becomes comic partly because it is an un-willed, *automatic* corollary of the unwilled metamorphosis (it was "unmistakably his own voice . . . but with a persistent horrible twittering squeak behind it like an undertone"). This source of comedy (automatism, "la mécanisation de la vie" in Bergson's formula) is also active, combined with comedy of contradicted expectation (*Erwartungskomik*), at the moment when Gregor for the first time finds himself with all his feet on the ground: at once, unreflectingly, un-expectedly, automatically, in ludicrous accordance with his insect nature and despite his alarm ("with a little cry") in the previous in-stant, he is filled with a sense of pleasurable well-being. From time to time throughout the story Kafka thus subtly reminds the reader that Gregor now *cannot help* acting and reacting in many respects like an insect (an "automatism of species" comparable to Bergson's "auto-matisme professionel"). Thus, for example, whenever (listening through the door) he hears the family discussing its reduced financial situation, he is overcome with shame and flattens himself on the cool leather sofa—this is human, but not the final detail: "Often he just lay there the long nights through without sleeping at all, *scrabbling for hours on the leather*." Similarly when he reflects with pride on his previous achievements for the family, and for a moment rises to the most advanced level of thought shown by any character throughout the story ("But what if all the quiet, the comfort, the contentment were now to end in horror?"), Kafka again deflates him with grim pre-cision: "To keep himself from being lost in such thoughts Gregor took refuge in movement and *crawled up and down the room*."

Gregor's tastes and habits change in a way he cannot account for and of which, still using human valuations, he is ashamed: his wide high room, for example, strangely alarms him and he prefers to force himself uncomfortably under the sofa. He is distracted from human interests and intentions by sudden animal impulses ("he could not resist snapping his jaws together at the sight of the steaming coffee"). As a human being, milk was his favorite drink, but now, when after lying hungry and bruised by his father's maltreatment he advances eagerly towards the bowl of milk which his sister has left for him, comedy of automatism (the insect-reaction) is again combined with

Erwartungskomik, this time in the form of acute disillusionment ("not only did he find it difficult to feed because of his tender left side—and he could only feed with the palpitating collaboration of his whole body—he did not like the milk either . . . indeed it was almost with repulsion that he turned away from the basin and crawled back to the middle of the room"). He can now only eat decayed food such as human beings find disgusting ("a piece of cheese that Gregor would have called uneatable two days ago," etc.). He is now less susceptible to pain and injury, as he notices (with exquisite innocence: "Am I less sensitive now? he thought, and sucked greedily at the cheese"): in other words, his biological level is now more primitive. His attitude to dirt in general, as to food, undergoes a corresponding regressive change: distressed at first by the accumulating filth and lumber in his room, he later crawls about in it "with increasing enjoyment." He now enjoys crawling for its own sake, and has the advantage over mankind of being at last able to run up the walls, or fall ("for mere recreation") from the ceiling. These features—the interest in dirt, the pleasure in crawling, and the further habit he develops of taking food into his mouth merely "as a pastime," spitting it out again hours later—all serve to emphasize the *infantile* character of the degraded state to which Gregor has symbolically returned; thus strengthening the latent aspect (adult—infant) of the implied comic comparison (human being—animal; living creature—automaton) and contributing to the comic aspect (*Herabsetzungskomik*) [8] of the story's main theme. Only one change in Gregor's tastes (his new appetite for music) is not similarly regressive—this we shall consider later.

The other main category of (tragi-)comic effects derives less from the physical than from the *mental* behavior, after the metamorphosis, of Gregor and the other characters. Again the basic source of comedy is a suggested comparison which reveals a disparity, a discrepancy, an incongruity: here, between the quantity of emotional and intellectual output that an experience such as the metamorphosis would in reality demand, and the quantity with which Gregor and the others appear to respond to it. This disparity, which is an extremely important factor both in the parabolic function of the story and in Kafka's (tragi-)comic technique generally, may be considered from several points of view. In the first place, it serves the purposes of a narrative technique that characteristically achieves its strongest effects by ironic understatement and obliquity: by describing an incongruous reaction to the metamorphosis, Kafka conveys its true though latent impact with far greater force than if he had attempted to express the required horror and amazement directly and rhetorically. Secondly, the disparity can be described in psychological terms as a defense-mechanism involving reality-denial and affect-displacement, and thus as analogous to either or both of two different (though basically similar) things each of which illustrates the humiliating (degrading) dominion of fear and desire over human reason, namely: (1) the abnormal mental behavior of psychotics and neurotics, and (2) the behavior of the mind in dreams (that is, in its normal flights into temporary psychosis). And thus (thirdly) the literary effect here is one of mingled horror and comedy. Gregor's "flat" reaction, as Kafka presents it, is horrifying because of its "uncanny" psychotic (e.g., schizophrenic) character; because it insidiously enlarges an implied rift between daily actuality and monstrous possibility; and because it casts dreadful and tragic light on human incapacity to appreciate disaster. It is comic, on the other hand, because it is mechanical and because it is like a reaction in a dream.

Kafka's stories have often been compared to dreams or nightmares, but the analogy has seldom been elaborated. We may here take the opportunity of inspecting the actual mechanics of the "dream-logic"— the pseudo-logic, the subrational thought—with which not only "The Metamorphosis" but Kafka's whole work is saturated.

Waking and finding himself supernaturally, unmistakably, and disgustingly transformed, Gregor shows concern only with the weather, his job, the train he has missed, and the best method of getting out of bed: in other words, he automatically *displaces* his attention on to inessentials, on to peripheral details of his situation, distributing and reducing his manifest emotion accordingly.[9] His reaction (rather similar to that of Georg in "The Judgment" in this respect) shows the typical Bergsonian comic "raideur"; and it is comic because (as a result of the disparity between the demand and the response, between the quantity of emotion produced in the reader by the narrative and the quantity apparently produced on Gregor by the event) empathy is first stimulated, then rendered superfluous, and so discharged in the form of laughter or its equivalent. Displacement, moreover, is a primitive irrational process, a typical unconscious device used in the formation of dreams, witticisms, and mental symptoms, and there is comic disparity between the automatic ease with which primitive thought ignores the demands of logic and the difficulty that rational (civilized, adult) thought has in meeting them; once again, laughter ensues from a relief of energy-tension (that required for the upkeep of logical inhibition).

Besides that of comic disparity, the story's opening paragraphs of course also have the effect of intense tragic irony in the dramatic sense. From the outset a clearer grasp of the real situation is made available to the reader than to the victim. To the former, the unseen spectator, the objective event is offered baldly in the first sentence; and this information is at once attended by its corollaries, the half-dozen lines of detail that complete the first paragraph. To say that Gregor is *unaware* that something monstrous has actually taken place would be to over-simplify: his question now, "What has happened to me?" is followed at once by the crucial recognition, "It was no dream." But this recognition, though confirmed by the further reality-test of looking round his familiar room, is immediately submerged; and as the first chapter develops, Gregor is shown clinging to the belief that his metamorphosis is a dream or other hallucination, while at the same time thinking and acting, in certain essentials, on the basis of a fear—even a latent knowledge—that it is real and could be perceived by other people. Kafka illustrates a very similar equivocal reaction at one point in "The Burrow," where the animal protagonist acts and argues on the *assumption,* before he is prepared to admit as a *hypothesis,* that the mysterious "noise" is caused by the approach of a single large enemy. In each case the discrepancy, the time-lag, is due to the protagonist's fear of recognizing an inacceptable but unalterable situation.

Gregor's gnat-straining begins with the third paragraph: he looks towards the window and notices the rain, which makes him "quite melancholy." He decides to sleep on for a little and forget "all this nonsense"; his inability to turn over evokes only a quite commonplace train of thought ("what an exhausting job," etc.) of the type to which his waking mind is conditioned, a perfectly banal stream of commercial-traveller consciousness, only momentarily interrupted when he notices the unaccountable white spots ("This getting up early, he thought, makes one quite stupid. A man needs his sleep"). A sense of crisis is first provoked in him by the discovery that he has slept through the signal of his alarm clock, and he begins to speculate whether he could plausibly excuse himself on grounds of indisposition. When he hears himself speak his defenses are shaken, and to avoid confirmation of his fear that the metamorphosis may be real he answers his family's questions as briefly as possible, and feels glad that his doors are locked. That he should have lost his human shape is not tolerable, "therefore" not true; the experiment that might prove it true must be avoided at all costs or at least postponed for as long as possible; he must continue as if nothing had happened and thus establish that all is as it was. The alterations are "purely imaginary"; "this morning's delusions" will gradually disappear when he gets out of bed; the strangeness in his voice is the first sign of a cold. The morning seems foggier than usual. "And for a little while he lay quiet, breathing lightly, as if perhaps expecting such complete repose to restore all things to their real and normal condition." He hopes that the noise of his fall on the floor will not alarm his parents; he wishes his father and the kitchen maid would come in and lift him out of bed and turn him over (but "in spite of his misery he could not suppress a smile at the very idea of it"). When the junior manager of his firm calls to enquire for him, he resents this as an aspersion on his conscientiousness, the very conscientiousness that today has made him "so tormented by conscience as to be driven out of his mind" and incapable of getting up. Both the firm and the family are making an unnecessary fuss. But he still refuses to speak until stung by the manager's reproaches. His policy then changes: he will show himself, and if they are not alarmed, then equally all will be well and he can catch the eight o'clock train. As the manager retreats aghast before him, Gregor reverts again to his only *accustomed* form of serious anxiety, the fear of losing his job; and as his numerous feet touch the floor he is filled with a sudden grotesque optimism: "he was inclined to believe that a final relief from all his sufferings was at hand."

These effects and many others of the same type fill the story's first chapter, after which Gregor is presumed to abandon (though still not completely) his forlorn pretenses, and achieves a certain pathetic resignation. The comedy of his first reactions is now reflected in the behavior of the family and other characters. Their very acceptance of the situation is as comic as it is appalling: at most they are distressed and physically nauseated, but they are too limited, imaginatively and intellectually, to be in any way fundamentally puzzled or shaken.[10] Even Gregor's mother at last grows used to the sight of him; and she clings for weeks to the hope that he may still recover from his "affliction." His sister does, as she says, try "to look after it and to put up

with it as far as is humanly possible . . . ." His father, further distorted into conformity with Kafka's own father-image, seems to think
that the metamorphosis is very much what might have been expected
of Gregor. The impassive charwoman treats him as some curious kind
of pet. The three lodgers, when Gregor first crawls into their view, are
at first amused and then indignant at what they call "the disgusting
conditions prevailing in this household and family . . . ."

Kafka's technique is thus seen to consist largely of skilful exposures,
cumulative revelations of a basic incongruity between situations and re-
sponses; it insistently explores the self-protective devices to which the
human mind has recourse at a level far below that of rational judgment.
In the successful dream (as in the successful psychosis) pain is pro-
hibited, disturbing emotion prophylactically drained away from the
experience to which it belongs; should it prove too intractable, the
attempt to sleep through it is abandoned. But in Kafka's stories the
defense is maintained, psychological disinfectants are placed at every
corner, the horror is repudiated, the extraordinary is absorbed into the
ordinary; and thus the doors of the madhouse of sleep never open, the
alarm clock rings in vain. The world in which Kafka's characters live
and die is one where reality-criteria are not applied—its inhabitants
dare not apply them. It is a world deceptively real, described with the
most detailed naturalism: yet somewhere a rent in this fabric uncovers
the glittering darkness of a nightmare region in which nothing is impossible.

In such a world, of course, logic is not needed and not wanted,
though argument is continually used. At the behest of desire and fear,
any hypothesis will explain, any pretext will serve, any excuse will
justify; and the more excuses, however incompatible, the better. One
of the most striking features of Kafka's whole work is his ceaseless
rummaging among the interminable possibilities of futile quasi-
rational elaboration; his studies of the law and of the Talmud no doubt
helped him here, as Charles Neider points out.[11] Kafka is the supreme
master of obsessional hairsplitting: if he is untranslatable, it is largely
because particles such as *ja, doch, vielleicht, etwa, sogar, allerdings,
schon, oder besser, zwar—aber, freilich—jedoch, wenn nicht—so doch,*
and all the other aids to logical refinement with which the German
language is so richly supplied, are the words he most constantly uses.
Kafka's world is one, remarks Austin Warren,[12] "in which everyone
is able, like Lewis Carroll's creatures, to argue long, ingeniously and

convincingly." Convincingly, that is, to themselves, for an important factor in the Kafkan comic technique is the comedy of unwitting self-contradiction (*Unsinnskomik* in a strict sense).

Examples from "The Metamorphosis" include the inconsequential succession of theories that form themselves in Gregor's mind as he attempts to rationalize his experience, hunting helplessly for explanations of the inexplicable (the metamorphosis is a dream, a cold in the head, a foolish hallucination induced by pangs of conscience, the magical outcome of malevolent detraction by his co-employees, etc.); and above all, his two long speeches to the junior manager, anticipated by the rather similar speeches of the junior manager himself and of Gregor's mother, whose voluble excuses for her son are full of comic-pathetic irrelevancies. The second of Gregor's two speeches, delivered as he clings upright to the open door ("'Well,' said Gregor, knowing perfectly that he was the only one who had retained any composure. 'I'll put my clothes on . . . . temporarily incapacitated . . . later on, when the incapacity has been got over . . . ,'" etc.), is virtually his last attempt to make himself understood verbally, and occurs at the moment when the others see him for the first time; thus the horrific effect here tends to overlay the comedy of the speech, which is also full of ironies so extreme that Gregor himself seems to be sadistically conscious of them. His first speech, however, brilliantly crystallizes the whole atmosphere of the first chapter in its absurd aspect. It is an elaborate self-exoneration, a kaleidoscopic succession of special pleas which nullify each other, such as for example the four pairs of anti-thetical statements with which he begins:

(1) He is unwell ("A slight illness, an attack of giddiness"), but now he is well again ("But I feel all right again").

(2) He is still in bed, but in the act of getting out of bed.

(3) He is still in difficulties ("I'm not quite so well as I thought") but already all is in order ("But I'm all right, really").

(4) His illness has taken him by surprise, his parents can vouch for his having been well on the previous evening; "or rather," there were signs of it the previous evening too, as his parents can attest.

This is comic because of the implied comparison between genuine logic and dream-logic. An example of the latter closely similar to Gregor's speech both in its tendency and in its effect is the story, quoted more than once by Freud, of the man who having lent a kettle to a neighbor complained that it had been returned to him with a large hole in the bottom. The neighbor disclaimed responsibility on the grounds that (1) he had returned the kettle undamaged, (2) it had been damaged before he borrowed it, and (3) he had never borrowed it. And exact parallels both to Gregor's speech and to this story are to be found in *self-exculpatory dreams* of which the classical example is Freud's dream of "Irma's injection." [13] In all these cases the desire to exonerate oneself overrides with *automatic ease* the law of contradiction (to which Gregor's one concession is the phrase "or rather"). But observance of this law, recognition that a cake cannot be both eaten and had, is a developmentally advanced achievement, learnt by the human child with difficulty and sorrow; and to the spectacle of a more primitive mental organism (whether in a child, a savage, a neurotic, a madman, or a dream) blithely defying reason's painful demands, the maturer mind reacts with laughter: the laughter with which life avenges itself on maladaptation; the release by which energy withdraws itself from unneeded effort, thought, or feeling; the automatic euphoria in which lost innocence takes refuge from experience.

Thus the comedy of Gregor's speech, as of all the other behavior in the story, is the comedy of primitiveness; and its tragedy lies in the fact that it represents not mere innocence, but yet another aspect of a degrading regression. It is significant that during the speech he is "beside himself," that "all this was tumbling out pell-mell and Gregor hardly knew what he was saying"; and still more significant is the reaction of his hearers, to whom it is *unrecognizable as the speech of a human being.* Gregor's processes of thought have sunk below the level of organization and synthesis, and it is to this *intellectual* degradation, among other things, that the physical loss of his human shape and voice is parabolically equivalent. His mother interprets what she has heard as a sign merely of illness, of accidental disorder; the junior manager, more dispassionate, recognizes it as the essential subhuman gibbering of a beast ("das war eine Tierstimme").

The junior manager, who is in some respects the realist of the story, here utters in four words Kafka's whole criticism both of himself and of mankind. The Kafkan mining and countermining in subrational darkness is something both personal and more than personal, both compulsive and more than compulsive: it not only expresses an individual neurosis, it is a satire and an accusation, gaining another

dimension of meaning from its correspondence with the known unfortunate facts of human experience in general. From the constant,
specious, sometimes even conscious rationalizations in which mankind
is and has been everywhere engaged—from the contrast, in a thousand
forms, between the rational and the pseudorational, Kafka derives
his basic theme, both comic and tragic,[14] which achieves its most terrible crystallization in "The Metamorphosis." Without once directly
mentioning it, Kafka here completely exposes the persistent primitiveness of man, the power of unco-ordinated unconscious processes
even over his highest faculties, the primacy of the "will" in Schopen-
hauer's sense, the degradation of reason.

The situation is of course not exhausted when conceived in terms
of this antagonism and perpetual struggle between instinct and reason
(or more accurately, since in practice only the irrational can overcome the irrational, between instinct condemned by reason and
instinct approved by it). Kafka adds another factor to this dualism
in the strangest and most moving episode of "The Metamorphosis,"
that of the violin, the climax of the last chapter. Gregor's "metamorphosis" has been, in all other respects, a degradation, a regressive,
retrogressive change. He can no longer support himself economically,
has lost all contact with the outer world (a situation stressed by the
removal of his furniture and pictures); he has become inarticulate,
evil-smelling, mechanical, instinct-dominated, and goes on his belly.
But whereas Gregor as a man had shown no taste for music, Gregor as
an insect is irresistibly drawn towards the sound of a violin. It is an
effect on which Kafka does not dwell, passing straight on to Gregor's
fantasy about his sister with which it is closely associated. We have
learnt earlier in the story that Gregor had intended to send Grete, at
his expense, to the college of music, thus using his position as economic
head of the family to make a positive claim on her, in opposition to his
parents' wishes. This comparatively innocent plan now reverts to a
more primitive form, expressed in an extraordinary complex of pa-
thetically erotic and obscurely aggressive impulses ("He was determined to push forward till he reached his sister . . . . she should stay
with him . . . . Gregor would . . . kiss her on the neck," etc.). But
this is preceded by two sentences that strike quite another note: the
mystical statement, "He felt as if the way were opening before him
to the unknown nourishment he craved"—a theme that Kafka was to
develop in later stories; [15] and before this, the sudden, momentary, but

crucial speculation: *"Was he an animal,* that music had such an effect upon him?" Has he become less, or more than human—merely infantile, or mature in a different dimension of maturity? Or is not illness a kind of holiness, and anguished primitive fantasy the substance of art and religion, and may not the energy of savage instinct serve the loftiest aims? Unobtrusively, Kafka implies here the question that "A Report to an Academy" and "In the Penal Colony" also ask, and also leave open.

The problem of how to correlate two quite different scales or dimensions of value—the ethical-humane-realistic-rational-scientific on the one hand, the aesthetic-mystical-romantic-religious on the other—is also, of course, the essential problem of Thomas Mann, to whom of all his contemporaries Kafka is said to have felt himself most closely akin. With Thomas Mann the recurrent formula, which sees him through the greater part of his work, is to condemn his protagonist on the first of these valuations while simultaneously (hence irony in various degrees) absolving him on the second. Of "The Metamorphosis" and "Death in Venice," two of the greatest *Novellen* of the twentieth century, each represents its author's saddest and bitterest act of atonement in this sense. Both are stories of degradation—outwardly the degradation of a human being turning into an insect, or of a respectable and distinguished middle-aged writer painting his face and following a boy along the streets—inwardly and essentially the degradation of the rational organism, the collapse of civilized values before the latent ("daemonic") forces of chaos. In both stories the protagonist is tragically isolated, and dies voluntarily in a spirit of renunciation. Both stories exploit a literary technique of sinister ambiguity, both are artistic *tours de force.*

The differences, however, between Mann's masterpiece and Kafka's are as interesting as their similarities. In Kafka's starker and grimmer story the artistic transfiguration, the Apollonian miracle, is achieved entirely without the help of romantic glamour. Aschenbach falls in love with a boy: but homosexuality in one form or another was something already consecrated by literary tradition—much of the greatest Greek art and literature had breathed it, there were illustrious Renaissance precedents, it had inspired Winckelmann and Platen, had lain under the surface in Wagner and Nietzsche, and had finally become the basis of a cult and been raised to high mythical incandescence by Stefan George. But Gregor Samsa's experience has no cultural legend to support it; no great figures from the past can be made to share his responsibility for it; it cannot enlist the sympathy traditionally accorded to passionate romantic love; it is not set against a background of Venetian splendors, Platonic echoes, Homeric seascapes, and "an immensity of richest expectation." Mann is more firmly related than Kafka to convention, to the external object, the world of reality and civilized society; and in all his most typical works, destructive diseases of the soul are safely provided with some physical correlative (typhus, cholera, tuberculosis, syphilis). Kafka is a more serious case than Mann, not merely in the sense that he died of tuberculosis instead of writing about it: he is more acutely isolated, more deeply involved in illness both physical and mental. He did not descend amid the stench of the Lost People; he was living there already.

And for this or for whatever other reason, he is as a writer more daringly and richly inventive than Mann: he does not add an aura of parabolic significance to narrative patterns already largely supplied by external accident, but creates wholly original narrative patterns of his own, unprecedented psychological parables of the highest intrinsic potency. The nightmare described in "Death in Venice," Aschenbach's "dream" of pagan eroticism and barbaric frenzy, is an elaborately written artificial literary vision, and when Mann introduces Aschenbach's last monologue by calling it "dream-logic," this description is quite inappropriate: he is merely apologizing in advance for a highly sophisticated train of thought reasoned at a conscious level on Mann's familiar lines. But Kafka's "dream-logic" is genuine. He is basically as autobiographical and repetitive as Mann, but less noticeably because more obliquely so. He retreats wholly behind his material instead of standing beside it and discussing its points with the reader. In Kafka there are none of Mann's analytical reflections, long or short: his far more economical, more furtive prose never pauses to sigh, to shake the head, to exclaim, "Who shall unriddle the mystery of the artist's nature and character?" (or, as the case may be, the mystery of being a Jew, or of Christianity, or of illness, etc.) This is the difference between Mann's "objectivity" and Kafka's; the difference, in fact, between their modes of self-consciousness. Mann regards "a human sense of one's own importance" ("menschliches Sichwichtignehmen") as a fundamental value, as (with the honesty which at times seems to surpass even his capacity for self-analysis) he confesses in the preface to *Meditations of an Unpolitical Man*—a book pervaded by an attitude that would have been impossible to Kafka. Kafka can no longer take his case, the more serious one, so seriously; his tragic awareness extends as far beyond seriousness as beyond mere self-persiflage and apotropaic nest-fouling. In Mann the process of withdrawal, of *Distanzierung*, is still incomplete and relative (and as such, no doubt, less morbid); in Kafka it is ambiguously absolute, seeming at times to be null and at times to be total. There is little evidence that Kafka believed intellectually in a transcendental God, but it is as God, or an inhabitant of Mars, might look on them that part of Kafka looks on the miserable Kafka affair and on the miserable human affair generally. It is in this sense, perhaps, admissible to call him, as Thomas Mann has called him, "a religious humorist." [16]

Humorous *Distanz* is an essential feature of Kafka's technique and of his greatness. As a storyteller it is this that enables him to exploit every possible effect of understatement, to accentuate horror by reporting it with terrible detachment: Gregor's situation, for example, is "his mishap" or "his present condition," and his family suffer "inconvenience" and "anxieties." Kafka's attitude is essentially a species of *Galgenhumor*, the humor, on a vaster scale, of the criminal who, led out to execution on a Monday, remarked, "Well, this is a good beginning to the week." [17] In principle, such humor, and indeed all humor, involves at least two participants though both may be aspects of one self: namely, the active subject in whom the humorous attitude operates, and the passive object(s) in whom the comic behavior or situation is observed. In the anecdote of the criminal, the object is the criminal himself in his comic aspect; in "The Metamorphosis" it is the manifest protagonist, Gregor. Gregor is (tragi-)comic but not himself humorous; the (tragic) humor of the story is an aspect of the attitude of the author (towards himself and mankind). [18] The same is the case in Kafka's other works. It is typical that in "The Metamorphosis" the manifest object of his humor should be an animal, as in "A Report to an Academy," "Josephine the Singer" (in the *Hunger-Artist* collection), "The Burrow," and "Investigations of a Dog." Interpreting his parable, we may say that Kafka observes human activities and interests as a human being might observe the scuttling of ants or beetles or mice, the burrowing of moles or badgers and the antics of dogs or apes; as a grown-up person, in fact, might observe the behavior of children; and what he observes he sees to be "purposeful and yet nevertheless purposeless or purpose-defeating, serious and futile yet nevertheless playful and futile." [19] This is Kafka's Martian *Distanzierung*, his God's-eye view. By the strictest standards, no doubt, such humor is not a truly realistic response to reality, but a schizoid self-division, a flight into divine superiority, displacement in yet another form, a massive displacement of emotion which emerges this time as the attitude of a grandly magnanimous imaginary parent. But whereas to comic behavior, such as Gregor's, we react with mingled amusement and pity, to humor we react with mingled amusement and admiration. Mankind values humor as a supreme defense against its environment, a triumphant excursion above mere reality and mere illusion, a reassurance and reassertion of the self in the face of hopeless odds. And in the last resort Kafka is at one with humanity's perhaps vain yet persistent struggle for "the conclusive amendment of all suffering." [20] In his later works, perhaps even in "The Burrow," there are clear traces of this irreducible sense of human solidarity—of a sympathy, even an admiration, that alleviates his bitterness.

NOTES

1. February 11, 1913; quoted by Charles Neider, *Kafka: His Mind and Art* (London, 1949), p. 74.

2. As Brod points out, Kafka also calls himself "vermin" ("Ungeziefer") in his letter to his father.

3. *Franz Kafkas Inferno. Eine psychologische Deutung seiner Strafphantasie* (Vienna: Internat. Psychoan. Verl., 1931; originally published in *Imago*, XVII [February, 1931], 41–103).

4. The species of insect is not clearly stated. As so often, Kafka strengthens his effect by ambiguity—a parallel case is the later (unfinished) story "The Burrow," told in the first person by an animal which is never described. Gregor becomes "ein ungeheueres Ungeziefer," which the charwoman later addresses as "Mistkäfer"; it is at least two feet wide, hardbacked, manylegged, brown, malodorous, eats household leavings at first but would perhaps prefer blood.

5. Gregor starves, however, partly because he himself feels less and less inclined to eat. Kafka concentrates on the theme of starvation and mystical sitiophobia in the very remarkable story, "A Hunger-Artist," which, like "In the Penal Colony" before it, uses "loss of public interest in the performance" to symbolize the defeat of a primitive fantasy by increasing reality-sense.

6. The general theoretical principles of comedy and humor applied in the present article are drawn mainly from Theodor Lipps (*Komik und Humor*, Hamburg and Leipzig, 1898), Bergson (*Le Rire*, Paris, 1900), and Freud (*Der Witz und seine Beziehung zum Unbewussten*, 1905, and *Der Humor*, 1928, in Volumes VI and XIV, respectively, of Freud's *Gesammelte Werke*, London, 1940–49). On this particular point, cf. Freud on "Bewegungskomik," VI, 216–21, and Lipps, pp. 51 f.

7. He remains able, however, to understand what is said, though his family do not realize this. From his increasing loss of the faculty of sight a mainly pathetic effect is derived, as when he props himself for hours by the window, "obviously in some recollection of the sense of freedom that looking out of a window always used to give him."

8. Cf. also Bergson on "dégradation."

9. Cf. a similar point made by Albert Camus in an article, "Hope and Absurdity," reprinted in *The Kafka Problem*, ed. by Angel Flores (New York, 1946): "The only thing which disturbs [Gregor] . . . is that his boss will be displeased by his absence. The legs and antennae of an insect grow from him, his spine arches, white spots appear on his belly, and . . . it causes him a 'faint vexation'" (p. 254).

10. As Austin Warren (in "Kosmos Kafka," *The Kafka Problem*, p. 67) remarks, "the chief horror of the story is, perhaps, that no one within it sees what happens as 'impossible': it is horrible, to be sure, but in various ways these people, who are obviously sane and simple, adjust themselves to a painful situation."

11. *Kafka: His Mind and Art*, pp. 27 f.

12. "Kosmos Kafka," p. 62.

13. Analyzed in *Die Methode der Traumdeutung* (1900); see *Ges. Werke*, II–III, 110–26. The dreamer argues that the persistence of his patient's symptoms is not his fault because it is (1) her fault, (2) due to an organic disease, (3) due to her widowhood, (4) the fault of the other doctor who gave her the wrong kind of injection.

14. This is pointed out by Neider, *Kafka: His Mind and Art*, Ch. II.

15. For example, in "A Hunger-Artist"; the obscure connection between music and food is also reflected in "Investigations of a Dog," one of Kafka's last unfinished stories.

16. In an article reprinted in *Der Monat*, June, 1949; originally printed in English as an introduction to the second American edition of *The Castle* (New York, 1941).

17. Quoted by Freud in *Der Humor*, from which the principles implied by the following descriptions of the humorous process are also taken.

18. Only occasionally does the humorous attitude of Kafka as latent protagonist seem to infuse itself into Gregor, as for example when he clears his throat as quietly as possible, "since this noise too might not sound like a human cough for all he was able to judge"; or when, at the denouement, in the process of turning to crawl back into his room, he pauses to let his sister recover from the further hysteria which this movement provokes, then "Perhaps I can go on turning round now, thought Gregor, and began his labors again."

19. Lipps, *Komik und Humor*, p. 23.

20. "The negation of a positive human value, which by this very negation is brought nearer and made more vivid and precious to us: such is . . . the inmost essence of tragedy. And such, too, is the inmost essence of humour."—Lipps, *Komik und Humor*, p. 234.

Basil Busacca

A Country Doctor

THE tales of Aesop, as everyone knows, have two substantive aspects: 1) the dramatic surface—taken either as itself or as coating for the "meaning"; 2) the "meaning," which has little to do, except nominally, with foxes and grapes, or pelicans and bottles. The *meaning* could be expressed in the *x*'s and *y*'s of symbolic logic more economically than in language, albeit less charmingly, because it is concerned with particular *relations* and not with specific *termini* (e.g., foxes, grapes). The formula of relations (the meaning) may, like a proverb such as "A stitch in time saves nine," be applied to any set of specific *termini* whose relations may be conceived as analogous: thus we tell the child who says that "spelling is silly," after he fails to spell correctly, that he should "remember the fox and the grapes."

The function of both aspects is comic. The stories of Aesop are droll tales significant of droll patterns of behavior which are available to rational correction. In reading the tales we are sufficiently detached from specific *termini* to recognize discrepancy from the rational even when such discrepancy is analogous to some of our own behavior. Aesop is an example of the comic poet, whose strategy, as Professor Julius Weinberg of the University of Wisconsin likes to put it, is to lift you up beside him, let you look down upon an analogue of your own irrational behavior, and give you a chance to say, in effect, "Just look at those ridiculous creatures. *I* would certainly never do anything so silly—and what's more I never will again!"

The world assumed by Aesop is rational and orderly. The only

45

variables are the sentient beings. But such a construction of the world has, in human history, stood only as Working Hypothesis A. Working Hypothesis B, equally ancient, assumes a world in which tragedy is natural and inevitable, assumes that order is not a fact of nature but a limited and fallible human construct. In the "B" world, which is perhaps as valid as the "A," any rationale of behavior which assumes a thoroughly orderly universe must be more or less mistaken, tragic to participate in, comic to view—if viewed, with detachment, from a "B" world standpoint.

Franz Kafka, who properly regarded his writings as comic, is clearly of the "B" world. That he is the subtle Aesop of that world (who lets one smile wryly at one's predicament in a tragic universe) is apparent from the facility with which his explicators have "proved" the analogies between given texts and a variety of political, moral, economic, religious, sexual, biographical, historical, and other contexts. Individual explicators fail only if they are bad workmen and mistake the essential relations or assign an x or y inappropriately, but almost all of them share a logical fallacy, which is to assume *not only* that the story of the fox and the grapes *can* refer to the child who can't spell, but *also* that it *can refer to no other situation.* The analogues offered by the explicators are perfectly sound; what is ridiculous is the insistence of each explicator that the others are wrong.

Therefore, since the vital matters for analogy are the patterns of relation, and not specific *termini* of relations, we shall attend mainly to the former here, and consider the latter only in a contingent role as "in the context of."

There is a pattern of relations, archetypal perhaps, which is familiar to readers of Kafka: that in which feelings of confusion, anger, and guilt follow upon the imperfect and partial recognition that, although the self ought to recognize and accept obligation toward any transcendent value, one may be confronted by the fact that what stands for such a value is not necessarily the value which it stands for, whether or not that value exists apart from what stands for it; and that, consequently, the only route to the transcendent value being through what allegedly stands for it, one may, by attempting to satisfy the obligation to the value, fail to realize the value itself.

One form of this pattern is the fantasy (questioning of friends leads me to believe that it is not uncommon in dreams) in which one is on a road (or in an elevator, or on a train) which is supposed to go to a destination it is imperative to reach; although there is no alternative route, one fears the possibility of having been misled, so that one will never arrive; as time passes and the goal is not perceptibly nearer, anxiety increases; one becomes frantic and fears even to pause for meals; until finally the tension becomes unbearable; *or* until one abandons one's self to the situation (in effect renouncing the destination), and damns one's self as a moral coward.

There seems to be no practical limit to the situations in life which can serve as referents for this sort of configuration: e.g., the predicament of the individual *vis-à-vis* the law court which is consecrated to Justice (in principle), but which, as an *institution,* evolves rules of procedure, patterns of custom, a whole body of bureaucratic machinery that is necessary to the institution, efficient in doing the housekeeping of the court, in perpetuating the institution, but is not necessarily of service to *justice;* as a result the individual deals with a court in which the mediate values (those necessary to maintain the institution) have become the *de facto* ultimate values, and *legal justice* has come to have two meanings—first, the institutional activity, and second, the ideal which the institutional activity is no longer able to serve (if indeed it ever did) precisely in the cases in which concern for the ideals of justice is most desperately needed. The petitioner to the court, therefore, confronts a paradox: the court is the only agency of legal justice; there is no way to secure legal justice through the court. As the only agency of justice, the court deserves the petitioner's respect; as the agency of actual injustice, it deserves his contempt; therefore, although the petitioner may be angry because the only agency of justice does not offer justice, he is prey also to anxiety and guilt, for the only way to justice *must* be the true way, there being no other.

The Church may be conceived to stand between God and Man in a similarly ambiguous relation. The Church is the only official agency between God and Man, but the Church's claim to direct communication with God is much less certain than its actuality as institution (well-characterized by Mr. Eliot in "The Hippopotamus"). For the supplicant, passionate to achieve God, the situation may be desperate: the Church, which is the official (and in this sense, only) route to God is demonstrably a route to its own institutional actuality and not, at least demonstrably, to Godhead.

Both Church and Court present the paradox of bowlegged bifurcation: the "false father" is the only father and therefore must be the true father.

As institution, every organization (church, party, business, bureau, and so on) develops an internal rationale (as against its ideal end) of forms, red tape, bureaucratic machinery—all self-perpetuating but largely irrelevant to the ideal end which the institution allegedly serves. Thus there are: economic systems which fail to keep the citizenry fed, sheltered, and clothed; businesses which no longer produce efficiently because "overhead eats up all the revenues"; political systems set up to provide democracy which destroy democratic processes in the effort to secure them; educational institutions which lose sight of educational ends in meeting "practical exigencies" such as enticing students to register and winning football games (no doubt there could be a complete, and perfectly apt, analogue to Kafka's work drawn from the academic situation).

The paradox is inevitable; for to achieve an end one must, whether one is an individual or an institution, come to some sort of terms with the territory between one's self and the goal. Insofar as one does so, one must recognize and accept values which have, in their own right, existence independent of the mediating role they have between one's purpose and one's goal. (Put in moral terms, the problem is very much like the dilemma so familiar in the novels of Henry James: if you are absolutely pure, you cannot act effectively; if you fail to act effectively, your purity is stained.) Thus to achieve an end by the only means available is also to be diverted from it. The end itself, consequently, has a double existence. Insofar as achievable, it is never ultimate. Insofar as ultimate, it is never achievable. Witness "The Burrow."

As achievable, the end is available by two routes, both ironic, since each is a form of denial of, through indifference to, the ultimate end. Both are apparent in *The Trial* as clearly as anywhere in the work of Kafka. The first is the way of the mundane: to be an efficient bank functionary, and not trouble one's head about the ultimate at all (thus to achieve the serenity of a complete, because limited, orientation— and the securities of animal faith).

This way becomes unavailable to K., partly because he has realized that the microcosm is not the macrocosm, partly because concern for his "case" unfits him for further success in the bank.

The second way lies within the tangible structure—the institution— which stands for the ultimate. It is the way of the priest who is satisfied that the Church pertains to God, whatever its failures; it is the way of the Anglo-Saxon lawyer who is satisfied that the courts lead to justice whenever possible; it is the way of the folk of the "Court" who so puzzle K., and the way of the castle functionaries in *The Castle*. All of them have a *modus operandi* rather than a solution.

The K. of *The Trial* avoids both ways, faces out the tragic irony of the ultimate, and is victorious over compromise and the impulse to accept false solutions—with the inevitable result that he is "destroyed."

The K. of *The Castle* tries to come to terms with the mundane, but without success. He has seen the vision; he cannot simply cultivate cabbages, nor can those who know him as alien, as one who has aspired to the Castle, really accept him as their own.

For the same reason, it is ironic to say that Gregor, in "The Metamorphosis," is "transformed" into an insect. Rather, he recognizes the insect-character of his life, symbolically realizes how remote is his way of life from the human norm. His instinctive wish to get on with his job and fill his role in the hive of commerce (consider his dialogue with the office representative) demonstrates, with bitter humor, how his former life was bounded by the terms of insect society. He is not more, but less, a bug in his new mien; for only the man who has found salvation knows himself as sinner; only the man who has gained wisdom knows his own ignorance: this is the irony of such salvation and such wisdom as men may achieve. Even Gregor's family dimly recognizes that his relation to them is an accusation, an indictment of their failure. Admittedly, Gregor does not entirely comprehend, but the reader should do so, at least after the picnic scene, with its paradox of two mutually exclusive truths: the serenity (and sub-humanity) of ignorance; the anguish (and human achievement) of self-knowledge.

In "A Country Doctor," which is usually accounted a difficult story for the reason that no single social context seems adequate to serve as analogue for it, the *primary* relations are comparatively simple. A man glimpses the "B" world, and is shocked out of "rationalistic complacency," out of the "A" world, for the shock transforms his sense of his own human role, revalues his past-present-future, jolts him into a new ontology.

His new *Weltanschauung* seems prescient because it recognizes an order of necessity invisible to the old:

Never shall I reach home at this rate; my flourishing practice is done for; my successor is robbing me, but in vain, for he cannot take my place; in my house the disgusting groom is raging; Rose is his victim; I do not want to think about it any more. Naked, exposed to the frost of this most unhappy of ages, with an earthly vehicle, unearthly horses, old man that I am, I wander astray. My fur coat is hanging from the back of the gig, but I cannot reach it, and none of my limber pack of patients lifts a finger. Betrayed! Betrayed! A false alarm on the night bell once answered—it cannot be made good, not ever.

Those are the concluding lines of the story. Contrast these which open it:

I was in great perplexity; I had to start on an urgent journey; a seriously ill patient was waiting for me in a village ten miles off; a thick blizzard of snow filled all the wide spaces between him and me; I had a gig, a light gig with big wheels, exactly right for our country roads; muffled in furs, my bag of instruments in my hand, I was in the courtyard all ready for the journey; but there was no horse to be had, no horse. My own horse had died in the night . . . .

There is nothing surreal (*surreal* from the "A" world standpoint) in the opening lines.

The "B" world intrudes almost immediately, when horses and groom are discovered in the pigsty, but is rejected with a comfortable cliché: "The servant girl was standing beside me. 'You never know what you're going to find in your own house,' she said, and we both laughed."

Both the rejection and the laughter are arrested by the behavior of the groom, an ambivalent figure who both aids and injures. Set off by the groom, the horses carry the man ten miles in a seeming instant; the blizzard stops; the moon appears; for nature has become the projection of a point of view.

Experience, as well as time and space, is telescoped. The patient is "seriously ill," is "sound and best turned out of bed with one shove," "might be ill," is "past helping." He is all seekers who have found, all who know their wound: "A fine wound is all I brought into the world; that was my sole endowment." His attitude toward the doctor is expressed by praying, "Let me die"; offering "smiling" welcome; sobbing, "Will you save me?"; crying, angry and contemptuous, "I have very little confidence in you . . . . What I'd like best is to scratch your eyes out."

The visit, the professional call, is clearly synecdochic—"I have been in all the sickrooms, far and wide"; the man is doctor, parson, lover, every guise of the god-surrogate that fails and knows itself false, in some sense, because foredoomed, caught in metaphysical demands beyond its power or any power: "the doctor is supposed to be omnipotent with his merciful surgeon's hand. Well, as it pleases them; I have not thrust my services on them; if they misuse me for sacred ends, I let that happen to me too." He is stripped of professional garb, and of the rationalistic illusion of self-determination as well: "you were only blown in here; you didn't come on your own feet"; he is corrupted in the attempt to purify: "they laid me down . . . on the side of the wound"; he is sinned against and sinning (e.g., in the defeat by, and abandoning of Rose to, the groom).

Like other tragic heroes of Kafka's comedies, whose new prescience cuts them off from the comfortable notion that speech is able to communicate real meaning, he recognizes the failure of "A" world language to communicate "B" world perceptions: "To write prescriptions is easy, but to come to an understanding with people is hard." Having gained a new world, he is lost in tragic wisdom and ontological loneliness: "Naked, exposed to the frost of this most unhappy of ages, with an earthly vehicle, unearthly horses, old man that I am, I wander astray." He has transcended the catalogs of science (consider the useless medical bag, and the worms of no phylum in the unnatural wound), and the rational superstitions of the schools: "a school choir with the teacher at the head of it stood before the house and sang . . . to an utterly simple tune: Strip his clothes off, then he'll heal us, / If he doesn't, kill him dead!" Knowing his failure, he must yet suffer the burden of ironic success—"O be joyful, all you patients,/ The doctor's laid in bed beside you!"—which underscores the ultimate indictment presented by the unearthly horses at the window, their whinnying a "noise . . . ordained by heaven."

Here, as in all literary art, what is of first importance is not the fable but the dramatic surface, the immanent qualitative reality of the experience of "A Country Doctor" itself. Taken as *oracle,* however, if one picks vocabulary from the "B" world, or as *slide rule,* if from the "A," the story may be particularized, for those who insist upon particularizations, in the local contexts of numberless analogues; for once the primary *relations* are apparent, there is no problem in providing *termini.* Consider the following examples:

Sampler A.—This is simply the paradox of the medical man. The doctor ignores, and in effect, sacrifices, his own household in order to accept the demands of professional life. Ironically, the sacrifice is wasted, becomes in fact almost criminal, precisely in those cases in which he attends patients who are mortally ill. As sooner or later he comes to realize unless he is a complete fool, his role is more absurd when he visits a patient beyond medical aid than when he calls on one "who doesn't really need a doctor," and in the former case, rather than the latter, it is charlatanism for him to go through the professional motions which reassure the family, because, in his helplessness, the doctor is, in effect, in the same bed with the patient. Taken against the whole universe of the situation, moreover, his professional services are multiply absurd—destructive of his home, of himself, and perhaps (in a more basic sense than the medical) of the patient, if for example the doctor is called in preference to the priest who might claim the last moments of the soul. Then the doctor's activity serves only to confirm the superstitious belief and/or cynicism of the citizenry toward medicine, and works to intensify his own increasing sense of the hollowness of his own pretensions, of his vulnerability to the horse-laugh of the gods, of the desperation of his loneliness.

Sampler B.—The so-called doctor is roused by homosexual desire. In the opening scene he admits to having ignored Rose, and his anger at the rapacious groom is coupled with the motive to have the groom accompany him on a ride. The death of his horse correlates exactly with the rejection of heterosexual desires, and the new horses, which are "magnificent," were concealed in what had been to him a pigsty. He is a doctor in the ironic sense of assuager of (sexual) pain, his own and his "patient's," and in his ambivalent relation to the patient's appeal, itself ambivalent, to "let me die," that is, leave me to my present sexual predilections, and "save me," that is, reconcile me to heterosexuality: resolved for the patient of course when he realizes the "doctor" is willing to accept the "wound." For the "doctor," the realization that he himself has accepted homosexuality, and has passed into another world (with all the reorientations that passage will require), is an awareness that begins slowly, but quickly accelerates as he feels himself alienated, naked, unable to return to "normal" life, betrayed.

Sampler C.—Obviously the story is an ironic History of the Jews. At a point when the motive power of the faith has been lost, when the relations between the Learned in the Law (the doctor) and the society

(Rose) have degenerated to the mere rituals of institutional house-keeping, there emerges—in what is symbolically the community of the unclean, the pigsty—the ambivalent messianic faith Christianity (Church of the Prince of Peace, and Church Militant). Although Judaism attempts to deal with the problem of the newer faith, it has lost its capacity for healthy growth; it exists in the hothouse atmosphere of the ghetto; the open spaces where the new religion thrives are to it only sterile and icy wastes. Even the faithful (the "patient") view their situation with resignation, or with desperation, or with skepticism. Thus the wound in the side of the false messiah (plotted, but not inflicted, by the Jewish hierarchy: "You brute . . . do you want a whipping?"), paradoxically, festers in the society of the ghetto. No matter, then, that the messiah was false. The wound is real, and so are the taunts from the fringes of the community, the echoes of the Gospels, taunting the faith which never achieved its own Messiah. ("Strip his clothes off, then he'll heal us,/ If he doesn't, kill him dead!/ Only a doctor, only a doctor.") The ghettos of the victims are the shards of the world of the chosen people, and tragedy eats like acid at the tables of the law: "Never shall I reach home at this rate; my flourishing practice is done for; my successor is robbing me, but in vain, for he cannot take my place; in my house the disgusting groom is raging; Rose is his victim; I do not want to think about it any more."

Sampler D.—We have here the situation which would occur if K.'s advocate in *The Trial* were to recognize that his semiofficial status was not only ambiguous but specious, that the logic he brought to K.'s case was irrelevant, that his detachment was merely the illusion of the legalistic mind—if, in short, he were forced to the realization that he is vulnerable to trial just as K. is. Like his client he would discover himself in a new dimension, but there would be this difference; for him there would be added the terror of the familiar-become-strange. He could not return to his profession, as K. could not return to the bank; and truly he could say of any successor to his practice that "he cannot take my place"—that is, he cannot understand what I now understand, and he cannot yet know how close he is to the two-edged gift of such understanding.

At this point, obviously, all the familiar analogues which have been posited for *The Trial, The Castle,* and no doubt "The Metamorphosis,"

William C. Rubinstein

A Report to an Academy

KAFKA's story, "A Report to an Academy," has never aroused much enthusiasm among his critics. To Charles Neider, "'A Report to an Academy' . . . aside from its bright satirical tone and its empathy for the ape, is merely an exercise, whose function is to satirize the spiritual in man. The education of the ape, his transformation into a human being, depends upon a system of repression and destruction of memories. Kafka, like Swift, implies that man is a beast." [1]

The comparison with Swift is implicit also in Brod's brief comment: "Or, what is still more horrible [than the degradation of "The Metamorphosis"], he lets the animal be raised to the level of a human being, but to what a level of humanity, to a masquerade at which mankind is unmasked." [2] This interpretation, that the ape is in some way a satire of humanity, is approved of by Herbert Tauber, who writes that the ape "is really a picture of the everyday man who expands himself in the superficial, who cannot fulfil his being and realize it in freedom, but whose first commandment is to adapt himself." [3]

Now there is no doubt that in general the story supports these explications, but this reader feels that there must be some more specific object of the satire than humanity. There seems to be a precision in the choice of the symbols which is not reflected in the analyses of the critics, possibly because they have not considered the story worthy of a full-length treatment. Then too, the "bright satirical tone" reveals an underlying savage bitterness, an almost personal anger, which

55

suggests that the story is more than "merely an exercise" in reversing "The Metamorphosis."

The interpretation put forward in this paper will, possibly, seem extravagant and even outrageous to many of Kafka's admirers. It is intended merely as a suggestion to be considered tentatively until some more satisfactory explanation of the symbols is made. If it sends old readers back to the story and inspires others to read it for the first time, it will have performed its function.

Since many of the readers of the novels are not familiar with "A Report to an Academy," a brief summary of it is given here.

An ape is lecturing to an academy on his life before he transformed himself into a human being. Unfortunately he can tell the academy very little about it, for, since his transformation, he has forgotten the past. He was captured in Africa, and his first clear recollections are of the cage in which he was confined on the boat to Europe. Here he suffered numerous abuses. The members of the crew spit in his face, laughed at him, prodded him with sticks, and burned him with their pipes. He soon realized that the only way for him to get out of his cage was to become a human being. With great effort he succeeded in doing this. The climax of his efforts came the day he was able to drink "schnapps," a feat which repeatedly nauseated him, but one on which the members of the crew placed the greatest importance—the ape could not understand why. After that his progress was very rapid, although marred once by the fact that one of his teachers, as a result of his contact with him, almost became an ape himself. Today he has a smug satisfaction in the thought that he has reached the intellectual level of an average European. He is very tactful about mentioning the abuses he suffered as an ape and obsequiously goes out of his way to excuse human beings for having inflicted them. In the evenings, he goes home to his mistress, a half-human, partially crazed ape.

The key to the interpretation of the story is the symbolic significance of the ape. In order to determine precisely what he represents, it might be well to begin with the most trying experience in his transformation and the one to which the most space is devoted in the story.

"My worst trouble," the ape tells the academy, "came from the schnapps bottle. The smell of it revolted me; I forced myself to it as best I could; but it took weeks for me to master my repulsion. This inward conflict, strangely enough, was taken more seriously by the crew than anything else about me."

One of the crew members considers it his special duty to teach the ape to drink from the bottle. "He could not understand me, he wanted to solve the enigma of my being." Very patiently, this human being repeats before the cage the ceremony of drinking the schnapps. The ape describes himself as "enchanted with my gradual enlightenment," but this "theoretical exposition" exhausts him so that he hangs limply to the bars of his cage.

Of course there is obvious irony in describing the spectacle of a man drinking a bottle of whiskey as an enlightening or theoretical exposition, but the very obviousness of it should put the reader on his guard. Kafka does not usually work for such crude effects. It is, therefore, quite possible that some deeper meaning is intended, a double irony of some kind.

In spite of his "theoretical instruction," it is a long time before the ape can drink from the bottle. Each time he is about to do it, revulsion seizes him, and he throws the bottle from his lips. His teacher alternately tortures and cajoles him. The ape cannot understand his revulsion, and both he and the teacher try to conquer it, for "we were both fighting on the same side against the nature of apes."

Finally, "one evening before a large circle of spectators—perhaps there was a celebration of some kind, a gramophone was playing, an officer was circulating in front of the crew," the ape succeeds in drinking the schnapps. Instantly his transformation, in spite of a few subsequent lapses, is made. He breaks into human speech, "and with this outburst broke into the human community." He now feels the previously mocking and hostile faces of the crew "like a caress over my sweat-drenched body."

What is the significance of this strange episode at the climax of the story? Why does the crew place such great importance on the ape's drinking the schnapps—an emphasis which the ape is unable to understand? Why does drinking instantly make the ape a human being?

It may be that in accordance with the usual interpretation Kafka considers drinking the most characteristic symbol of human degradation, and, therefore, the ape is accepted as soon as he has learned to drink. But such an interpretation seems rather weak. The ape's teacher is not a drunkard, and intoxication does not seem to be the aim of his drinking. The drinking is rather a ritual, for the ape must learn not merely to drink, but to follow every movement and gesture of his teacher in doing it.

This ritual drinking on which such great emphasis is placed, which must be preceded by theoretical instruction, which is given during "a celebration of some kind," and which instantly transforms the ape into a human being accepted by the crew, is far more likely, it seems to this writer, to be a symbol for the sacrament of Communion, which is itself a symbolic act denoting the acceptance of Christ. By drinking the schnapps, the ape, or whatever he represents, becomes a Christian and is welcomed joyously by the assembled celebrants of the rite. If this interpretation is correct, the story is really about a conversion.

But who is the convert? Obviously his conversion is not a sincere one. He wants to be a human being only so that he will not be spit on, burned, or kept in a cage. Although the schnapps bottle revolts him to the last, he drinks in order to be accepted as human. His obsequiousness before the *real* human beings of the academy, even after his transformation, makes him a despicable figure. He is quite possibly a Jew who has allowed himself to be converted to Christianity in order to escape persecution.

Is the symbolism of the rest of the story consistent with this interpretation? The ape tells the academy that he could never have accomplished what he has, "had I been stubbornly set on clinging to my origins. . . ." He is satisfied that the "strong wind that blew after me out of my past" has slackened. He is very angry at the people who point out his resemblance to another ape. He tells his audience that he cannot remember his life as an ape, but this turns out to be a lie, for he remembers quite vividly the various torments he endured.

The motivation for the lie is his craven reluctance to accuse the members of the audience of having persecuted him. He can hardly avoid doing this if he remembers his past in any detail. Thus when he does mention some of these torments, he is careful to excuse his tormentors. His teacher burned him, but the ape now realizes that he did it with the best of intentions. The scar he bears was—"let me be particular in the choice of a word for this particular purpose, to avoid misunderstanding—the scar made by a wanton shot." Although he was intolerably cramped in his cage, that is apparently the way apes are kept and that is all there is to it. As a matter of fact, he could not "risk" talking about his past at all "if I were not quite sure of myself and if my position on all the great variety stages of the civilized world had not become quite unassailable."

The ape comes from the Gold Coast, but he has no personal recollection at all of his life before his capture. "For the story of my capture

I must depend on the evidence of others." His "own memories gradually begin—between decks in the Hagenbeck steamer, inside a cage." Here he must "stay motionless with raised arms, crushed against a wooden wall." Although it may seem extravagant, the early life of the ape is probably that portion of pre-European, Jewish history for which he must rely on the Old Testament, the evidence of others. All he can remember personally is his life in the cage (the ghetto, specifically, but more generally the whole situation of European Jews at this time).

Since life in the cage is unbearable, the ape must find some way to get out of it. Two courses are open to him: to attempt an escape to freedom (Zionism), or to become a human being (assimilation and conversion). The dangers of the first course prevent the ape from ever considering it seriously. He is afraid he will drown in the ocean, and even if he does manage to get back to his home, what is there to prevent his recapture?

Actually he does not want freedom, but merely "a way out" of the cage. So he decides to become a human being "even though these men in themselves had no great attraction for me." After his conversion, he has several lapses, and, in order to avoid being put into the zoological gardens, on his arrival in Hamburg he embarks on a strenuous program of training. He engages teachers for himself and puts them into five communicating rooms. "By dint of leaping from one room to another" he takes lessons from all five at once. Who these five teachers are it is difficult to say. Possibly they are the four evangelists and Paul, but this is only a desperate guess.

At the end of his lecture, the ape again congratulates himself on his transformation. "In itself that might be nothing to speak of, but it is something insofar as it has helped me out of my cage. . . ." But in spite of his progress, he goes home in the evening to "a half-trained little chimpanzee . . . [with] the insane look of the bewildered, half-broken animal in her eyes," a look which the ape "cannot bear."

There is some interesting bibliographical evidence which may have a bearing on the interpretation of the story. According to Angel Flores, "A Report to an Academy" first appeared in the collection, *A Country Doctor.*[4] Brod, however, without giving any details, mentions that there was an earlier publication in a magazine called *Der Jude.*[5] The story first appeared in the eighth number of the second volume of this magazine. It was the second part of a pair called "Two Animal Stories," the first part of which was the short piece, "Jackals and Arabs." [6]

Der Jude was conceived and published by Martin Buber, a leading Zionist. In the opening number (April, 1916), there was a declaration of purpose: to spread and promote knowledge of Judaism. Throughout the eight years of the magazine's history, it dealt exclusively with Jewish problems, usually from a Zionist viewpoint. While there is not the slightest reason to suppose that Buber would not have published a story by a friend of his friend Brod, unless it explicitly furthered the views of the magazine, the appearance of "A Report to an Academy" in *Der Jude* does add, however little, to the probability that the story dealt with the problems of European Jewry.

The Jew who, for some ulterior motive, allowed himself to be converted was a popular villain in the Yiddish literature of Europe. Kafka mentions in his diary (October 4, 6, 8, 1911), for example, seeing a play, *Der Meshumed* (*The Apostate*), in which Seidemann, a converted Jew, is also the murderer of his own wife and the would-be murderer of his daughter's fiancé. Bad as the play was, it made a profound impression on Kafka, for he devoted several pages of the diary to a summary and analysis of it. It probably furnished him with the first sketchy outlines for the two "assistants" in *The Castle*,[7] and after being transmuted in his artistic consciousness might very well have emerged as "A Report to an Academy."

NOTES

1. Charles Neider, *The Frozen Sea* (Oxford, 1948), p. 81.

2. Max Brod, *Franz Kafka: A Biography,* tr. by G. Humphreys Roberts (New York, 1947), p. 135.

3. Herbert Tauber, *Franz Kafka: An Interpretation of his Works,* tr. by G. Humphreys Roberts and Roger Senhouse (New Haven, 1948), p. 71.

4. Angel Flores, *Franz Kafka: A Chronology and Bibliography* (Baltimore, 1944), p. 8.

5. Max Brod, "Epilogue," in Kafka's *Penal Colony,* tr. by Willa and Edwin Muir (New York, 1948), p. 318.

6. Franz Kafka, "Zwei Tiergeschichten: Schakale und Araber; Ein Bericht für eine Akademie," *Der Jude* (Berlin: October and November, 1917), II, 488, 559–65.

7. This suggestion is made by Brod in the notes to the *Diaries* (for the entry of October 4, 1911).

R. W. Stallman

A Hunger-Artist

"A HUNGER-ARTIST" epitomizes Kafka's theme of the corruption of interhuman relationships, as one of his critics defines it. It is one of his perfections, if not his best story, and it belongs surely with the greatest short stories of our time.

Realism of detail within a framework of symbolism, to quote Max Lerner, is Kafka's unique quality and his special gift to modern fiction. The world of a Kafka story is one of mystery, the mysterious being obtained by a realism pushed to the extremes. As a critic of *The Castle* points out, Kafka subjects his details "to a transmutation which makes them seem to compete with each other in enveloping us with some weighty secret." The weighty secret remains a mystification for many readers, even for Einstein. "I couldn't read it for its perversity," he is reported to have remarked upon returning a Kafka novel to Thomas Mann. "The human mind isn't complicated enough." One critic of "The Burrow" describes that story as "in itself a 'burrow' of the most complicated construction," with an ingenious system of intertwining tunnels of which he interprets the "inner fortress" alone, "whence the whole structure can be overlooked."

"A Hunger-Artist" is an allegory, but Kafka's method is quite different from that of such an allegorist as Bunyan. In *Pilgrim's Progress* each character represents the trait, virtue, or vice which his name signifies—Christian, Faithful, Envy, Lord Hategood, and so on. Bunyan manipulates these characters through a story whose every element has a direct meaning in his moral parable. Further, these meanings are constant throughout the story: Faithful is always faithful, Envy is always envious, Apollyon is always the epitome of evil, the town of Vanity Fair is so called because "*all* that is there sold, or that cometh thither, is vanity." In the allegories of the quite different but equally familiar *Gulliver's Travels* the same constancy of image is found. The rope-skipping Lilliputians satirize political preferment; the dispute between the Big-Endians and the Little-Endians satirizes theological controversy. Both sets of terms are equally fantastic, but the one having to do with egg-breaking has no connection with the one having to do with rope-jumping. There is no overlap of meaning from one unit into the next.

Kafka's method is very different. He employs symbols rather than allegorical images. He assigns multiple meanings to his realistic or fantastic details; their significance is therefore not constant, nor can they be paraphrased back into point-by-point equivalents. As D. H. Lawrence puts it, "an allegorical image has a *meaning*. Mr. Facing-both-ways has a meaning. But I defy you to lay your finger on the full meaning of Janus, who is a symbol." Kafka employs continuous symbolization. Therefore we find his images meaning different things not only at different times, but *at the same time*. There is a constant interweaving of symbolical meanings, an overlapping of allegorical patterns. As we shall see, it is possible to read the meanings of "A Hunger-Artist" on at least three different levels; there is never a time when we can say that any of its elements means precisely and exactly this.

The same thing is true of the story pattern. Bunyan and Swift employ narratives that proceed in logical order from their assumptions. Bunyan assumes that Christian will make a journey through a land which never existed to a City not of this life; Swift assumes the tiny world of Lilliput and the gigantic one of Brobdingnag. Having postulated these, however, they stick to their facts; the frame of reference is always constant. It is no accident that *Pilgrim's Progress* and *Gulliver's Travels* have been read as adventure stories by generations of children happily ignorant of allegory and satire.

Kafka is no more bound by precision in his narrative than in his symbols. He has a fantastic genius for imparting a sense of everyday reality while completely ignoring everyday logic. His symbolic objects do not conform to the nature of objects in the actual world; they are subject not to the determinate laws of nature, but rather to the laws of that unique world in which they have their special function. The hunger-artist hires himself out to a great circus, an enormous, complex, and efficient machine which nevertheless contrives to forget his existence so completely that he is finally discovered only by probing into the "putrid straw" of his "empty" cage. Obviously this is a circus of fantasy; like the rest of Kafka's "facts," it is an imaginary phenomenon that belongs to a dream world. In "A Hunger-Artist" the laws of physics and biology are defied, the facts of human existence distorted. Though all the details are apparently simple and commonplace, they become, on closer examination, elusive, charged with multiple significance. It is impossible to keep Kafka's facts as facts or to suppress or minimize their metaphorical character.

The present essay attempts to open up the cage of Kafka's meaning in "A Hunger-Artist." [1] But first, as a starting point for our analysis, here is the story at its literal plane, a matter-of-fact account stripped of interpretation:

The story is about a once-popular spectacle staged for the entertainment of a pleasure-seeking public: the exhibition of a professional "hunger-artist" performing in a cage of straw his stunt of fasting. His cage's sole decoration is a clock. His spectators see him as a trickster and common circus-freak and therefore they expect him to cheat, to break fast on the sly. But fasting is his sole reason for existing, his life purpose; not even under compulsion would he partake of food. For him, to fast is the easiest thing he can do; and so he says, but no one believes in him. Because the public distrusts him, he is guarded—usually by three butchers—and prevented from fasting beyond a forty-day period, not for humane reasons, but only because patronage stops after that time. His guards tempt him with food and sometimes mistreat him; yet they breakfast on food supplied at his expense! A great public festival celebrates his achievement, and thus he is "honored by the world." But when he is removed from his cage he collapses in a rage, not from hunger, but from having been cheated of the honor of fasting on and on and on and of becoming thus "the greatest hunger-artist of all time." Though emaciated almost to the point of death, he quickly recovers and after brief intervals of recuperation performs again and again.

Nowadays, however, he has been abandoned for other spectacles. People visit his cage in the circus tent, but only because it is next to the menagerie. His spectators are fascinated by the animals. All's changed: there is, apparently, no clock, and the once beautiful signs to announce the purpose of his act have been torn down. Now no tally is kept of the number of fasting days achieved. There are no guards. "And so the hunger-artist fasted on without hindrance, as he had once dreamed of doing . . . just as he had once predicted, but no one counted the days; no one, not even the hunger-artist himself, knew how great his achievement was and his heart grew heavy." Thus the world robs him of his reward. Indifference replaces admiration and on this note he expires. He is buried with the straw of his cage and replaced by a panther, who devours fiercely the food he naturally craves. The people crowd about his cage.

We notice that the facts in this "matter-of-fact" account are not in themselves complete or sufficient, and that our attempt to take them at their matter-of-fact or literal level is quite impossible. They seem to compete with each other and to thrust us beyond their literal properties into the plane of their allegorical significance. That clock seems to be simply a clock; it does not apparently represent anything else. And yet no literal meaning can be ascribed to that bizarre clock. It strikes the hour just like a real clock, but (so to speak) it does not appear to tick. The life of this hunger-artist is unclocked. He exists outside time, and periodically he survives starvation sieges no ordinary man could endure. (Actually, a calendar would be the logical means for reckoning the artist's fasting days.) As for the other facts, these objects likewise suggest symbolic significance. It is impossible to reduce Kafka's facts to a single self-consistent system of meaning. The trouble is that his meanings emerge at several planes at once, and the planes are interconnected. No complete paraphrase is possible.

We cannot confine Kafka's meaning to a single circle of thought. The plight of the hunger-artist in his cage represents the plight of the artist in the modern world: his dissociation from the society in which he lives. By this reading of the story, "A Hunger-Artist" is a sociological allegory. But we can also interpret the hunger-artist to represent a mystic, a holy man, or a priest. By this reading the story allegorizes in historical perspective the plight of religion. A third possible interpretation projects us into a metaphysical allegory: the hunger-artist represents spirit, man as a spiritual being; the panther, in contrast, represents matter, the animal nature of man. If the story is translated into metaphysical terms, the division is between the spiritual and the physical; into religious terms, between the divine and the human, the soul and the body; into sociological terms, between the artist and his society. Kafka's blueprint—the groundplan of ideas upon which he has built this structure of parables—is toolmarked with these three different systems of thought.

Consider first the story as an allegory of the dilemma of the artist. He is set in contrast to the multitude. The people who attend his exhibitions of fasting cannot comprehend his art. "Just try to explain the art of fasting to someone! He who has no feeling for it simply cannot comprehend it." The artist starves himself for the sake of his vision. He has faith in his vision, faith in himself, and integrity of aesthetic conscience. As the initiated alone understood, "the hunger-artist would never under any circumstances, not even under compulsion, partake of any nourishment during the period of fasting. His honor as an artist forbade such a thing." It is his vision, solely this, which nourishes him. Of course the artist can "fast" as no one else can do. It's not everyone who is an artist. We concede, "in view of the peculiar nature of this art which showed no flagging with increasing age," the claim he makes of limitless capacity for creating works of art. But if his public is devoid of any sympathetic understanding of the artist and of his art, if his public has no faith in him, how then can he cling to this faith in himself? It is because his public is an unbeliever that the artist is in a cage (the cage symbolizes his isolation). Society and the artist—each disbelieves in the other. And so the artist comes to disbelieve, finally, in himself; he cannot survive in isolation.

The hunger-artist is emaciated because of the disunity within himself, which is the result of his dissociation of soul from body, and because of the disjunction between himself and his society. It is his denial of the world of materiality that is the source of his gnawing doubt and "constant state of depression." He repudiates half of life, and the multitude repudiate him. The public reject the emaciated body of the artist for the healthy body of the panther—they reject art for life itself. These two occupants of the cage, the purely spiritual and the purely bestial, represent, then, the dual nature of man. The people outside the cage, with whom he is also contrasted, crave the same food as the panther. For them, as for the beast, their joy in living issues from their throat—and from their belly. These human and bestial beings represent the sensuous physical realm of matter. They are all-flesh, whereas the hunger-artist is no-flesh. In the one we have pure matter; in the other, pure spirit. But the hunger-artist, as pure soul, is a failure. Though he is apparently free from those gnawing dissatisfactions which our purely physical appetites create in us again and again, nevertheless he is not entirely free from the claims of the body, from the claims of matter, from the claims of the world in which he lives. At the same time that

artist. It is time that triumphs over the very one who denies the flux
of time, which is our present reality. The clock in his cage is a mockery
of the artist's faith in the immortality of his creative act or vision, a
mockery of his faith in his art as an artifice of eternity. The tragedy of Kafka's hunger-artist is not that he dies, but that he fails to
die into life. As he dies he seeks recognition from those whom he
has all his life repudiated: " 'I always wanted you to admire my fasting,' said the hunger-artist." It is his confession that spirit has no
absolute sovereignty over matter, soul has no absolute sovereignty over
body, and art has no absolute sovereignty over life. In "Observations
on Kafka" James Burnham defines Kafka's metaphysics: "His world is
split by the absolute Manichaean division into Good and Evil, which
is identified with the division between Light and Darkness, Spirit and
Matter . . . . As with all Manichaeans, the ambivalence remains: He
[Kafka] longs for Matter, for the evil natural social world, at the same
time that he denies it; he is appalled by Spirit even while he must seek
it absolutely." Kafka's hunger-artist represents Kafka's doctrine: "There
is only a spiritual world; what we call the physical world is the evil
in the spiritual one, and what we call evil is only a necessary moment
in our endless development." "A Hunger-Artist" is a kind of critique
of this doctrine. Matter here triumphs over Spirit.

Throughout the story the author laments the passing of our hunger-
artists, their decline and extinction in our present-day civilization. But
nonetheless throughout the story all the logic is weighted against this
hunger-artist's efforts at autarchy. In his last words we are given his
confession that the artist must come to terms with life, with the civilization in which he lives, the world of total reality. "Forgive me, all of
you," he whispers to the circus manager, as though in a confessional
before some priest. And they forgive him. They forgive him for his
blasphemy against nature. The hunger-artist seeks Spirit absolutely;
he denies the "evil natural social world" at the same time that he longs
for it. And this is his dilemma, even as it is ours. It is not possible for
man to achieve a condition of pure spirituality, nor again is it possible
for him to achieve a synthesis of spirit and matter. As the agent of
divine purity the hunger-artist is a failure. His failure is signified, for
instance, on the occasion when he answers the person who has explained his emaciation as being caused by a lack of food: he answers
"by flying into a rage and terrifying all those around him by shaking
the bars of his cage like a wild animal." This reversion to the animal

divests him momentarily of the divine, and it also betrays the split-soul conflict within him. His location next to the menagerie serves as reminder that the claims of the animal body are necessary claims upon the soul and cannot be denied. And this is true even though matter is wholly evil (i.e., "the evil odors from the stalls," etc.); complete separation from reality can never be obtained. (Compare the idea of "complete detachment from the earth" as it figures in "The Burrow.") Pure Spirit is as vacuous as Pure Matter.

In the same way that Kafka's sets of facts can be translated into allegorical terms at the philosophical and aesthetic levels of meaning, so too in terms of the religious allegory the multiple meanings of his facts overlap. Our post-Renaissance world has discarded the philosopher, the artist, and the mystic. The hunger-artist as mystic-faster is dead. Call him priest or artist, he has been rejected by the "pleasure-seeking multitude" and replaced by other amusements; for instance, by the exhibition of a live panther. It was different in times past. For example, in the Middle Ages and in the Renaissance he "lived in apparent glory, honored by the world." Then he had his patron. (The patron of the artist was the impresario.) He had his critics, the butchers who guarded him out of the public distrust of his creative act. And he had his historians, the attendants who recorded his creative act or kept count of his remarkable performances. In those times he was at least admired for his achievements as an imitator of life. In his cage he imitated a panther: ". . . deathly pale, dressed in black tights, his ribs protruding powerfully, sometimes nodding politely and answering questions with a forced smile, even thrusting his arm through the bars to let them feel his emaciation . . . and paying attention to no one . . . looking straight before him with eyes almost closed. . . ." But what a poor imitation of real life he presented! In those times he was at least celebrated (albeit, not without hypocrisy), honored by rituals conscientiously enacted upon appointed fast days. Consider this hunger-artist as mystic-faster or priest. At one time, everyone attended his services daily. Regular subscribers sat, as in church pews, "before the small latticed cage for days on end." Everyone pretended to marvel at his holy fast. Actually, however, not one worshiper had faith. Nevertheless, despite this sham of faith in him, he submitted again and again to crucifixion by these pretenders to faith. He was a martyr for his divine cause. The multitude, because "it was the stylish thing to do," attended his "small latticed cage"—they attended it as they might a confessional box. But the multitude, since it does not understand what Faith is, has no sin to confess. The hunger-priest hears no confession. (Ironically it is he who, in dying, confesses.) In short, all mankind—apart from a few acolytes to his cult, disbelieves this Christ who many times died for man's sake. And when he dies, see how these disbelievers exploit the drama of his death. Here is Kafka's parody on the drama of the Virgin mourning the loss of her Son.

But now there happened the thing which always happened at this point. The impresario would come, and silently—for the music rendered speech impossible—he would raise his arms over the hunger-artist as if inviting heaven to look down upon its work here upon the straw, this pitiful martyr—and martyr the hunger-artist was, to be sure, though in an entirely different sense. Then he would grasp the hunger-artist about his frail waist, trying as he did to make it obvious by his exaggerated caution with what a fragile object he was dealing, and after surreptitiously shaking him a little and causing his legs to wobble and his body to sway uncontrollably, would turn him over to the ladies, who had meanwhile turned as pale as death.

The ladies who so cruelly sentimentalize over his martyrdom represent sympathy without understanding; a sympathy which is devoid of understanding is mere self-sentiment. One of the ladies weeps—but not for him. She breaks into tears only in shame for having touched him. "And the entire weight of his body, light though it was, rested upon one of the ladies, who, breathless and looking imploringly for help (she had not pictured this post of honor thus), first tried to avoid contact with the hunger-artist by stretching her neck as far as possible, and then . . . she broke into tears to the accompaniment of delighted laughter from the audience . . . ." It is a mock lamentation that these two Marys perform. What a difference between the theme of the Virgin mourning the loss of her Son as treated in Kafka's parody and as depicted in the famous *Avignon Pièta* or in Giotto's *Lamentation*.

It is thus that the religious and the metaphysical and the aesthetic meanings of "A Hunger-Artist" coincide: (1) Christ is truly dead. Our post-Renaissance world has discarded the act of faith from its reality. (2) For the mystic, as for the artist, there is no resurrection because today not spirit but matter alone is recognized. And as we have seen, it is recognized, this triumph of matter over spirit, even by the dying mystic, who ends a skeptic and a defeatist (not unlike Kafka himself): I had to fast, because I could find no food to my liking. Fasting is my destiny. But " 'if I had found it, believe me, I should have caused no stir, I should have eaten my fill just as you do, and all the others.' Those were his last words, but in his glazed eyes there remained the firm, though no longer proud, conviction that he was still fasting."

NOTE

1. This essay represents a revised version of the original published in *Accent* 8 (1948) and reprinted elsewhere. The text of Kafka's story used here is the translation by M. L. Nielsen, first published 1946 in *Rocky Mountain Review*.

Carl R. Woodring

Josephine the Singer, or the Mouse Folk

KAFKA's fictions spiral metaphorically. Reading "Josephine" alertly is in one aspect like putting back together the leaves of a disassembled cabbage through which a supernaturally hungry worm and snail have bored separate holes. In the restored cabbage, each hole of continuous meaning leads from suggestion on one area of the surface inward through tightly curled leaves to a firm pith and out again through leaves of connotation to the outermost and largest leaf. Each leaf curls in metaphorical relation around other leaves. Analytic passage through "Josephine" can follow—in a wormlike way—either the songstress herself or the mouse folk among whom she sings. The botanist in his laboratory may devise other means of analysis, but only by proper alignment of holes through the various leaves can the lay reader of Kafka possess and enjoy the continuity of reference.

Thomas Hardy divided his novels into tragedies, romances, fantasies, and ingenuities. Distinguished somewhat similarly, Kafka's fictions could be called perplexities, frustrations, affections or acceptances, and agonies. "Josephine" belongs to the group of affections and acceptances. This story of an heroic, conceited, scorched soul has pathos without agony. It bears another striking trait of Kafka's later stories. In nearly every fiction by Kafka, symbols can have a separate aura in separate leaves or areas of reference. In the later stories, the meaning passes from leaf to leaf in such a way that a given symbol may, in any one leaf, successfully symbolize itself. In only a petty or a figurative sense could the surveyor in *The Castle* be said to symbolize a surveyor, but in "Josephine" a singer is masterfully symbolized by a singer; here an artist is an artist is the artist.

Josephine regards herself as the only artistic singer among mouselike people. The narrator has noticed that the people's casual piping in workaday moods is almost, but not quite, like Josephine's unique kind of piping. The folk, too pressed by troubles to care deeply for music or other art, nevertheless give considerable attention and respect to Josephine. They take a group pride in her talent. Feeling in her own conceit that her art cannot be understood by the crowd, that in the absence of understanding she deserves clear and permanent recognition, that she strengthens the people in crises more than they in their fatherliness protect her, Josephine has for a long time petitioned fruitlessly to be exempted from all mundane work. Spasmodically she has worked, balked, petitioned, sung with more feeling; the people have refused firmly. Recently in her struggle she has adopted such unworthy methods as cutting short her grace notes. Just now she has disappeared, she will not sing. The narrator, one of those thought of as her opposition, can see no course for Josephine now but descent to oblivion.

At its pith, "Josephine" concerns a soloist and leading actress, or "male impersonator," attached to a Jewish theatrical troupe singing plays (operas) in Yiddish, of the kind to which Kafka had become attracted in 1910 and especially in 1911, when he first saw Mrs. Klug and Mrs. Tschissik perform at the Café Savoy in Prague. The mouse folk make up the stilled audience for such a troupe. This small mouselike group (only the title declares them actually to be mice) by its mousiness and its cohesive isolation carries the referent outward to the Jewish people—Jews in the congruent circles of Prague, of Eastern Europe, of the world today and back through their racial history. ". . . Josephine's thin piping amidst grave decisions is almost like our people's precarious existence amidst the tumult of a hostile world." And "among our people there is no age of youth, scarcely the briefest childhood." There seems to be once a Zionist reference to the Diaspora, to the difficulties of living dispersed. The mice's racial dreams need to be interpreted and expressed.

If the reader moves from café or theater to the synagogue, Josephine sings as the cantor: "Was her actual piping notably louder and more alive than the memory of it will be? Was it even in her lifetime more than a simple memory?" P. P. J. van Caspel, by a brief article in *Neophilologus,* 1953, would make the songstress represent the Hebrew prophets, specifically Jeremiah. (In German *Jeremias* has the same number of letters as *Josefine.*) Josephine's earliest namesake was rather Joseph, interpreter of dreams; perhaps her most important was Joseph K. of *The Trial.* Regarding Kafka's meaning as essentially religious, Herbert Tauber would read in the songstress' piping the reduced art of prophecy among modern Jews. True, half-believing prediction and half-hearted prayer typify a modern assemblage, but the story "Josephine" is not, I think, primarily religious. In Josephine one may find the Yiddish writer of belles-lettres, a Sholom Aleichem, a Morris Rosenfeld, a Joseph Lateiner. The Zionist writers, whatever their language, bring us nearer to the periphery, and Jewish novelists still nearer. For Josephine sings just such unorthodox, unique creations as this fiction in which she appears, and represents at the same time the universal artist.

Recent critical writing about Kafka has contained considerable reference to totemism. Without abandoning his previous identification of Josephine as a prophet, van Caspel in 1954 noted the characteristics she shares with totem animals in primitive rituals of Australia, as described by Durkheim. Her totemic identification with the folk, as even the *or* of the title may indicate, is an intense relationship of artist to audience, almost equally fitted to theatrical performer, Zionist writer of novels, or universal artist.

Josephine likes to sing in the midst of unusual social distress or confusion. When, on such occasions, she stamps, swears, and bites because "she stands there in ceremonial state for quite a time without a sufficient audience," she symbolizes by her temperament the individual artist, but the charming metaphor of her ceremonial state asks that she be viewed also as representative of an original art, possibly in process of formulation by a coterie—if it is not quite singing, yet it possesses the dignity and integrity of other music. For such an artist, the narrator might have given the example of Franz Kafka. Those who would make a monomaniac of Kafka never admit by their analyses that he took his writing seriously. He sought to create the ceremonial out of the original.

Words and also artless fictions fill popular periodicals and the mouths of the people. To be consumed like Kafka and his friends with the seriousness of art is to raise your piping out of this mediocre conformity, but not necessarily to reach the level of classical narrative. Yet "we really do listen to her in a sense, probably much as one listens to a trained singer." A pure artist would have no audience. As Kafka has the narrator put it, "May Josephine be spared from perceiving that the mere fact of our listening to her is proof that she is no singer."

Josephine's claim to strengthen the people in time of stress does not lack merit, but her attraction of audiences when danger is almost imminent—the folk say saucily—has hindered timely precautions. (We folk now call it the treason of clerks.) Josephine has apparently struggled, like Kafka, for a job with a single shift, leaving her free for art after two in the afternoon. Following Kafka, she has longed to be free of all such work; but the narrator, also following Kafka, appreciates the reluctance with which concessions have been granted to artists as individuals who use brittle temperament as an excuse for delinquency. The narrator tries, almost with success, to understand how it is that an artist serves society without giving social service. If he rejects Shelley's "unacknowledged legislators of the world," he does not stoop to W. H. Auden's mere registers of the *Zeitgeist,* prettifiers of inevitable social currents. He does not doubt Josephine's value, he just does not know what her value is.

In this narrator, Kafka has assumed an unassuming mask. He speaks always of "we," as one of the mouse folk, but also as one of those mistakenly thought to form Josephine's opposition. He declares that in fact she has no opposition. The narrator's set—lawyers, physicians, other professional men, say, the informed but uncultured—have the intelligence to observe Josephine with sympathy, not enmity. As the songstress subtilizes from the Yiddish stage singer to the universal artist, the audience expands to the citizenry of the twentieth century. What reader besides Josephine fails to recognize himself, humanized a bit, in the narrator? Whose masses in our century are not—a little less humane—Kafka's mouse folk? By one of the best specific ironies of the story, the further Kafka moves the reference away from the café performances toward the problems of literary art and the universal plight of the artist, the more he particularizes the sense of an audience in assembly: "At her concerts, especially in times of stress, it is only the very young who are interested in her singing as singing . . . ."

In his fictions of naturalistic surface, Kafka triumphs through completely realized situation, increasingly fantastic and increasingly unbearable. Because of the animal myth suggested in the title, fantasy is present in "Josephine" from the beginning, as in "The Metamorphosis." This later fiction is more daring in method than "The Metamorphosis." A metaphorical character sketch, "Josephine" abjures the traditional techniques of immediacy. The exposition requires most of the space; relaxed, we follow the expository voice of the Philistine narrator; action comes late and no scene ever develops. We want Josephine to have her way, not merely because she bears the burden of all art on her frail shoulders, but also because she is she herself in this story. So urgently do we want her to act that we approve when, limping speciously onto the stage, she protests that injury from work will require her to cut short her songs; we even feel that we too, like the Philistine narrator, would fail to perceive the serious difference when pique leads her to curtail her artistic techniques. "Since I am nothing but literature and can and want to be nothing else," Kafka wrote in August, 1913, purportedly to the father of his fiancée, "my job will never take possession of me; it may, however, shatter me completely . . . ." Thus it is with the self-dedicated singer.

The triumphant virtue of "Josephine" is characterization. Where most of Kafka's heroes satisfy an obsessive need to suffer, Josephine opposes with stubbornness and dignity, in the name of art, the mild if firm authority of the public. Her cathartic defeat is received calmly, as such an indifferent elegist as hers would receive it. Kafka accepts her alienation as well as her probity. He accepts her inept and confused arrogance. And, through the sympathetic Philistine, he communicates his affection for her.

In one sense, my analogy of the cabbage refers to an utter illusion. Kafka's symbols have as specific referents only themselves. In "Josephine" he makes little use of a favorite tactic of his, the suspended fact, the crucial point where he withdraws the "Open sesame!" with a "probably," or with a "but this has never been accepted." Yet in "Josephine" as elsewhere he deliberately thwarts binocular vision; he bores the holes of meaning slightly out of alignment. Thus we return from the excitement of big game and flea hunting, as he intends, to the remarkable metaphors themselves. Josephine is Josephine, skillfully blurred.

Clement Greenberg

At the Building of the Great Wall of China

CHINA acquired a special place in Kafka's imagination as the image of a vast yet isolated continuity in space and time; as a vision of swarming, anonymous generations that succeeded each other in time eddying outside history; and as the idea of a highly unified social entity whose geographical parts were nevertheless remote from one another and from their common center. Thus China became the name of Kafka's figure of speech for Diaspora Jewry.

The Great Wall, being interpreted, stands on one level of meaning as the "fence" of Jewish Law, or Torah, which the rabbis themselves referred to as a fence or wall. Their Law protects the exiled Jews not only from the profane, but from history—Gentile history, which is the only kind there has been since the destruction of the Second Temple. Gentile history, because it tends to no Jewish solution, remains meaningless vicissitude, without place or interest for the genuinely human.

Like Jewish Law, the Chinese Wall has come into being discontinuously. The Law is supposed to provide for every contingency, but contingency is infinite; hence the Wall, which can never be more than finite, must remain forever incomplete and vulnerable. For this reason there is "legendary" uncertainty as to whether the Wall has been really finished. Though the narrator expresses skepticism about this uncertainty, it is only enhanced by the somewhat inconsistent indications of time he himself gives in his essay. The narrator passes his last ex-

77

amination in primary school at the age of twenty, just when the Wall is being started; the work of building it "could not reach completion even in the longest lifetime," yet at the moment of writing it appears to be long finished—why else express skepticism as to the rumors that it is still incomplete?

"Fifty years before the first stone was laid" all China is set to studying the art of building, and especially bricklaying. Similarly, all Jewry was set to the studying of the Law and the sharpening of logic years before Torah replaced Palestine as the Jewish homeland. As China had its surplus of architects and masons, so Jewry came to have its surplus of logicians; yet without an over-supply of "technicians" and the patient, circumscribed toil to which they could be made to submit, the fence of the Law could not have been raised to such an imposing height, nor could such large areas of life have been embraced within it.

The Chinese in the southeastern provinces, where the narrator lives, "almost on the borders of the Tibetan Highlands," do not really need the Wall because their remoteness suffices to protect them from the northern nomads. But this remoteness also protects them from history, or deprives them of it, because history is made in Pekin, likewise in the far North—the North being the scene of history in general: sacred history in the capital, Pekin, and profane history among the nomads along the frontier. Pekin vibrates with many meanings: the "high command" is seated there, at the feet of the Emperor, here a symbol for God, or for one who, like a high priest or prophet, is in direct communication with God. So vast is the land and the spread of time over it that the Chinese in the South, like the Jews in their exile—or like humanity itself islanded in sense experience and rationality—can have no knowledge of either the historically or absolutely contemporary. They live according to laws and decrees handed down thousands of years before. No wonder faith has become weak in the South, and at the same time very rigid. "There is perhaps no people more faithful to the Emperor than ours in the South, but the Emperor derives no advantage from our fidelity."

Israel, outside history in the Diaspora, marking time until profane history runs its haphazard course, is of little service to the God of History who is Jehovah. In the beginning, Israel was commanded to turn away from Nature, whose time is heathen because repetitious, and to seek salvation and solution in irreversible, teleological, historical time. But with the loss of Zion, the Jews lapsed from history to live solely in the Law, which became a man-made but equally repetitious substitute for Nature, reviving in even intenser form the circularity of heathen, mythical time that it was supposed originally to overcome. This it did by perpetually celebrating and retelling the incidents of a chapter of history long over and done with. "Long-dead emperors are set on the throne in our villages, and one that only lives in song recently had a proclamation of his read out by the priest before the altar. Battles that are old history are new to us, and one's neighbor rushes in with a jubilant face to tell the news." Thus Israel, which had discovered history, became in the Diaspora the ahistorical people par excellence, more fanatical and petty in its conservatism than any earth-rooted peasantry.

Kafka constantly chides the Jews for their abandonment of history. He is aware that they did not choose to leave history, and that the "essential responsibility" might lie with the "government" for not communicating its will with sufficient directness and steadiness to the "farthest frontiers of the land." In other words, God no longer reveals himself or his wishes. Nevertheless, the Jews have in the long run become too content to stay outside history, despite the physical dangers to which this exposes them, and they have even begun to insist on staying there. ". . . a certain feebleness of faith and imaginative power on the part of the people . . . prevents them from raising the empire out of its stagnation in Pekin and clasping it in all its palpable reality to their own breasts, which yet desire nothing better than but once to feel that touch and then to die." This also alludes to the anemia of Judaism as a *felt* religion.

However, its very feebleness of imaginative power enables Israel to survive in its exile. "All the more remarkable is it that this very weakness should seem to be one of the greatest unifying influences among our people; indeed, if one may dare to use the expression, the very ground on which we live. To set about determining a fundamental defect here would mean undermining not only our conscience, but, what is far worse, our feet." Ghetto Jewry lacks religious as well as historical curiosity; its "feet" are the petty daily concerns—business, logic-chopping, and gossip—which absorb minds indifferent to public issues. However, if Jewry is not curious about religion, it is still curious about God, only not in a theological sense; and this kind of curiosity, together with its immersion in the day-to-day, serves to keep it from heretical thoughts. Remarkably few sectarian differences have appeared among the Jews in their dispersion.

But the Great Wall should not be interpreted too consistently or closely in terms of its Jewish meaning. It alludes to the entire human condition, in the sense Kafka has of it as being walled around by ignorance reinforced by irony. His great power is to fabulize general observations, to find situations and images of behavior in which to figure forth broad conclusions of a kind that ordinarily resist the art of fiction. Conclusions about his fellow Jews in particular are extended to cover humanity in general by virtue of being so fabulized. The movement from the particularly Jewish to the universally human goes on always, and many things in "The Great Wall of China" open out into art only because they are carried by this movement, in which the allegorical meaning is kept shuttling between two or more contexts.

Thus the Wall stands for many more things than Jewish Law. Religion dissolves into culture, and culture is seen as humanity's effort to keep the formless at bay. Culture is also illusion: illusion piled on illusion. A scholar proposes that the Wall serve as the foundation for a more successful Tower of Babel to be built according to the methods of modern technology. Other intellectuals, the foremen of the work gangs, better educated than the laborers they supervise, are more aware of the possible illusoriness of the project, and need special measures of relief to keep them from despairing of its aim, of their own immediate work, and of the world. The mass of the Chinese, however, do not have such troubles; culture proceeds over their humble heads.

The art of "The Great Wall of China" consists most immediately in the interweaving of motives that enter as ideas rather than as acts or events. As is usual with Kafka, the evenness and closeness of the interweaving require that we look a second time to discern the emphasis of the pattern. This, as I see it, comes just short of halfway in the narrator's essay, and all that goes before and after circles towards it. I refer to the parable of the river with its admonition as to the point at which speculation upon the "decrees of the high command" ought to stop. Kafka has the traditionally Jewish distrust of theology, and the aversion to inquiry into the nature or ultimate purpose of Being—"but not because it might be harmful; it is not at all certain that it would be harmful. What is harmful or not harmful has nothing to do with the question." In compensation, the positivistic intellectual—and Kafka is one in his way—has all the more curiosity about the way the world actually works. The narrator pursues his inquiry on the plea that it is purely historical. The plea is that of the post-religious, modern Jewish intellectual.

Kafka asks again and again: what is it that made me what I am? Among the things that made him what he is, the Jewish past bulks large, the Diaspora Jewish past. That past could conceive of history as only in a much remoter past and in the form of what amounted to legend. This may explain in part why Kafka cast his own history of the history-less Diaspora in legendary form. But it does not follow from this that the content of that form is legendary. In fact, it is hardly fiction.

Jarvis Thurston

The Married Couple

> "Faun's flesh is not to us,
>   Nor the saint's vision.
>   We have the press for wafer;
>   Franchise for circumcision."
>   Ezra Pound, "Hugh Selwyn Mauberley"

To speak of Kafka's novels and stories as "myths," myths for our time, is instructive, especially when we consider the warmth with which critics of various nationalities have offered their variant readings, but "myth" implies the futility—and, sometimes, even the sacrilegiousness—of attempting an interpretation. And I know of no contemporary writer who more quickly provokes one to interpretation than Kafka. Though I agree with those critics, Claude-Edmonde Magny, for instance, who protest against the allegorist who offers us a conceptual scheme in place of the Kafka story, I do so not because their interpretations are without merit but because they are too limited. It must be granted that there is in Kafka a strand of realism, "the stuff of everyday life," usually comic and satiric, which achieves its perspective through incongruity (not unlike Swift in this respect); but there are other strands which, by the patterning of symbols, force the reader into conceptualizing if he is to make more than a limited entrée into the story.

Clearly Kafka is no Bunyan; he links, rather, with such multi-leveled, imagistic poets of the metaphysical as Dante, Yeats (of

"Byzantium"), and Stevens (of "The Emperor of Ice-Cream") who use very concrete detail for the exploration of rather abstract meanings. Whether an imagistic poet or a "metaphysical poet in symbolist narrative" (as Austin Warren has called Kafka), any writer who forgoes authorial commentary (Kafka limits himself to the vision of the main character, or has his protagonist tell his own story) must employ devices which provide the reader with some kind of interpretive key. Two such devices most frequently used by Kafka are symbol and incongruity, the clearly recognizable symbol (Kafka's symbols are "public," not researched) and the patently incongruous act. Without such devices images can mean almost nothing and almost anything; with them a writer may confine the area of possible meanings, limit what "more" than the literal we may reasonably see. Using the key provided by the few obvious symbols that Kafka characteristically provides, we can penetrate the surrounding symbols, but not without an increasing lack of certainty as we proceed; we should not be too surprised if we find ourselves on another floor, but still, we hope, in the same house. As exemplum let me explore Kafka's "The Married Couple," admittedly one of his slighter pieces, but containing practically all that is essentially Kafkan.

On the surface the story seems to be almost meaningless: a man whose business is bad calls upon a prospective client at his home, is unsuccessful in coming to terms with him, and leaves, feeling dejected but realizing that "one must keep going." This surface meaninglessness—if the reader trusts the author—and the incongruities of some of the events described ought to cause the reader to abandon any attempts, at least tentatively, to take the story very literally. It is, however, an unmistakable symbol near the end that lifts the story to a generalized meaning and forces a re-examination of other details that had previously been taken as literal: "he lay down for the time being in his son's bed; a pillow was made beside his son's feet with two cushions hastily brought by his wife. *After all that had gone before I found nothing particularly odd in that*" (italics added). Here we obviously have the author calling attention to an important matter. When two people lie in the same bed it is customary for them to lie with their heads at the same end; here the father's feet are at the son's head, and the son's feet at the father's head. Placing one's self at someone's feet has been for thousands of years a symbol of obeisance, a token of reverence and submission. Customarily it is the father who is the head of the family; the son is his subordinate. In the Kafka story the relationship of father and son is paradoxical. Certainly it should be no unwarranted leap for the reader to link this with the Christian paradox of the relationship of the Father and the Son: "He that hath seen me hath seen the Father . . . . Believe me that I am in the Father, and the Father in me."

Once we have been assured—by an unmistakable symbol—that the story, at least on one level, is concerned with a religious theme and that it explores the theme by the use of symbolism, many of the details of the story begin to be more meaningful. N. symbolizes God, his son Jesus Christ, his wife the Virgin Mary (this identification will be qualified). The agent, then, seems to be a member of some religious sect (a Christian, a Jew, or a representative of both). Who, then, is the "I," the protagonist of the story? He seems to be secularized modern man in search of faith and certainty. Offhand these identifications may seem quite arbitrary, but it is doubtful if any others will explain so fully the details of the story. Let me support this by a closer examination of this very short story.

Exactly what business the protagonist is in we do not know: Kafka very carefully keeps his terms generalized—"business in general," "business relations," "business matters," "business call"—so that the particularity of any specific business will not force him into ludicrous ingenuity in handling the symbolic level of his story. "Business," wide-ranging in meaning (rightful work, personal concern, affair, transaction, etc.), has sufficient relations to the world of religion in its hierarchic structure, its unpredictability, its abstraction to make it a suitable framework for religious symbolism and permit, at the same time, an ironic commentary upon modern man, living in a civilization very much dominated by mercantile and commercial activity, in the buying and selling of the goods of *this* world.

The secularization of the world which has accompanied man's investigation of his physical universe needs no documentation. Until relatively recent times man had hopes that his sciences would lead to final truths, but his pursuit of Becoming has left him uncertain about Being. His disillusionment, his confusion about values, his pessimistic view of his role in the world are registered in contemporary literature, art, and music. In "The Married Couple" Kafka takes as his theme disillusioned modern man in search of his soul.

Kafka's narrator lives in an illogical world: "in the present unstable state of affairs often a mere nothing, a word, will turn the scale, and in the same way a mere nothing, a word, can put things right again." Such a world of hazards leads to anxiety and neuroticism, for unless a given act is followed by a predictable consequence man cannot make sense out of his choices. Kafka's narrator does not try to seek N. until business is very bad (that is, he makes no attempt to establish, or re-establish, his relationship with God until he is desperate). During his youth he was a believer in God, but he has gradually, unintentionally, drifted away from Him (this we can take as both personal and universal history). N. has grown somewhat infirm of late because his existence is a matter of faith and in modern man faith has become weak, so weak, Kafka says, that one has to seek him personally, at his home, for he rarely is to be found in his "office," that is, the church which is dedicated to his worship.

In the second paragraph we begin to learn a little more about the personality of the teller. Though "it was really no time for paying calls," too near the dinner hour, he selfishly sets out, and instead of returning home after he has been informed that N. is in the bedroom of his ill son, he goes in anyway, and with his overcoat and hat. The rudeness of this act would seem to be denied by his being "requested to go there" and by his hesitation, but the incongruity of the act is one of the interpretive keys to the story. Many of the narrator's statements indicate an awareness of manners, secular rituals (business should be conducted in offices; there are appropriate times for making calls; overcoats should not be worn in bedrooms; hats are not put on in the house, etc.), but even those he does not take seriously. His hesitation only underlines the rudeness, by showing he is aware of the proper behavior. More importantly, he is unable to understand that in N.'s house secular rituals are without significance. Moreover, he interprets religious symbols secularly: a death-and-resurrection is a "dissembling"; the positions in the bed are merely another oddity among the many he has encountered since entering N.'s house.

The narrator seeks for a relation with N. but certainly with no humility; in fact, he considers the search a "disagreeable visit." The only reason that he goes at all is that "business is bad." His case of samples of the goods which he desires to sell to N. we may consider as samples of his acts and beliefs.

There are some suggestions in the story that both the narrator and the agent are Jewish, but there are also suggestions which point toward a Christian identity, or, more commonly, to both simultaneously. A positive identification as Christian or Jew would unnecessarily limit the meaning of the story. This ambiguity accounts, in part, for a number of details. The narrator thought he had to deal only with N., but when the Son shakes his fist, he realizes that he can no longer regard the Son as only a "secondary factor" in his plans; the agent's putting on and taking off his hat in the presence of N. reminds one that in prayer the Jew covers the head, the Christian bares it; as she is the mother of N.'s son, the saintly mother symbolizes the Virgin Mary, yet her devotion to the Father and not to the Son carries a suggestion of Jewish patriarchy; the symbolic "death" and "resurrection" happens to the Father, not to the Son. The incongruities in these symbolic relationships preclude the story's being taken as solely a Jewish or Christian parable of a search for faith. Besides indicating that the narrator's quest involves both Judaism and Christianity, these incongruities are necessary for maintaining a reasonable consistency at other levels of meaning—and are ramps leading to these other related levels.

In the description of the second paragraph we can hardly avoid noticing that N.'s son has the short beard usually seen in traditional pictures of Christ. N. himself is more majestic than his son, but "grown thin because of some creeping malady," the malady of man's loss of faith. He is wearing a fur coat, a symbol of his aristocracy, his lordship. His wife, the Virgin Mary, in her selfless devotion, scarcely notices the others. Observe that she has difficulty removing the coat because of "the great difference in their height." Though she is the Mother, her rank is below that of the Father or Son. She almost vanishes under the coat.

The agent is sitting comfortably by the son's bed in a "beautiful ample overcoat." He has prospered, at least materially (at one level, the sitting by the son's bed and the ample overcoat suggest the historical prospering of Christianity). The narrator's envy reveals that his own coat is probably neither beautiful nor ample, and not so good a protection from the inclemencies of the world, physical or spiritual. The agent's coat, not unlikely, is religious vestment, "the garment of salvation"; its ampleness, in the familiar symbolism of coats, suggests the historic extensions of ritual and theology (Christ's seamless coat of the New Testament subsumes Joseph's coat of the Old, and Christ's coat, in turn, becomes more ample in Pauline Christianity).

In the long third paragraph the teller discloses himself as proud, impatient, arrogant, and rude. He ignores the agent, begins his proposal ("without ceremony," secularistically) at the moment N. indicates a desire to talk with his son, and harangues his listeners as if he were in his own office. Though he is self-analytical enough to be aware of his imperfections and his impoliteness, he rationalizes his behavior by saying: "Well, every man has his bad habits, yet I can congratulate myself on mine when I think of the agent's." He judges the agent's behavior severely—"surely such conduct must be called unpardonable"—but does not see the beam in his own eye; the agent has done little more than put his hat on and off. The teller thinks himself very shrewd ("but there are people whom that trick with the hat might have put off completely"). Regardless of whether or not he recognizes it as ritual act, the teller sees the trick with the hat as heckling. (Kafka commented about the Chassidic rites he once attended with Brod: "Looking at it closely was like observing a wild African tribe. Crude superstition.") The teller is observant, as his account indicates, but his conceit constantly causes him to misinterpret the events observed, or, at least, to consider a very limited number of possible interpretations. He does not consider the possibility that his proposals, his bargainings with God, are so outrageous that the agent puts on his hat as if to leave, a gesture indicating his inability to tolerate the teller's outrages.

He also misinterprets N.'s staring blankly into space as if he were not listening; we suspect that N.'s impassivity is the impassivity that accompanies sorrow and pain so great that it passes beyond expression. Although the narrator prides himself on taking in "quite well" N.'s unreceptiveness, he offends by still further bargaining: if you will do this for me, I shall do that for you. In his world of buying and selling he is so far from the Judaeo-Christian ideal of submitting his will to God's that he can attempt to come to terms with God only by bargaining—by making "advantageous offers." Selfishly he is even frightened by his own concessions. (The narrator's bargainings seem not unlike those of religious questers who would join a congregation if it would modify or abjure various rituals and doctrines.) And then he tells us that he was motivated in his proposals as much by a desire to triumph over the agent as to establish a relationship with N. Since the agent has stopped his heckling, the trick with the hat, and has "folded his arms across his chest," the narrator feels that he has "given a severe blow to his designs." He does not consider the possibility that the agent has resigned himself to hearing him out, knowing that the narrator will not find what he seeks.

The narrator describes N.'s "stroke": "he was trembling and his body was bent forward as if someone were holding him down or striking him on the shoulders," which is exactly what the narrator has been doing verbally. He has so little faith in N. that the minute he feels his cold hand, that is, cold to him, he assumes that he has died. "So it was all over." He then sentimentalizes the "death" by saying, "Still, he was a very old man. We would be fortunate if we all had such an easy death."

With unquestioning faith N.'s wife takes up her husband's hand, which is not cold to her. N.'s explanation about having fallen asleep out of boredom, boredom because of the teller's importunities, his brashness, his shallowness, his lack of faith, is interpreted by the teller as being some kind of dissembling. The evening paper, which N. glances at but does not read, is a record of human activity such as one can find in the daily newspaper, a record of murder, infidelity, greed, pride, triviality. While he is glancing at the newspaper N. makes "unpleasant observations" about both the teller and the agent, about their "business methods," the manner in which they wish to establish a relationship with him.

Upon meeting Frau N. as he is leaving, the narrator has twinges of sentimental nostalgia and tells her that she reminds him a little of his mother: "Whatever people say, she could do wonders. Things that we destroyed she could make whole again. I lost her when I was still a child." The word "mother" functions here in a double sense. The narrator desires the security and faith of childhood, the time when his mother could be depended upon to make things *whole again*. The mother also stands for the unquestioning religious faith which he lost when still a child. Frau N.'s silence about being likened to his mother (she would certainly not feel pleased about her Son being likened to the narrator) is explained by the narrator as being due to deafness. He egoistically feels that she would have been more communicative if she had not confused him with the agent, but we suspect that to the faithful, selfless Frau N. there is little difference between the waiter and the seeker. Neither is a man of much faith. In their eyes, the eyes of modern man, N. is infirm, his son sick. The waiter waits "for what time would bring," but the seeker half-heartedly seeks that which can only be found by a selfless devotion. He is quite sure that his searches will come to nothing ("now at last, it seemed to me, my moment had come, or rather it had not come and probably would never come") and, of course, they do. And so there is nothing else for him to do but "keep going."

In making this religious interpretation of the symbolism of "The Married Couple" I find that I have frequently offered supporting evidence, sometimes quite unintentionally, from other possible interpretations. The incongruities of certain actions and symbols are stairways leading to other floors; the few public symbols tell us what house we are in. Let us look briefly at a few of the other floors.

One level of interpretation is the philosophic. "The Married Couple" is a parable of any search for Truth. The "I" tries to find reasons for why things are as they are, offers explanations for this and that, but is not at all sure that the explanations are right. The meanings of certain actions he cannot understand at all; for instance, he dismisses the positions in the bed with the statement: "After all that had gone before I found nothing particularly odd in that." Kafka's protagonist, like all of us, is faced with the problem of understanding himself and the world about him—and there is much that seems to defy explanation, much that is irrational in the behavior of those whom he meets, and much that is irrational in his own behavior. At times he congratulates himself upon his sharpness, his ability to see himself and to see through others, but it is a pathetic kind of bravado. Something is wrong, for the mission is not accomplished, and he can only keep going. Like all of the human race, Kafka's hero is a strange combination of traits: a reasoning creature, he reasons endlessly, and without too much profit; though he is proud and arrogant about the little that he thinks he knows, he is confused in a world he never made; but he is also pathetic and admirable in that he keeps going.

Another level, the psychological, centers around the human need for "relations" with other human beings, the attempt to find the "home" lost in one's childhood, the attempt to overcome one's essential aloneness. In that respect the married couple (at the religious level the married couple seems also to stand for the relation between Father and Son, the linkage of Judaism and Christianity) contrasts with the "I," to whom it seems that only he has failed to establish relationships. Even the rival agent seems to the protagonist to *belong*. He is envious of the agent's "sitting comfortably . . . in his beautiful ample overcoat."

Each of us living in his cell of subjectivity feels that others have achieved the belongingness denied to us. (Of interest, at this level, are Kafka's remarks about marriage in the "Letter to His Father": "Marriage is certainly the pledge of the most acute form of self-liberation and independence. I should have a family, the highest thing that one can achieve, and so, too, the highest thing you have achieved . . ."; why Kafka could not marry is reflected in the family relationships in "The Married Couple," but this is of more importance to the biographer than the critic.)

The last level which I wish to name is the cultural-historical, a level which links with the high burlesque of a Swift or a Chaplin. "The Married Couple" is a comic and satiric commentary on a world whose history parallels the narrator's movement from a childhood where there was a mother to make things "whole again," to an irresolute adulthood whose only link with love and faith is a sentimental nostalgia for the past. In the person of the narrator Kafka satirizes a secular and commercial civilization—competitive, crass, arrogant, and essentially absurd—which strides up and down in that last sanctum of privacy, the bedroom, making its sales pitch and regretting the lack of the— "usual cigarette."

These other possible interpretations, merely hinted at here, are not mutually exclusive. God's ways are mysterious, but so are man's; they symbolize each other. It is characteristically Kafkan that the levels of "The Married Couple" should fuse and reinforce one another.

Part Two

THE NOVELS

Mark Spilka

Amerika: Its Genesis

"ALWAYS this one principal anguish," wrote Kafka in 1915: "If I had gone away in 1912, in full possession of all my forces, with a clear head, not eaten by the strain of keeping down living forces!" Here is the recurrent dream of escape from his father, from the oppressive job in Prague, and from his own inner torment. The destination is almost anywhere: a room of his own, a job with a distant uncle, a flat in Berlin, or, in 1912, an entirely new life in America. He had begun writing his first novel in that year, and, in a burst of creative power, he had projected an imaginary trip across the ocean to a land he had read about, through Whitman and Franklin, but had never seen. From Whitman he had probably received an expansive sense of acceptance, of inclusion within the great democratic embrace, which is the keynote at the close of *Amerika.* In Franklin he had probably found an image of an earnest and morally sensitive young man, thrifty and industrious, who was able to make his way in the world despite early handicaps. This same young man had escaped from an oppressive family situation, yet he had continued to respect his father's wisdom and to look upon him with affection and regard. From Franklin, then, came the notion of a land where fathers and sons might live in mutual trust and consideration. For this reason Kafka had recommended the *Autobiography* to his own father, and there is some evidence of its influence on the actual structure of *Amerika.*

In his memoirs, for example, Franklin speaks of his decision to leave Boston altogether, so as to avoid further trouble with a harsh elder brother: "I determin'd on the point, but my father now siding with my brother, I was sensible that, if I attempted to go openly, means would be used to prevent me. My friend Collins, therefore, undertook to manage a little for me. He agreed with the captain of a New York sloop for my passage, under the notion of my being a young acquaintance of his that had got a naughty girl with child, whose friends would compel me to marry her, and therefore I could not appear or come away publicly." In Kafka's novel the hero is "a poor boy of sixteen, who had been packed off to America by his parents because a servant girl had seduced him and got herself a child by him." Franklin was seventeen at this time. Like Karl Rossmann, he had arrived in New York "without the least recommendation to or knowledge of, any person in the place, and with very little money in [his] pocket." Unable to find work as a printer, he had set out for Philadelphia, leaving his "chest and things" to follow him by sea. Traveling by boat or on foot, stopping at inns or at the home of a kindly old woman, he had entered that city in a bedraggled state, and had continued so until the arrival of his chest and clothes. Then (again like Rossmann) he was able to find a job and to make his way through hard work and frugality. Yet he was often the victim of deceitful friends. The governor took a liking to him, for instance, and made lavish promises: he would set him up in business as a printer, or he would give him letters to those who could. But as Franklin learned, he had no money to give and no credit with anyone. There were also younger friends who drank heavily at his expense, and who frittered away his business or his funds. When he loaned some of his brother's money to one of them, he never got it back. His father had warned him earlier that he was too young to manage business affairs, and he admitted now that he had committed a grave error, and that his father "was not much out in his judgment."

In spirit and form these early adventures resemble those of Karl Rossmann in *Amerika*. In each case there is the story of a seduction (which is true for Karl, though a ruse for Franklin); there is the separation of a young boy from his family, and then later from his chest of belongings; there are attempts at thrift and industry which are thwarted by deceitful friends; and finally, there is a confirmation of a father's wise prediction, for on giving him his box, Karl's father also asks: "How long will you keep it?" More important than all this, however, is the principle by which Franklin explains his "errata" in a discussion of the moral precepts which preserved him "thro' this dangerous time of youth, and the hazardous situations I was sometimes in among strangers remote from the eye and advice of my father, without any willful gross immorality or injustice that might have been expected from my want of religion. I say willful, because the instances I have mentioned had something of *necessity* in them, from my youth, inexperience, and the knavery of others."

The principle of necessity is important here, for it helps to explain one of the most difficult concepts in Kafka, that of "sinfulness without guilt," which is so often ignored by his critics. For the moment, however, we must leave this problem in abeyance and turn to other works which might have influenced Kafka. For there is some evidence that Charles Dickens was another source of his interest in America, although no one has given the point much credence.

Indeed, Klaus Mann finds it strange that "in Kafka's mind the figure and the work of Dickens were vitally connected with the American atmosphere and landscape." [1] But the connection is scarcely strange, since Dickens had traveled twice to America himself, had written a book about it called *American Notes,* and had even devoted a long portion of *Martin Chuzzlewit* to the American scene. John Forster spends ten chapters on these visits in *The Life of Charles Dickens,* a book which Kafka seems to have read and from which he might even have turned to the travel book itself, or to the novel which followed. [2] At any rate, there are points in the novel worth noting. When young Martin Chuzzlewit goes to America, for example, he leaves his lady-love behind him and is accompanied on the journey by his friend and servant, Mark Tapley. On the trip across, master and man are shown together in "the unfathomable depths" below decks. Here Tapley exhibits his perennial jolliness and helpfulness, which are later to work a profound change in his selfish master. In other words, the trip abroad is really a spiritual quest, and Martin's need for his servant's qualities is, to this extent, like Karl Rossmann's need for the burly stoker in *Amerika.*

A more suggestive parallel is the Eden Land Corporation, although Dickens' equivalent for the Nature Theatre of Oklahoma turns out to be a swamp, not a Paradise, and its inhabitants are compared with "a gang of convicts in a penal settlement." Yet the promise it holds seems peculiarly American. Its agents describe it as lovely and wholesome, a place "where man is bound to man in one vast bond of equal love and truth." Consequently, they have reserved it for "Aristocrats of

Natur' "; but since Martin and Mark have money, they easily qualify as aristocrats and receive their share in the settlement. Once they arrive there, however, they are stricken by fever. First Mark nurses Martin to health, and then Martin attends his servant when his strength gives out. By doing so, he is finally able to exorcise his selfishness. In this sense he is made more whole, as Karl Rossmann is presumably made whole in *Amerika*.

We must turn to *David Copperfield,* however, for the most telling source of Kafka's vision of this country. Let me repeat only the most relevant passage from his diaries: "Dickens' *Copperfield*. 'The Stoker' [Chap. I of *Amerika*] a sheer imitation of Dickens, the projected novel even more so. The story of the trunk, the boy who delights and charms everyone, the menial labor, his sweetheart in the country house, the dirty houses, *et al.,* but above all the method. It was my intention, as I now see, to write a Dickens novel, but enhanced by the sharper lights I should have taken from the times and the duller ones I should have got from myself. . . ."

The exciting elements here are the five points which Kafka singles out in *Copperfield,* and his fascination with Dickens' method. The five parallels have already been explicated by E. W. Tedlock, Jr., in a splendid article called "Kafka's Imitation of *David Copperfield*." Tedlock confines himself to the acknowledged parallels, however, and fails to connect them with the sweep of Kafka's novel. For the purpose of this essay, let me show how this connection applies to only one of the five items.[3]

When Copperfield decides to run away from the Murdstones, and from the oppressive job at the warehouse, he asks a strange young man with a cart to carry his trunk to the coach office. The young man agrees for a sum, and then rattles off with the box and all his money. David runs after him, in bewilderment and chagrin, but he is unable to catch him. As Tedlock shows, this episode corresponds with Karl Rossmann's many difficulties with his box, some of them at the hands of two mechanics, Delamarche and Robinson, whom he has met along the road to Rameses. But the parallel seems more extensive than this. As David travels to Dover, for instance, he is forced to sell his jacket for a mere fourpence at a second-hand clothes shop. A day later he is accosted by a ferocious tinker and his wife. The tinker demands his money, looking so sternly at him that David fears he can see the money in his pocket. Then the man pulls a silk handkerchief off David's neck, and strikes down the woman when she tries to give it back. In *Amerika* the more or less ferocious Delamarche and his passive companion, Robinson, take Rossmann's newest suit and sell it to an old woman who deals in clothes. When they stop at an eating house, Karl is forced to pay the bill; but he is afraid to reveal where he keeps his money, in a secret pocket. Later that night, after the two tricksters have rifled his box, Karl searches them and finds one of his scarves in Robinson's jacket. A bit earlier, moreover, while standing at the counter in the Hotel Occidental, he thinks of an even more telltale incident: "It seemed a universal custom here to plant your elbow on the counter and rest your head on your hand. Karl could not help remembering how his Latin teacher Doctor Krumpal had hated that posture, and how he would steal up silently and unexpectedly and knock your elbow off the desk with a playful rap of a ruler which suddenly appeared from nowhere."

The schoolmaster in *Copperfield* is Mr. Creakle, whose name corresponds rather closely to that of Dr. Krumpal, and whose behavior seems almost identical: "Here I sit at the desk again on a drowsy summer afternoon. . . . I sit with my eye on Mr. Creakle, blinking at him like a young owl; when sleep overpowers me for a minute, he still looms through my slumber, ruling those ciphering books, until he softly comes behind me and wakes me to plainer perception of him with a red ridge across my back."

As these parallels indicate, it was the entire trip to Dover which fascinated Kafka, and not simply the incident of the trunk. It was the image of a young boy, caught up in a series of external traps while traveling along strange roads, which attracted him, for he had probably found a similar pattern in Franklin's memoirs. Thus, when Rossmann arrives at the Hotel Occidental, he is dressed in an old suit of clothes and looks dirty and bedraggled; the same is true of Copperfield when he arrives in Dover, and of Franklin when he arrives in Philadelphia. In short, the three journeys are more or less identical in spirit and form. It seems fairly possible that Kafka fused what he found in Dickens with what he knew about Franklin, that he enriched the trip to Dover with Franklin's mishaps at the hands of dissolute friends, and with his own insights into adolescent misfortune.

In discussing Dickens' method (which attracted Kafka "above all"), Tedlock rightly points to the element of "moral and emotional ambiguity" in each writer's work, and to their common use of "the technique of the grotesque." Yet he defines the grotesque as the mere "distortion of reality," a kind of arbitrary distortion, apparently, for the purpose of expressing ambiguities. Unfortunately, this fails to account for the child's view of the universe which seems to characterize these novelists. Indeed, the very fact of the childhood point of view *explains* the grotesqueness of their worlds, which is neither distortion nor realism, but an apprehension of reality, a way of getting at the truth, though only one way among others. And beyond this, it accounts for the particular form of ambiguity which Kafka dealt with in *Amerika,* and which Dickens dealt with in his favorite novel: that of sinfulness without guilt, which holds special meaning for the adolescent child.

In his introduction to *Amerika,* Klaus Mann speaks of its resemblance to Dickens as "only accidental and superficial": "The adolescent heroes of the English master-novelist have to endure suffering and adventures because the world is wicked. But Karl Rossmann . . . is harassed by more profound and complicated dangers: the problem of guilt *as such,* the mystic curse of Original Sin follows him over the ocean. . . ." Mann seems to treat each artist in blanket fashion here, as if Dickens had never developed beyond the world of *Oliver Twist,* or as if Kafka were forever writing *The Castle* and *The Trial.* Rossmann is viewed as another K. or Joseph K., a bit younger perhaps, but apparenly just as guilty of Original Sin. Yet in comparing *Amerika* with *The Trial,* Kafka himself speaks of "Rossmann and K., the innocent and the guilty." The distinction could scarcely be clearer, but there is little provision for it in Mann's thought and few other writers have followed up the lead. Parker Tyler has argued that Karl is "essentially *innocent*" because of his real moral action, "whereas the symbolic action of K's subjectively ambiguous world establishes his guilt." [4] This is a good description of the movement of each novel, yet it seems to obscure the sense of Kafka's world. A more careful appraisal is needed, one which begins with the premise which is central for Kafka: namely, that sinfulness is a state of being "quite independent of guilt."

In other words, Karl Rossmann is sinful but innocent, as is any child or adolescent in Kafka's world. He has not yet reached that "certain point in self-knowledge" when he will either have to admit and accept his limitations, or transcend them, or take on guilt by denying them. He is not a young adult, like Gregor Samsa or Georg Bendemann or

Joseph K. He is sixteen years old, and he has never been confronted by the fact of his sinfulness, in concrete form, as Gregor is confronted by the abominable state of his own being, or as Georg is confronted by his father's judgment, or Joseph K. by the Inspector, on his thirtieth birthday. In *The Trial*, for example, the priest explains the legend of the doorkeeper, who stands before the Law and guards it from the man "for whom alone the entrance is intended": "One must assume that for many years, for as long as it takes a man to grow up to the prime of life, his service was in a sense an empty formality, since he had to wait for a man to come, that is to say someone in the prime of life, and so had to wait a long time before the purpose of his service could be fulfilled . . . ."

This is the important principle: at the "prime of life" a man is able to grasp the facts of his own creation. In the meantime he is simply sinful without being quite responsible for it, or even aware of it. But what does Kafka mean by sinfulness *per se*? Is it a "mystic curse," as Mann vaguely implies? Or is the answer sharply Freudian? In his diaries, for instance, Kafka cites the nethermost and uppermost levels of the mind, and the filth and dissimulation which exist at each level. By dissimulation he seems to mean something like the Freudian concept of ambivalent motivation; and by filth, the incestuous longings, the aberrant sexuality, and the deepseated hatreds of the young child, who comes "dripping into the world with this burden." In the early fiction this burden is seldom given much metaphysical depth: one is sinful (and later guilty) before the human rather than the divine tribunal—a point which Kafka makes about a week before admitting Dickens' influence on *Amerika*. But in *The Trial* and *The Castle* and the later parables, both sinfulness and guilt are clearly metaphysical in depth. So there is a development in Kafka's thought which critics often overlook; and there are stages and progressions, as well, in his concept of guilt, whether social or metaphysical.

But if this is true, then the attraction to Dickens becomes more comprehensible. For in Dickens there is also a progression from adolescence to young manhood, or from "sinful innocence" to acknowledged guilt. Franklin's concept, that he was never willfully evil as a boy, but evil only out of *necessity*, because of "youth, inexperience, and the knavery of others," seems helpful here. For it describes the sort of crimes which Dickens' heroes often commit, in the course of growing up. And the point is, they do commit crimes, they do make appalling mistakes, out of necessity rather than willfulness; for on the one hand, the child is inexperienced and impulsive, while on the other, the world is full of wicked Murdstones, charming Steerforths, and doll-like Dora Spenlows, and involvement with such people is inevitable rather than fortuitous. The process is inescapable, that is, in one form or another, and every child inherits it as part of the human condition. Still, until he can comprehend this for himself, he is not responsible for his inheritance; and the adults who would make him so are doing him an injustice. When David funks his spelling lessons, he needs help more than he needs a beating; and when he bites Murdstone's hand, he commits the "crime" not deliberately but impulsively, so that his five-day imprisonment seems exorbitant. In later life, however, David comes to see his own culpability. When his blind affection for Steerforth leads to the seduction of young Em'ly, he admits his own "unconscious part" in the calamity; and when his love for Dora Spenlow ends in a disastrous marriage, he admits his own dissimulation. "The first mistaken impulse of an undisciplined heart," he calls it, and these words recur to him whether he is awake or asleep. So Dickens' hero suffers from the errors of his own "undisciplined heart," and not merely because "the world is wicked," as Klaus Mann suggests. Most of these errors work grievous harm upon others; all of them bring pain and disquiet upon himself; and all of them are connected with his youth and inexperience.[5]

In a more complicated way, the same holds true for Kafka's hero in *Amerika*. While Rossmann works at the Hotel Occidental, he is visited and exploited by the drunken Robinson. When the drunkard crumples in a corner, Karl foolishly tries to hide him in the employees' dormitory. But he fails to cover his absence from the lift completely, and the Head Waiter discovers it. Karl is fired in short order, and even his erstwhile protector, the Manageress, seems convinced of his guilt. In the meantime, Robinson has been knocked out by the other lift-boys and thrown out of the hotel. As Karl attempts to leave, he is manhandled by the Head Porter. To complete the farce, Robinson then blames him for his damaged state. Karl is to blame, of course, both for leaving the lift untended and for Robinson's misfortune. Yet his sins were committed out of necessity, and there is simply no one in the hotel who is willing to recognize the fact, and to offer counsel and forgiveness. "It's impossible to defend oneself," Karl thinks, "where there is no good will,"

Or where there is no parental indulgence. For with Kafka as with Dickens, the necessary crime should be forgiven, and the child's sinfulness balanced by his youth, his inexperience, and the knavery of others. This was the attitude which he found articulated in Franklin, and which made him recommend the *Autobiography* to his father; this was the principle which he also found in Dickens, and which made him turn to Dickens, rather than Dostoevsky and other novelists, during the composition of *Amerika*. In each case, it was the image of a growing boy, sinful but innocent, who deserves the indulgence of his elders and who travels along strange roads, which caught and held his attention.

As I have tried to suggest, the problem of sinfulness is intimately connected with the child's view of the universe. Without knowing it, the child is divided against himself. He seems to suffer from external penalties, brought down on his head by harsh parental figures. But actually he is also governed, with Dickens, by an "undisciplined heart," and with Kafka, by what amounts to an undisciplined unconscious. He contributes to the general scheme of pain and suffering, and his enemies are as much within as without.

Thus, in one sense, his pilgrimage through life is an attempt to achieve internal unity, or at least self-knowledge. Perhaps the two goals should be divided evenly between the two writers, for with Kafka, self-knowledge is not enough: like psychoanalysis, it can only reveal the full extent of hidden degradation, but the cure for this remains elusive. With Dickens, however, self-knowledge seems to instigate a conscious effort towards redemption; there is forgiveness and an amelioration of pain, as at the end of *Great Expectations,* and he seems willing to settle for this moderate solution. Kafka asks more and ironically achieves less. But neither artist solves the problem of the divided self.

Amerika is Kafka's boldest statement of the problem. The slightest of three puzzling novels, it is also the clearest in structure and intention. The novel opens, for example, with an image of Karl's relation to his unconscious self. He plunges down into the bowels of the ship, as if plunging into the depths of his own being. There he meets a stoker, and the very name suggests a source of life and power. Karl has stopped before his door by chance, and he has begun to hammer on it unthinkingly: "What are you hammering at the door for, like a madman?" asks the stoker. "I've lost my way," Karl replies, and a bit later he thinks, "Perhaps I should join up with this man . . . where am I likely to find a better friend?" That the stoker is part of Karl's being, and a part he ought to "join up with," seems fairly likely. Thus the moment Karl swings into the man's bunk, he remembers that he has left on deck the box his father gave him: "Can't you do without your box?" his new friend asks. "Of course not," Karl responds. Yet his need throughout the novel is, in essence, to do without his box, to escape exorbitant dependence on his parents, and to achieve some kind of harmony with those powerful inner forces which can serve his life or destroy it.

This seems to be Karl's dilemma, then: the box or the stoker, dependence or autonomy, childhood or maturity. At the end of the first section, when he is forced to leave the stoker, Karl bursts out crying and kisses the man's hand, "pressing it to his cheek like a treasure which he would soon have to give up." Then, as he leaves the ship: "It was now as if there were really no stoker at all"; and Karl strongly doubts whether his uncle "would ever be able to take the stoker's place." Karl is dependent on his uncle now, as if on a father; he is under his control, and in this sense he is also under the control of the potential filth within him. Yet with the stoker he seems most clearly in command of his own energies. He defends him before the assembled authorities in the ship's office, where the stoker looks upon him "as if Karl were his heart to whom he was silently bewailing his grief." Their case is weakened, however, when he begins to wrangle with Karl, and the ship's authorities agree (rather significantly) that "a man like the stoker could not be too severely repressed." The stoker seems to collapse under this opposition; but Karl, who still operates under the impetus of newfound energies, feels "more strong and clear-headed than perhaps he had ever been at home." He fails to see that the seeds of his own undoing are within him, and that the stoker's collapse presages his own: "If only his father and mother could see him now, fighting for justice in a strange land before men of authority, and though not yet triumphant, dauntlessly resolved to win the final victory! Would they revise their opinion of him? Set him between them and praise him? Look into his eyes at last, at last, these eyes so filled with devotion to them? Ambiguous questions, and this the most unsuitable moment to ask them!"

At the peak of his strength he falls back upon his parents for approval: this is ambiguity indeed, and it sets the pitch for the rest of the novel. For the efficient little Schubal now steps in and presents his case. As the Chief Engineer, he is the cause of all the stoker's complaints. Karl has already assumed "that the confrontation of Schubal and the stoker would achieve, even before a human tribunal, the result which would have been awarded by divine justice, since Schubal, even if he were good at making a show of virtue, might easily give himself away in the long run." But Kafka gives this thought an ironic twist, since it is Karl who is now "given away" as his uncle discovers his identity and recites (with evident relish) the embarrassing facts of his seduction. Then the stoker's case is decided in terms of discipline, rather than justice, and Karl departs under the complete control of his uncle. For the rest of the book, he too will appear before the human tribunal, he too will receive harsh discipline instead of justice, and punishment instead of love.

As this last thought suggests, the novel actually does proceed through Dickensian situations: Karl defends a poor stoker "before men of authority"; his rich uncle offers him a nebulous career, then casts him out among vagabonds who tramp the road; for a time he works industriously in a large hotel, until he is again cast out to the vagabonds and trapped in a squalid apartment; then finally he escapes to a more democratic realm, in the Nature Theatre of Oklahoma. But along with this surface pattern of social disruption, Kafka seems to borrow a much more psychological pattern from Dickens, and to intensify it to suit his own needs. I refer to the proliferation of parental authorities and external traps which characterizes both *Copperfield* and *Amerika*. Hence Edgar Johnson's list of surrogate parents, in the former novel: "They are all dissolutions and refusions of Dickens' own actual parents or of facets of his feelings about them, separated from each other and for the most part not related to David at all, so that without filial disloyalty David may feel toward them in the different ways Dickens did toward his father and mother. Each of these people symbolizes one sharply differentiated aspect of Dickens' merged and contradictory sentiments about John and Elizabeth Dickens." Johnson goes on to develop these points in more detail, citing David's oedipal attraction to his mother and Nurse Peggotty, his consequent hatred of the wicked Murdstones, his lack of security with the irresponsible Micawbers, and his desire for acceptance by his aunt and the gabbling Mr. Dick, who provide him with his *only* solid refuge. Indeed, as Johnson rightly observes, this dearth of happy homes is startling in Dickens; his warm celebration of family life "has created a glow in which readers overlook how relatively seldom he portrays what he praises." [6]

Yet there was one reader who surely caught this point, for this same succession of unhappy "homes" recurs in *Amerika,* as if Kafka too had projected various aspects of his parents into fictional situations. Thus Uncle Jacob is a successful businessman and a "bully of humility," like Kafka's father: "And let me tell you I started it all myself thirty years ago. I had a little business at that time near the docks and if five crates came up for unloading in one day I thought it a great day and went home swelling with pride. Today my warehouses cover the third largest area in the port." Kafka had a heavy dose of this from his father. In his famous "Letter," he cites remarks that positively wore grooves in his brain, like: "When I was only seven I had to push the barrow from village to village"; "We were glad when we got potatoes"; "I was only a little boy when I was sent away to Pisek to go into business"; and finally, "Is there any child that understands such things today?" Uncle Jacob is just as doubtful about Karl's understanding: when the boy tries to praise him for his achievement, he breaks off the conversation. At other times he bursts out with loud exclamations or decisive pronouncements; or he tries to instill self-distrust in Karl, in the manner of Hermann Kafka:

> "You see . . . what a lot of trouble this visit of yours has caused already."
> "I'm very sorry," said Karl, "but I'll be back again in a minute," and he made to rush away. . . .
> "You'll miss your riding lesson tomorrow. Have you called it off?"
> "No," said Karl; this visit to which he had been looking forward so much was beginning to be burdensome, "I didn't know —"
> "And you mean to go in spite of that?" asked his uncle.

Pollunder and Green suggest still other aspects of the elder Kafka. Both are tall, stout gentlemen, and such massiveness as theirs seems to depress Karl as much as it had depressed young Kafka, when he had undressed beside his father at the bathing beach. Even Green's eating habits are suggestive. When he puts a slice of pigeon into his mouth, his tongue takes it in charge with a flourish. Karl feels sick when he sees this, even as Kafka had been sickened by his father's rapacious appetite.

There are other splinterings. At the Hotel Occidental, the Head

Waiter and the Head Porter treat their underlings as enemies. They deprecate their achievements, dismiss them on impulse, and use discipline instead of justice to keep them in line. When a sheet of paper falls from the Head Waiter's desk, Karl pounces on it and hands it back to him: but the man receives it calmly, "as if it had flown of its own accord from the floor." The Head Porter also bullies Karl with threats and harsh reproofs and cutting sarcasm. Such traits are neatly summarized in Kafka's "Letter":

In my childhood other businesses did not concern me. But you I heard and saw shouting, cursing and raging in the shop, in a way that in my opinion at that time had not its equal anywhere in the world. And not only cursing, but other sorts of tyrannizing. For instance, the way you would push goods you did not want to have mixed up with others, knocking them off the counter . . . and the assistant had to pick them up. . . . You called the employees "paid enemies," and that was what they were too, but even before they became such you seemed to me to be their "paying enemy." There, too, I learnt the great lesson that you could be unjust; . . . it made the business insufferable to me, reminding me far too much of my relations with you.

Here Kafka views his father's business in much the same way as Dickens views the warehouse episode in his own life. He works his father's traits into the hotel episode, even as Dickens uses his ordeal in *Copperfield* and connects it with his father through Murdstone and Micawber. "The business and you became one for me," writes Kafka in his "Letter," and then extends the proposition to include the world: "Hence the world was for me divided into three parts: into one in which I, the slave, lived under laws that had been invented only for me and which I could, I did not know why, never completely comply with; then into a second world, which was infinitely remote from mine, in which you lived, concerned with government, with the issuing of orders and with annoyance about their not being obeyed; and finally into a third world where everybody else lived happily and free from orders and from having to obey."

The principle here is divisive and static, but if we make it linear and progressive, the results are startling: a boy lives in one world which is controlled by the authorities of another; he wants to go beyond them, to a third realm where everybody lives happily and free from orders; to get there, however, he must pass through a series of traps and predicaments set by his elders. Viewed in this light, *Amerika* becomes an intensely subjective pilgrimage toward social and personal redemption. As Karl moves down the road, he must suffer through a series of ambiguous conflicts with parental figures; but he will redeem himself through suffering (rather than "real moral action," as Parker Tyler holds), and in this way he will qualify for the great Nature Theatre at the end of the road. The process is really akin to psychological growth: it begins with a very consciously articulated "rebirth" in the Senator's rooms, where Karl displays a kind of innocent bisexuality; but he escapes from this at the country house and moves on to his oedipal attraction for the Manageress, at the Hotel Occidental; when her fidelity to the "father" (the Head Waiter) is established, Karl is rejected, and the whole oedipal situation becomes repulsive: he tries to break away from the gross parental figures in Brunelda's rooms. So the novel becomes a kind of modern pilgrim's progress, a picaresque allegory with the usual symbolical depth one finds in Kafka. First, there is the literal conflict, and beneath this, its irrational depth and significance. Yet because the progression is linear, and because the tribunal is human rather than divine, there is no religious depth to the experience. Karl suffers *toward* redemption, but as we shall see later on, redemption simply means integrity of being, in a world not especially characterized as infinite. The father is still Kafka's father, in a dozen guises. He is not yet God.

At best, one might give the experience an intellectual cast, a loose allegorical meaning. In this sense, the whole American journey can be likened to the Hotel Occidental, which is clearly a metaphor for Western society. Karl works *in* the hotel; he does not approach it as K. approaches the Castle or Joseph K. the Law. In fact, the law here is given a distinctly human significance, as Karl mulls over his dismissal: "It had happened with a rapidity he had not expected, for after all he had worked here for two months as well as he could, and certainly better than many of the other boys. But obviously such considerations were taken into account at the decisive moment in no part of the world, neither in Europe, nor in America; the verdict was determined by the first words that happened to fall from the judge's lips in an impulse of fury."

Europe and America, then, are governed by the impulsive fathers of the triumphant middle class; in such a world Karl Rossmann tries to work his way towards manhood, as Franklin and David Copperfield had worked their way to positions of responsibility. But in Kafka's Europe the fathers are too well established: they not only cast out the sons and treat them like enemies or servants, they also fail to provide a place for them, at the end of the hazardous journey towards manhood. In America, however—in the America of Franklin and Whitman and of an older Dickens—there is still an open world at the end of the road, where the child can establish his maturity "free from orders and from having to obey."

Consider the last two ordeals in *Amerika*, both as steps in this progression and as brilliant extensions of the splintering process. At the Hotel Occidental Karl is fired for leaving his elevator untended for two minutes. The man who fires him, the judge at the human tribunal, is clearly a father-image. The woman who protects him, the stately and kindly Manageress, is very like a mother to the homeless boy. As we shall see in a moment, she is partly drawn from Kafka's mother, while the servant girl Therese is probably based on one of Kafka's sisters; indeed, there is even a hint of rivalry for the "mother's" favor, since the girl is afraid, at first, that Karl will take her place as secretary to the Manageress. Once this misapprehension is removed, however, they establish an ambiguous rapport: "'You are so clever at wakening people,' said Karl. 'Yes, some things I can do,' she said, ran her hand softly over the bedclothes in farewell, and rushed off to her room."

Plainly Therese's presence adds greatly to the oedipal quality of the hotel scene. When Karl is being fired, she stands beside him, along with his motherly protector, to form a kind of oedipal front against the callous Head Waiter. But at this point Karl is taught one of the drastic lessons of childhood, as the Manageress deserts him, out of choice, and agrees with the Head Waiter's decision. She thinks of Karl as "a fundamentally decent lad," but she is also in love with the Waiter, and their long association is given the cast of an actual marriage: "The Head Waiter, whose knowledge of people I have learned to prize in the course of many years, and who is the most trustworthy man I know, has clearly pronounced your guilt, and I must say it seems undeniable to me." During the "trial" itself, the Waiter stands behind her and smooths her lace collar; he smiles at her "in a way that obviously had nothing to do with Karl"; and he seizes her hand and fondles it, surreptitiously, as Karl bows out of the room.

Here is one of the "lights" from his own experience which Kafka used to enhance his Dickens novel. In *Copperfield* he had apparently noticed Dickens' attitude toward David's mother, who is portrayed as

Murdstone's prisoner, and who finally dies, as it were, from the blight of his companionship. Meek and submissive, she assents to all his decisions against her own true feelings. When Murdstone proceeds to whip David, she runs forward to check him, but Miss Murdstone restrains her and she can only stop her ears and weep in protest. During his five-day imprisonment, David is allowed to visit the parlor during prayers; but there his mother turns her face away in shame. Kafka would have liked this situation, but he probably would have sensed the element of wishful thinking in it. His own mother had defended him in this manner, yet as he instinctively suspected, and asserted in his "Letter," she was fundamentally allied with his father: "It was, incidentally, a true instinct the child had, for with the passing of the years Mother became ever more closely allied to you . . . she did more and more completely, emotionally rather than intellectually, blindly adopt your judgments and your condemnations with regard to the children . . . ."

This is, of course, Karl's discovery about the Manageress, and it leads to a distinct improvement upon Dickens. For if David retains the image of the loving mother, Karl seems disillusioned with his motherly protector, and he is further astonished when even Therese accepts his guilt, so that he leaves the hotel with both of these ties in question. In the next episode (his last ordeal) he is trapped in the apartment of the lusty Brunelda, and the change of scene implies an important change in Karl himself. He wants desperately to break with his obsessions now, and to achieve his sexual maturity. Hence the singer Brunelda seems at first like an object of sexual repulsion, and at the same time, like an image of motherhood. As one critic observes, there are children swarming all through the great apartment house; but more telling than this, the scene combines some of the most painful emotions from Kafka's childhood. Karl is badly beaten and shoved out onto the balcony, for example, while Brunelda and Delamarche remain inside and sleep on a "pile of clothes, blankets, curtains, cushions and carpets." During his own childhood, Kafka had complained petulantly for water one night, and his father had swooped down on him and carried him out to the balcony, where he was left alone for a while in his nightshirt. Clearly the terror and significance of this image (which affected Kafka for years afterward) have been woven into the Brunelda episode. But he connects it now with the bed of parental figures, and this recalls his nausea at his parents' double bed in the stale room at home, with its used sheets and nightshirts ready for wear: he feels "indissolubly joined with all that loathsomeness: it still clogs [his] feet which want to run, they are still stuck fast in the original shapeless pulp." Karl too wants to run, but his feet are stuck fast in the parental lovenest: in Brunelda his loathing for sex is at last connected with his desire to possess his mother; in Delamarche his hatred for his father is connected with the same desire. They act out his obsession, yet he genuinely wants to break away from them and from the stale room in which they live; for at this point he takes comfort in the reflection "that he was still young and that someday or other he was bound to get away from Delamarche; this household certainly did not look as if it were established for all eternity." The lines at once suggest the allegorical nature of Karl's dilemma. "This household" is his father's house.

After the Brunelda episode there are two fragments, the drift of which is hard to determine. But as Charles Neider points out, Delamarche and Robinson are missing in the second fragment, Brunelda seems meek and submissive, and Karl has become more masterful. He has also apparently shaken off his loathing for the woman: "Karl is protective, even gentle and loving," writes Neider; "he behaves as though he were a lover." [7] It may be, however, that Karl has simply lost the desire to possess his mother, for the woman before him seems more like a sexless hulk than a mistress. Whatever the case, the absence of the two mechanics is significant. They resemble K.'s two assistants in *The Castle*, who are described by Louis Adeane as being identical with K., or with part of his being: "they 'represent' . . . the position of the Id., and this being so all their manoeuvres become explicable." [8] It does not seem surprising, then, that Karl is first separated from the stoker, and then dragged about or imprisoned by Delamarche and Robinson: for when he fails to utilize the powers within him, they turn rampant and seem to take charge of his life. Significantly, it is the parental figure who separates him from the "stoker" and thus exposes him to the two "mechanics," by whom the engine of the unconscious is not stoked but exploited.

It seems significant, too, that the mechanics are rather dissolute figures, the one active and violent, the other passive and childish. In *The Trial* the two warders reveal similar traits, as do the two assistants in *The Castle;* yet, as K. tells the latter, "for me you're only one man." In the same way the two vagabonds seem like one man, or like two aspects of the same inward self. They are not men of authority, like most of the male figures in the novel; and when they do receive authority, they seem to act out Karl's desires. Thus Karl sleeps out on the balcony with the passive Robinson, while Delamarche revels inside on the parental bed. Yet all three are after the same object—the singer Brunelda, whom Karl considers repulsive on the conscious level, but whom he finally treats with loving care. Perhaps it is even relevant that Karl moves with Brunelda to a cleaner apartment, once the mechanics are gone, away from the stale and filthy room where, like Kafka before him, he was so patently stuck fast in his "original shapeless pulp."

Consider also the crucial box-motif which runs through the novel. This is a further instance of the objective dramatization of internal problems. As most critics agree, the box represents Karl's strong dependence on his parents. Like the cap and the flabby umbrella, it symbolizes his childish ineffectuality, or the sense of personal incapacity he has brought with him from Europe. Of course, Karl *is* an adolescent, and his reliance on his parents would seem normal enough, under different circumstances. But there is nothing normal about his present dilemma: he has been cast out of his home for a sin he scarcely committed, much less understood. He has been impressed by his parents with a sense of his own worthlessness, and he looks to his box for the comfort and approval they deny him. He wants to *receive* their favor, but they have deprived him of all normal support, and he can only get it abnormally from those objects which remind him of his family.

So the box and the umbrella, and the adolescent's cap, are the measure of Karl's insecurity. When he loses them, he is left with a sense of his own nothingness; while he has them, he depends on worthless objects for qualities which might have been nurtured within him, had his parents been more loving—so that he is as fearful with these things as without them. On the boat there is a suspicious Slovak who is "merely waiting for Karl to be overcome by sleep [Karl thinks], so that he might manoeuvre the box away with a long, pointed stick." At the country inn there are sleeping vagabonds who wait for the same chance. The source of comfort is deceptive: it produces internal anxiety in the place of self-reliance, and eventually it leads to arrested adolescence, as with Eduard Raban in "Wedding Preparations in the Country."

Karl's box explains this danger by its very contents. Besides clothes and money, it contains a stale Veronese salami and a photograph of his parents. The salami is a gift from his mother, and because of its shape and pervasive smell, it seems to function as an image of sexual repulsion: "If he could not find some way of eliminating that smell, he had every prospect of walking about for months enveloped by it." The photograph shows his father standing "very erect" behind his mother, with one hand clenched to a fist, while the mother slumps in her chair. In another photograph which he had left at home, however, both his father and mother eye him sharply. What these images suggest is borne out in the novel: his repulsion for sex is rooted in his love for his mother; his insecurity, in his father's sharp disapproval and his phallic power; his later disillusionment, in the mother's basic loyalty to her husband. The box itself is the father's old army chest, a symbol of his manhood, which he wants to impose upon his son by force and example. "How long will you keep it," he says in jest, but this is also his way of filling Karl with self-distrust. Because of such anxiety, Karl continually fails to keep the chest; he performs foolishly because he lacks self-confidence. But there is really no danger of losing the box, for parental figures will always give it back to him. Hence Karl can afford to be without his box at Uncle Jacob's, for he is "entirely dependent" there on his uncle's kindness. As he leaves the country house, however, his box and all its contents are restored to him (thanks to the "censor-figure," Schubal, who is always the agent for authority). A day later the two mechanics rifle it and steal his parents' photographs: as the unruly agents of his unconscious, the box is theirs to tamper with, and they amply demonstrate the falseness of its protective powers. But with the help of a waiter from the hotel, Karl retrieves his box and puts himself under the protection of the Manageress. Later on, he veritably enters the box itself, in Brunelda's rooms, and again there is no need for it: the external figures now replace the internal burden and dramatize its contents.

So throughout the book Karl is plagued from within, by the forms of his own sinfulness, and from without, by the injustice of parental figures. Yet by the closing chapter he has won his way, through suffering and apparent growth, to the recruiting camp for the Nature Theatre of Oklahoma. He has arrived, that is, at the heterosexual stage of his development, since he now successfully climbs the ladder to the angel Fanny, on a stage where spirit is deliberately aligned with flesh—

for at the recruiting camp there are devils as well as angels. And there is even an image of future parenthood, at the end, as a father pushes a perambulator at the head of the new recruits.

The social theme is also emphasized, since at this particular theatre "everyone is welcome," no matter how destitute or disreputable. The key to the proceedings, however, is Karl's use of the word "Negro," when he is asked his name. Bergson points to the comic meaning of this word, for by the logic of our dreams, "a negro is a white man in disguise." [9] So it is a disguise, or a rigid, protective surface, which Karl adopts; he returns to the burden of insecurity, with its familiar mixture of pain, anxiety, and false assurance. But note the management's reaction to his lapse:

"Negro?" said the chief, turning his head and making a grimace, as if Karl had now touched the high water mark of incredibility. Even the clerk looked critically at Karl for a while, but then he said: "Negro" and wrote the name down. . . . The head of the bureau, controlling himself, stood up and said: "You are engaged then, for the —" but he could not get any farther, he could not go against his own conscience, so he sat down and said: "He isn't called Negro."

The clerk raised his eyebrows, got up himself and said: "Then it is my duty to inform you that you have been engaged for the Theatre in Oklahoma and that you will now be introduced to our leader."

Here the paternal figure is contradicted, and Karl is taken on in spite of his past burdens and his present relapse. The child is granted the privilege of his own pain; the lapse is indulged; there will be time enough to correct it later on, in Oklahoma. Yet the correction is already at work, for as the assembled crowd runs along to the train, Karl makes a crucial observation—"no one carried any luggage; the only thing that could be called luggage was the perambulator, which the father was pushing at the head of the troop."

The box is gone. Maturity and wholeness are now possible. The book ends with an image of natural grandeur, for the dream-world has finally collapsed:

The first day they travelled through a high range of mountains. Masses of blue-black rock rose in sheer wedges to the railway line; even craning one's neck out of the window, one could not see their summits; narrow, gloomy, jagged valleys opened out and one tried to follow with a pointing finger the direction in which they lost themselves; broad mountain streams appeared, rolling in great waves down on to the foothills and drawing with them a thousand foaming wavelets, plunging underneath the bridges over which the train rushed; and they were so near that the breath of coldness rising from them chilled the skin of one's face.

Fittingly enough, this concluding image has its counterpart near the end of *Copperfield,* as David wanders through the Swiss and Italian Alps and enters a valley enclosed by remote heights of snow. His wife and his erstwhile friend are dead, and he feels burdened by accumulated sadness. But the natural scene has a softening influence on him.

The bases of the mountains forming the gorge were richly green; and high above this gentler vegetation grew forests of dark fir, cleaving the wintry snowdrift, wedge-like, and stemming the avalanche. Above these were range upon range of craggy steeps, grey rock, bright ice, and smooth verdure-specks of pasture, all gradually blending with the crowning snow. Dotted here and there on the mountain's side . . . were lonely cottages, so dwarfed by the towering heights that they appeared too small for toys. So did even the clustered village in the valley, with its wooden bridge across the stream, where the stream tumbled over the broken rocks, and roared away among the trees. . . . All at once, in this serenity, great Nature spoke to me, and soothed me to lay down my weary head upon the grass, and weep as I had not wept since Dora died!

Kafka might have had this passage in mind at the end of *Amerika.* In his note on *Copperfield,* he speaks of the German writer, Robert Walser, who resembles Dickens "in his use of vague, abstract metaphors." Walser's brief vignettes abound with such images: a young man moves through a dreamlike natural setting; he drinks in the freshness and beauty of mountains, streams, and forests; and then suddenly he feels overwhelmed by a sense of oneness with the world. This is the sort of thing which Dickens attempts here, and which Kafka seems to deliberately refine: for instead of great Nature's voice there is only the chill from the stream on "the skin of one's face." Yet there is more to the Dickens episode than this. For David receives a letter now from Agnes—worthy, patient, loving Agnes—which has some bearing on *Amerika:* "She gave me no advice; she urged no duty on me; she only told me, in her own fervent manner, what her trust in me was. She knew, she said, how such a nature as mine would turn affliction to good. She knew how trial and emotion would exalt and strengthen it. She was sure that in my every purpose I should gain a firmer and a higher tendency, through the grief I had undergone." This is lofty, abstract language, but the way in which Agnes receives David, with trust and without demands, resembles the ending of *Amerika*. She is clearly the agent of his redemption, and their marriage represents the end of his long quest for maturity.

These are arbitrary endings, from the standpoint of the author's grasp upon reality. Kafka never describes the crucial stage in Karl's transition; Dickens falls into barren language, and remains unconvincing in his portrait of the faithful Agnes. But as images of redemption these endings serve their purpose; they suggest that suffering works a gradual change in a man, if an occasion for love and trust is provided when the change seems imminent.

NOTES

1. Klaus Mann, introd. to *Amerika* (New York, 1946), p. vii.

2. In his diaries Kafka speaks of "reading about Dickens," and then launches into a brief metaphor on the "locomotive of inspiration." A similar metaphor occurs in Forster's account of the composition of *Nicholas Nickleby*, in his *Life of Charles Dickens*. The *Life* appeared in Germany by 1875; it would have been available to Kafka, who, as Max Brod tells us, "preferred reading biographies and autobiographies to anything else."

3. Tedlock's article appears in *Comparative Literature*, VII (Winter, 1955), 52–62. He accounts for the other parallels as follows: the charming boy—Steerforth and Mr. Mack; the country sweetheart—Dora Spenlow and Clara Pollunder; menial labor—David's work at the warehouse and Karl's at the hotel; dirty houses—the tenement where Em'ly is rescued and the apartment house where Karl is trapped. These are convincing parallels, though as I hope to show elsewhere, Rosa Dartle is the real model for Clara Pollunder.

4. Parker Tyler, "Kafka's and Chaplin's 'Amerika,'" *Sewanee Review*, LVIII (Spring, 1950), 307, 310.

5. There are also oedipal "sins" in Dickens which Kafka consciously exploits; but since my space here is limited, I have confined myself to the more obvious level of "sinfulness" in *Copperfield*.

6. Edgar Johnson, *Charles Dickens: His Tragedy and Triumph* (New York, 1952), II, 678–79, 685.

7. Charles Neider, *The Frozen Sea* (New York, 1948), p. 104.

8. Louis Adeane, "The Hero Myth in Kafka's Writing," *Focus One* (London, 1945), p. 51.

9. Henri Bergson, *Laughter* (London, 1913), p. 41.

Lienhard Bergel

Amerika: Its Meaning

AMONG Kafka's novels, *Amerika* has received least attention and least critical approval. The book is usually regarded merely as Kafka's first effort in the novel form, a trial run that remained largely unsuccessful. The only merit critics have found in the book has been that it foreshadowed his "greater" novels: fragments here and there seemed to be embryonic *Trials* and embryonic *Castles*. Compared with the other novels, *Amerika* seemed old-fashioned; as one critic put it, the "dream-distortions" that make the later novels so fascinating, so "expressionistic," are missing; the public associates Kafka with the unexpected, the weird and fantastic, and is disapppointed to find a novel that is fairly traditional in form and makes sense rather easily.

Against this point of view, the reverse may be argued: Kafka is artistically most successful where his technique is least bizarre and most conventional. Kafka reaches his highest achievements in the fable, a framework that permits him to write a story which, at least on the surface, does not differ essentially from the traditional fictional forms of realistic provenience. "A Hunger-Artist," for instance, is at first glance a fully coherent brief biography devoid of dream-distortions; similarly, "The Burrow" conforms outwardly to the traditional animal story form. Where Kafka distorts, he is frequently, not always, fumbling artistically; the emotional experiences that provide the raw material for his work have not undergone sufficient esthetic transformation: "the man who suffers and the mind which creates" are still too closely identified. It is therefore not surprising that Kafka's artistic failures

have evoked most discussion: here is grist for the mills of psychoanalytic and existentialist interpretations. It is an indirect confirmation
of the artistic solidity of *Amerika* that the novel has proved comparatively impervious to interpretations of this kind (which may be
one reason for its neglect) and equally unrewarding for sociological
investigations; a distinguished Marxist critic found the book "dis-
appointing" and "incomprehensible."

In *Amerika,* Kafka resorts to the oldest form of realistic fiction, the
novel of adventure, and its modern offspring, the novel of education,
joining with these the traditional motif of the simpleton who is sent out
to experience the world. Upon this inherited framework he imposes a
typically modern novelistic situation, the hero between two continents,
the emigrant from the old to the new world. Thus a firm realistic structure is established which makes it possible for Kafka to unfold to the
fullest his unique artistic ability to raise ordinary human situations to
the symbolic level, and which makes it unnecessary for him to resort to
the fantastic and absurd in the scaffolding of the fable.

This fusion of the realistic and the symbolic prevails from the beginning: the theme of the emigration from Europe is fused with that
of the end of childhood: America is the new world of adult existence
which must be conquered or endured. With the exception of Hof-
mannsthal, no contemporary German writer has presented this theme
with such dramatic symbolism, avoiding mere psychological analysis.
For Karl Rossmann the old world is the world of music, of impractical,
humanistic studies, which, like his baggage, are only a hindrance in
the new world where he has to learn business English. The statue of
liberty which greets him upon entering the new world carries a sword;
and never during his stay there does he cease to feel the new freedom
as worthless, and even a burden, and to experience it as a threat to his
individual and even physical existence. His innate European decency
and loyalty are no match for the American freedom of muscular self-
assertion. America, the world of adulthood, appears to him as mech-
anized, brutal, and practical, enormous masses in seemingly senseless
motion. The recurrent image of American life is the endless, impersonal
traffic, moving along on broad, straight streets and quickly absorbing
into its stream any new vehicle. The other significant symbols for
America are all institutions in which large masses of people are thrown
together by chance or practical necessity: the ship, the office, the
apartment house, the hotel, the Nature Theatre. This depersonalized

world can function only by replacing individual relationships with organization and the artificial order of empirical classification: Karl Rossmann's European clothes appear ridiculous in the new surroundings and are replaced by the uniform that prevents him from breathing freely.

Karl Rossmann's first encounter with America is on the boat: in the stoker episode. When he tries to help his recently acquired friend, he becomes aware of the conflict between "justice" and "discipline." He fights for the justice of a cause that cannot be clearly formulated because it is based on an intangible, subjective feeling of human decency, not amenable to practical classification; this experience is repeated, with himself as the defendant, at the end of his hotel career, when he learns that it is impossible to reveal and to explain to others all one's inner motivations if they are to be judged by impersonal justice rather than confidence among individuals. Karl Rossmann's ordeal resembles that of Dmitri Karamazov before the court: the inner world of subjective feelings and the outer world of practical organization cannot be reconciled; it is significant that Dostoevsky also conceives the plight of his hero as resulting from a conflict between East and West. Attempts have been made to explain Karl Rossmann's trial in the hotel in terms of the later novel; but the two situations are similar only in the outward circumstance. *The Trial* lacks completely the Dostoevskian aspect of the episode in *Amerika;* there the world is truly irrational, the individual is persecuted by inscrutable powers, while in *Amerika* the issues and the motivations of both sides are, at least to the reader, perfectly clear, just as they are in *The Brothers Karamazov.* On the one hand is Karl's feeling of loyalty which it is difficult for him to defend, on the other hand the head waiter's justifiable desire to maintain order among the lift-boys and insure efficient service for the guests of the hotel. Karl's wrongdoing consists in behaving spontaneously, "childishly," rather than as a member of a uniformed group, while his actions are necessarily judged in relation to that group and the larger organization to which it belongs. In the dramatization of this conflict between subjective and objective justice, and of the crisis in human relations brought about by the absence of confidence, Kafka is thematically close to one of his favorite stylistic models, Heinrich von Kleist.

Throughout the novel, this conflict remains unsolved and widens into the larger one in which Europe and America, the inner and outer world, become irreconcilable. Karl Rossmann's fate in America resembles more and more that of the Hunter Gracchus, who "fell" from the freedom of childhood into the restricted world of everyday reality and now, dead, drifts endlessly through it, washed ashore here and there and then continuing his voyage over which he has no control. There is this significant difference, however: Karl Rossmann never loses hope of gaining a foothold in America and, some time in the future, of becoming a respected citizen of a country that repels him emotionally and rejects him physically. His ideals remain the successful immigrants, his uncle and the Manageress. Yet what attracts him to them is the fact that even though they measure up completely to the robust requirements of American citizenship, there is still a remnant of Europe left in them. The uncle does not object to his nephew's love of music, he merely wants him to restrain it. He knows how dangerous to "adjustment" it is to watch American traffic too long; and he thinks little of those manifestations of American efficiency that border on the childish and ridiculous, such as the desk with its variable pigeonholes. It is Karl's European background that establishes a bond between him and the Manageress; if she has succeeded in integrating herself, it has only been at the expense of her health.

Karl soon realizes that the new continent must be conquered where it reveals its seemingly most repugnant aspects, in the city. The break with his uncle results from his excessive readiness to interrupt his practical education and succumb to the attractions of the country of Mr. Pollunder's villa. There is freedom from the restraints of the busy city life, but also lack of protection in the drafty, unfinished country house; and, most important, there is Clara. In this novel, as in so many of Kafka's other writings, women are presented as demons and vampires, ready to overpower and violate the male: the servant who forced his emigration to America; Pollunder's promiscuous and athletic daughter; and Brunelda, the overweight Circe, who exists at the fringe of respectable society. Not only are the women responsible for his expulsion from the world of Europe, but they interfere with his adjustment to America.

Thus the normal ways of associating himself with America, marriage and a profession, are closed to Karl Rossmann. If the hero of an educational novel fails to become educated, the story reverts to that kind of fiction from which it originated, the novel of adventure. This retrogression carries with it a shift in emphasis: the hero recedes somewhat into the background, while the world around him grows in importance. It has frequently been observed that *Amerika* has more realistic and social content than any other of Kafka's writings. Thus the episode dealing with the death of Therese's mother has hardly a parallel in Kafka's other works, and the frequently occurring descriptions of hierarchies with the concomitant phenomenon of bootlicking have here a distinctly social, realistic significance and are without the mysterious and mystifying connotations of the later novels. The sequence that Max Brod has given to the preserved scenes of the novel observes a logical development of embracing wider and wider areas of reality. After his contact with the smaller, private organizations of office and hotel, Karl Rossmann becomes acquainted with the larger, more comprehensive, public institutions. The election campaign that he watches from Brunelda's balcony affords him an insight into some basic processes of the modern democratic state and, after a gap in the story, he is attracted by the all-embracing organization of the Nature Theatre in Oklahoma.

The traditional interpretation is that this final episode promises a harmonious, happy ending: at last Karl Rossmann finds a berth for himself, at last he is accepted. According to Max Brod, the author himself intended this novel to be "more optimistic" and "lighter" than anything he had written thus far, with the Nature Theatre episode conceived as resolving the earlier dissonances. However, as Paul Valéry remarked, "an author's interpretation of his own work has no more validity than that of anyone else." Furthermore, Brod refers to Kafka's intentions for the completed book; what is preserved are only fragments. The critic must base his reading on what he has actually before him, and not on what the author might have written but never did write. Finally: Kafka's oral remarks to Max Brod are contradicted by the title by which the author refers to the book in his diaries: "The Missing Person" (*"Der Verschollene"*). This title indicates that Kafka saw his hero lost among the anonymous, amorphous masses of the new continent: not a particularly cheerful fate.

An unprejudiced reading of the Nature Theatre episode will reveal that the pessimistic-satirical tenor of the novel prevails to the end.

After Karl Rossmann's encounter with American democracy, he is exposed to the lure of the other comprehensive social organization, the church, symbolized in the enterprise of the Nature Theatre. In this episode, Kafka uses symbols similar to those which will appear again in "A Hunger-Artist": the show business representing organized religion. There is no institution other than the church that can promise a place, employment, and security to everybody, as does the Nature Theatre. The placards through which that enterprise hopes to gain recruits are written in a style which is a mixture of evangelizing and advertising, emphasizing the unique opportunity offered and, most significant, threatening damnation to those who "refuse to believe." Not one of those who have been recruited has yet seen the blessings promised on the placards; the future happiness can be attained only after a long journey and has now to be accepted on faith. The church that attempts to win Karl Rossmann is the church in its contemporary situation: few join the fold. The constant blowing of trumpets is confusing and the enormous display of devils and angels at the entrance repels rather than attracts; the angels are impressive in size, but their heads are small. The musical instruments are not bad in themselves, but they are poorly played. In the Nature Theatre episode, Kafka has written one of his most subtle satires. The Nature Theatre is pure organization, and it is in this that its American character is revealed. In its actual functioning the Nature Theatre does not differ essentially from the boat, the office, or the hotel. Here Karl Rossmann encounters the same mass enterprise, the same system of classification, the same bureaucracy to which he is accustomed. In some respects the administrative machinery is even more refined: there is a special office for former European intermediary students. Here too is the same impersonal treatment, the same impatience with the special case lacking identification papers, and here too the same haste: the walk to the train has to be made running. The prospective employees of the Nature Theatre behave exactly like those who did not heed the call: in the train Karl bears silently the coarse teasing of his card-playing companions. If Karl Rossmann accepts the invitation of the Nature Theatre, he does so in a mood not of impatient hope, but of resignation, and with significant reservations: he confesses that he does not consider himself suited to be an actor, the central occupation in a theater; he will be satisfied with inferior technical work. What is even more important, Karl Rossmann refuses to give his real name; he prefers to continue his existence as the "missing person" he became when he first abandoned his European identity. This is the "truly enchanting perspective that opens itself with paradisiac charm in the final chapter," as the most recent German edition of *Amerika* claims in its advertisement.[1]

Outwardly, *Amerika* remains a fragment; in its inner form it is complete. Kafka might have added other episodes providing further opportunity for satirical explorations of the new world; but undoubtedly these would have been mere elaborations of the basic theme; his hero would remain the same. The novels that follow continue the basic motifs of *Amerika:* alienation, the abortive struggle to become "Americanized," the brutality of "America." The forms become more and more fantastic; the themes remain the same. Kafka's neglected novel is an indispensable introduction to his work, for only *Amerika* provides the explanation for the world in which the two other novels take place: America, though it is not specifically mentioned, is their theater of action. Seen from this point of view, the stylistic difference between *Amerika* and its successors becomes meaningful, the shift from a relatively realistic presentation to one that becomes more and more fantastic and distorted. The initial stages of this process can already be discerned in *Amerika:* the further West Karl Rossmann goes, the further Europe recedes, the more grotesque his experiences become. It is a world that can be endured and accepted with resignation at best, but any genuine form of participation becomes impossible. Karl Rossmann's position as a lift-boy is symbolical in this respect: he learns the manual operations necessary to run the elevator, but he is never permitted to see and thus to understand the central mechanism. The world outside remains forever alien and is therefore perceived as increasingly fantastic, bizarre, and threatening.

The image of America that Kafka unfolds in his first novel has a remarkable resemblance with that given by some other European authors, e.g., George Duhamel, Emilio Cecchi, and Cesare Pavese in his novel *The Moon and the Bonfires;* it is a picture that stands in the sharpest contrast to the visionary Americanism symbolized by Walt Whitman. Yet, surprisingly enough, there may be a link between *Amerika* and *Leaves of Grass,* a book with which Kafka was acquainted. On the surface, America is conceived similarly in both books: the enormous dimensions of the new continent, its anonymous masses driven by gigantic energies, its muscular virtues, and its proud contempt of Europe. However, in Kafka's novel, these themes are transposed in a most unexpected way, because the values ascribed to the different aspects of American life are completely reversed: what Whitman praises as the special distinctions of the new world, is for Kafka an object of unspeakable horror. Kafka's *Amerika* is *Leaves of Grass à rebours.*

One of the basic themes of *Leaves of Grass* is the relationship between the new and the old world; in *Amerika* this tension provides the structural symbol for the whole book. It is not beyond the range of possibility that this framework may have been partly suggested by Whitman.

Thus Kafka's novel receives a new significance: interwoven with the theme of the transition from youth to manhood is that of the relationship between the old and the new world as historical realities; the two themes are organically intertwined. *Amerika* has nothing in common with psychological novels of adolescence of romantic inspiration; in a very precise and prophetic way, Kafka was historically aware that in the twentieth century the process of emerging from childhood must take place in an Americanized world. Karl Rossmann knows instinctively that reaching genuine maturity requires competence as well in the new world of technology. Unlike so many heroes of nineteenth-century novels of education, he plans to become not an artist but an engineer. If he ever shows heroic qualities, it is in his dogged determination to become a real American; not once is he even tempted to go back to Europe. He is fascinated by the spectacle of American efficiency, physical prowess, and self-assurance; at the same time, however, he is repelled by it. He cannot identify himself with America because the new world has too thoroughly eliminated all traces of the old; it is a Europe with an added dimension: the dimension symbolized by Whitman. Karl Rossmann "can't go home again" to the music of Europe, neither can he become an engineer in America. Thus the novel ends in an impasse.

NOTE

1. In a recent article, "Zur Struktur von Kafkas Romanen," *Tijdschrift voor levende Talen,* XX, No. 5 (1954), pp. 1–18, H. Uyttersprot likewise rejects the traditional, optimistic interpretation of the Nature Theatre episode, a reading for which Max Brod is largely responsible. Uyttersprot sees in *Amerika* "an intentional caricature of the most venerable species of the German novel, the novel of development and education; to be sure, it is a development that is presented, but its direction is downward. The novel describes step by step the destruction of a man of good will who

is finally stranded in the most god-forsaken and ill-reputed corner of America, in Oklahoma of all places. Oklahoma, that 'state-within-a-state,' the name of which, 'the beautiful country,' is a snare and a delusion. The last phase of the story takes places in this sterile, uninhabited desert; this is the last refuge of the humiliated and injured, of the misfits, the unemployables and the hopeless cases. Here Karl Rossmann will disappear without a trace—a 'missing person.' "

Herman Uyttersprot

The Trial: Its Structure*

It has often been stated that the sequence of chapters in *The Trial* is not fixed; it has indeed been asserted that several chapters are interchangeable like building blocks. Is this contention tenable? Is it impossible to trace a continuous thread? Must we abandon from the start all attempts to find a logically developed, plausible plot?

If we are not, indeed, to abandon such attempts, our first step must be to question the present arrangement of the chapters, an arrangement for which Max Brod, not Kafka, is responsible and upon which Brod himself (in the epilogue to the third German edition) has thrown some doubt.[1] If we begin with the first four chapters, we soon discover a relationship between Chapters I and IV so intimate as to suggest that IV should actually appear between I and II.

In Chapter I, on the evening of the day of Joseph K.'s arrest, he argues angrily with his landlady, Frau Grubach, over her suspicions concerning Fräulein Bürstner, with whom he would like to become better acquainted. Then follows the conversation with Fräulein Bürstner in her room at 11:30 that night, abruptly interrupted by their realization that the landlady's nephew, the Captain (still nameless at this point), is an involuntary eavesdropper. This realization evokes anxiety in Fräulein Bürstner, and in Joseph K. vague feelings of guilt and concern. Now Chapter IV—as shown by indications of time, events that occur, and the emotional state of the protagonists—constitutes a

* Condensed from a translation by Konrad Gries, Edmund P. Kurz, and Inge Liebe.

direct continuation of this incident. It begins with the information that "in the next few days K. found it impossible to exchange even a word with Fräulein Bürstner." And he at first refuses to speak to Frau Grubach, but on Sunday he ends his sulking. In so doing he relieves the suspense under which she has lived, fearing that he was permanently angry; and he discovers that the Captain has betrayed nothing to her about the conversation with Fräulein Bürstner, thus dispelling his own fear on that score. These two questions raised in Chapter I are, then, resolved in Chapter IV; and Frau Grubach's statement in IV— "I kept asking myself"—ties in directly with I. Furthermore, K. meets the Captain for the first time in Chapter IV—"This was the first time that K. had seen him close at hand"—a fact which is difficult to explain if there are more than a few days between the two chapters; for otherwise K. would surely have met him previously in the small boarding-house, where "on Sunday almost all the boarders had their midday dinner . . . ."

The indications are, then, that the Sunday in Chapter IV, the Sunday upon which K. ends his sulking and speaks to Frau Grubach, is the first Sunday after the day of his quarrel with her and of his conversation with Fräulein Bürstner—which was, of course, the day of his arrest. Yet at the beginning of the present Chapter II we learn that the first interrogation in K.'s trial is to take place "next Sunday"; and when that Sunday arrives, he says, "Some ten days ago I was arrested . . . ." This, in other words, in Chapter II, is the *second* Sunday after the arrest, apparently one week *after* the events of Chapter IV. And it is worth noting that only something of this kind can account for K.'s ability in Chapter II to invent a joiner called Lanz—"the name came into his mind because Frau Grubach's nephew, the Captain, was called Lanz"—even though, in the present arrangement of chapters, he learns the Captain's name for the first time in Chapter IV.

Let us now turn to the fragment (perhaps a brief chapter) called "The District Attorney," which Brod believes should have followed immediately upon Chapter VII—its "opening lines are written on that sheet which contains a copy of the final sentences of that chapter"— and to another fragment called "Journey to His Mother."

Careful analysis will show that "The District Attorney" actually belongs at the very beginning of the novel: it could even serve as the first chapter or as a kind of prologue. The atmosphere that pervades it might be described as that of a pre-trial stage; for there is no hint of danger, no suggestion of a trial. Joseph K.'s position in life and at the bank seems entirely normal and unshaken. The circle of friends in his favorite tavern, as depicted in this fragment, corresponds exactly with that of the beer hall mentioned in Chapters I and II and nowhere else; and nothing in the novel seems to demand the sudden reappearance of these friends five chapters later at the end of Chapter VII, where Brod would put them. Precisely the same is true of the influential Hasterer, who appears in the fragment and to whom Joseph K. refers as to a personal friend in Chapter I and whom the Deputy Manager mentions as one of K.'s friends in Chapter II; with the additional, surprising fact (if we are to imagine this as part of Chapter VII) that in the fragment the Manager expresses surprise upon hearing of the friendship between the two: surely by this time he would know about it.

Furthermore, in "The District Attorney" we are informed that Joseph K. "was deprived of his mother's affection, who, half-blind, was living out of town, and whom he had last visited two years ago." If we compare this with the first lines of the unfinished chapter "Journey to His Mother," we can easily derive the exact chronology of the novel:

Suddenly, at lunch it occurred to him that he wanted to visit his mother. Now *spring was almost over* and with it the *third year* since he had seen her. She had begged him at that time to visit her on his *birthday;* despite many obstacles he had acceded to her wish, and he had even promised to spend every birthday with her, a promise, however, which he had *twice* failed to keep. Therefore he did not now want to wait until his birthday, although it was only a matter of *two weeks,* but rather to visit her at once . . . . His mother's eyesight was almost totally gone, but Joseph K. had been prepared for this for several years by the doctor's reports. [My italics.]

According to "The District Attorney," then, Joseph K. last saw his mother two years ago, when she was half blind. In "Journey to His Mother" it has been nearly three years since he saw her, and she is now almost totally blind. There is, therefore, an interim of about a year between the two fragments—namely, the fateful year, the year of the trial, which began with K.'s arrest on his thirtieth birthday and ended on the "evening before [his] thirty-first birthday . . . ." "The District Attorney" therefore cannot be inserted after Chapter VII as suggested by Brod, for at that point Joseph K. has at most a few months of life left him: Chapter VII takes place on a morning in

winter, and Joseph K. dies in the late spring or the first days of summer
—as we know from the above passage (where two weeks before his
birthday spring is "almost over"), from a specific reference to spring
in the first chapter ("That spring K. had been accustomed to . . ."),
and from descriptive details in the last chapter ("the foliage of trees
and bushes rose in thick masses").

Strong proof that the birthday mentioned in "Journey to His Mother"
is indeed his thirty-first and that at this time he therefore has only
thirteen days to live resides in K.'s emotional state throughout the fragment, where we see him as a person nearly destroyed by the arduous-
ness of the trial in its final stages. He is guilty of a "general plaintive-
ness and an endeavor to indulge in all his desires." He is sentimental
at a time when it might cause him to miss something important—that
"opportunity for intervention [personal intervention in the trial] which
might now occur any day, any hour" and for which, in Chapters VII
and VIII, there is such a fervently expressed need. There are also indications here of that constantly growing and clearly realized inability
to maintain, in the face of his trial, his position at the bank and in
everyday life, the inability which constitutes the heart of his difficult
inner struggle in Chapters VII and VIII. "Now much occurred against
his wishes," which is to say that his position at the bank has been
weakened (just as his reputation has suffered). He consoles and deceives himself: "Joseph K. still was one of the most important officials
at the bank . . . he still could take away a letter from one of the
officials, by name of Kullich, who even had connections with the court,
and without any excuse, tear it to pieces." Yet Herr Kühne, a subordinate clerk, rudely accepts Joseph K.'s directives with his face turned
sideways—"as if he were condescending to permit this ordering about
on the part of Joseph K. only from the goodness of his heart."

These two fragments—one dealing with the days before the arrest,
the other with the final stages of the trial—lead us on to discover, with
surprising completeness, the rest of the chronology. We are now able
to arrange all but one of the important events in their proper order.
"The District Attorney" belongs not after Chapter VII, where in its
present form it would destroy the coherent development of the action,
but at the beginning of the novel, either as a prologue or as Chapter I.
In all probability "Journey to His Mother" was intended as the penulti-
mate chapter: Joseph K., condemned to death, tearful, self-indulgent,
abandoned even by his mother, presumably receives neither help nor
consolation from her. All that now remains is mute resignation to his

fate, the calm acceptance of the inevitable, shown by the composure
with which he receives his executioners in the last pages of the novel.
And the basic, over-all chronology is clear. On his twenty-eighth birthday K. visits his mother for the next-to-last time, and he agrees to visit
her each year on this day. On his twenty-ninth birthday he fails to keep
his promise. On his thirtieth birthday, the day of his arrest, he fails
again. Two weeks before his thirty-first birthday he wants to make up
for his neglect, and presumably he pays his visit. Thirteen days later
he is executed.

The next step is to determine the order of events—and thus the order
of the chapters and fragments—within the year of the trial. We know,
to begin with, that this year begins and ends in late spring (or, perhaps,
very early summer). We can, on the basis of hints about the season
that we have already noticed, place K.'s birthday—the beginning of
the trial (Chapter I) and the end of it (Chapter X)—towards the end
of May or the middle of June, shortly before the summer solstice. If
we examine the other chapters for similar hints, we get, with one
exception, a perfectly consistent picture of seasonal progress through
the year.

In Chapter IV, which for other reasons we have inserted after
Chapter I, there is nothing (beyond one reference to a house standing
in the sun) to help us here.

Chapter II takes place, as we have seen, about eleven days after
the arrest and puts us into the early part of summer: as K. hurries
along to the suburb he sees men in shirtsleeves leaning out of open
windows, women at other windows airing the bedding, children playing
in the street, a man with bare feet reading a newspaper, a young girl
in her night-jacket at the well, laundry being hung up to dry, a fruit-
dealer crying his wares to the people at the windows. It is the picture
of a suburb in summer.

That Chapter III is precisely a week later is clear from the opening
sentences: "During the next week K. waited . . . and when no appointment was made by Saturday evening, he assumed that he was
tacitly expected to report himself again at the same address and at the
same time. . . . [Now the interrogation chamber] was really empty
and in its emptiness looked even more sordid than on the previous
Sunday." And the summer weather is suggested by the comment that
"the sun beats on the roof here and the hot roof-beams make the air
dull and heavy."

Chapter V (which in the new arrangement follows III) begins "a few evenings later," but there are no references to the weather or the seasons.

The hints in Chapter VI are slight, yet they suggest that we are still in summer: K.'s uncle wears a Panama hat and stands for several hours in a light rain with no mention, in his bitter complaints, of being cold.

Chapter VII, however, takes place "one winter morning." The season is twice specifically designated as winter (though it is also once inexplicably called "an awful autumn"), and there are numerous comments upon the cold and the snow. It is furthermore apparent that K., in his musings at the beginning of this chapter, looks back upon a fairly long association with the advocate whom he first met on that summer evening in Chapter VI: now "it was more than a month since Huld had sent for him, and even during the first few consultations . . . ."

There is no clear reference to weather or season in Chapter VIII, but the commercial traveler (Block), who almost prides himself upon having a trial already five and a half years long, says to K., "Your case is six months old, isn't it? Yes, that's what I heard. An infant of a case!" This would of course place the action of the chapter in December.

Thus far everything has moved as it should. But the episode in Chapter IX—which in the old arrangement falls between a day in December (Chapter VIII) and a day in late spring (Chapter X)—takes place in autumn: the "prevailing wet autumnal weather" is very much in evidence. Either this chapter is out of place or there is a *two-year* period between the arrest on K.'s thirtieth birthday and his execution the evening before his thirty-first birthday! The following tentative solution, based simply upon the progress of the seasons, suggests itself: Chapter IX should appear immediately before Chapter VII.

But does such a change hold up under closer scrutiny and, if so, how does it alter our understanding of the novel? There are at least two important arguments in favor of the old arrangement: Max Brod, Kafka's intimate friend and literary executor, established it; and a cathedral (the scene of Chapter IX), a blessed, solemn place, seems at first glance to provide a peculiarly ideal background for K.'s last struggles and an ironic contrast with the action of the final chapter. Brod himself, however, destroys the value of the latter argument when he says, in his epilogue to the American and the first German edition,

"Franz Kafka regarded the novel as unfinished. Before the final chapter . . . various further stages of the mysterious trial should have been described." If this is true, then any purely aesthetic notions we may have about the juxtaposition of Chapters IX and X must give way. And there are of course some fragments—"Struggle with the Deputy Manager," "Journey to His Mother," and "The House"—which seem in fact to be Kafka's attempts to describe those "various further stages" of the action related to the trial. "Journey to His Mother," especially, with its precise information about the time—only thirteen days before the execution—fits smoothly into the novel immediately before Chapter X. "The House," we know, must follow the unit composed of Chapters VII and VIII; for it deals with Titorelli, the painter whom K. met on that winter morning in Chapter VII, and it speaks of him as K.'s close, almost intimate friend, thereby suggesting that a reasonably long period of time has passed since the December day of Chapter VIII. Yet there is still no evidence other than the autumnal setting of Chapter IX to suggest that the cathedral scene does not belong even closer to the end of K.'s life than does his journey to his mother. We must look more closely at the substance of the novel.

Whatever might be the meaning of the novel, it is certain that the year-long struggle between the incomprehensible trial and normal life —between those powers that would destroy and those that would preserve life, or, reduced to simpler terms, between the court and work (K.'s duties at the bank)—is the axis around which everything revolves. Until his thirtieth birthday Joseph K. lives for his work, his position, without any obstacle and with all his powers. We have already seen how the fragment called "The District Attorney" shows him as the completely unhampered and successful head clerk. On his thirtieth birthday the trial appears (the disintegrating delusion, the persecution complex, the obsession, the neurosis?); but at first, for months even, the danger is underestimated as it only slowly undermines the ability to work, the joy found in work. For example, even as late as the last lines in the fragment "To Elsa," which probably belongs between Chapters V and VI, K. has the power to forget about the court: "thoughts about the Bank began, as in former times, to absorb him completely."

K. resists the corrosive power of the court at first mildly, carelessly, in high spirits, even challengingly (see "To Elsa"), then more and more frequently and violently. But the trial slowly overpowers him, paralyzing his ability to resist, inducing at last a state of apathy and lack of will. At first K. recognizes what is happening, but the recognition grows fainter until he succumbs to the hostile power of the court "without knowing . . . ." If this struggle, with K.'s resulting disintegration, is progressive, close attention to it should tell us something about the sequence of chapters; and, indeed, if we read Chapters VII and IX carefully, we are struck by the fact that the disintegration is far more pronounced in VII than in IX.

In Chapter IX K.'s position with the bank is still safe, basically unaffected by the trial. He is still considered an efficient clerk whom his superiors trust not only with "honourable" business missions but with the responsibility ("that K. would once have felt to be an honour") of entertaining an Italian colleague whose "influential connections . . . made him important to the Bank . . . ." K. is, to be sure, deeply troubled. He knows that he is no longer "able to make the best use of his office hours," he sees himself "continually threatened by mistakes intruding into his work from all sides," he thinks "now that all his energies [are] needed . . . to retain his prestige in the Bank," and he cannot help "suspecting that there [is] a plot to get him out of the way while his work [is] investigated . . . ." But nothing in the chapter suggests that his superiors are actually aware of his decreasing value to them; and he cannot know "if there [is] even the smallest ground for his suspicions . . . ." The fear he has of not being allowed, after a business trip, to return to the bank is "a fear which he well knew to be exaggerated . . . ." His worries are, in other words, great; but he knows that he must fight against exaggerated and even unfounded apprehensions, that he must exert himself, force himself to work. Furthermore, he still has the necessary energy, the will to fight. In front of others—though not before his own conscience—he still asserts himself with determination. On the whole, it is his work and not the trial which as yet forms the center of his activities. Even when away from the bank he thinks about his duties there, aware, as he is, of his weakening ability to work properly. This is of course a sign that he is no longer normal, is already pathological: before the trial he could freely enjoy his leisure. Still, until the conversation with the priest late in the chapter, a conversation in which K. becomes involved almost against his will, there is little mention of the trial as such. His thoughts revolve around his duties at the bank.

Now let us turn to Chapter VII, where in contrast to IX, we find a shattered, tortured, self-torturing individual, one who is irresolute, apathetic, wholly unable to work. Consider the very first lines: "One winter morning—snow was falling outside the window in a foggy dimness—K. was sitting in his office, already exhausted in spite of the early hour. To save his face before his subordinates at least, he had given his clerk instructions to admit no one, on the plea that he was occupied with an important piece of work. But instead of working he twisted in his chair, idly rearranged the things lying on his writing-table, and then, without being aware of it, let his outstretched arm rest on the table and sat on with bowed head, immobile." The following pages are concerned with K.'s thoughts as he sits there shamelessly neglecting the interests of the bank and its clients, interests which were once so close to his heart. He is unable to rouse himself until eleven o'clock: "he had wasted two hours in dreaming, a long stretch of precious time, and he was, of course, still wearier than he had been before." When at last he grants one of the long-waiting clients (the manufacturer) an interview, he is unable to pay attention, though he knows this to be an "important piece of business"; and he is actually relieved when the hated Deputy Manager steals the client away, a theft that he would never previously have allowed. But now he is glad to be alone: "he had not the slightest intention of interviewing any more clients [there are several who have been waiting all morning for him] and vaguely realized how pleasant it was that the people waiting outside believed him to be still occupied with the manufacturer, so that nobody, not even the attendant, would disturb him. He went over to the window, perched on the sill, holding on to the latch with one hand, and looked down on the square below. The snow was still falling, the sky had not yet cleared. For a long time he sat like this, without knowing what really troubled him . . . ."

Chapter VII shows us a man who is no longer able to keep his mind on anything but himself, his own difficulties. Things have gone so far that it is no longer, as in Chapter IX, the trial which seems to him to interfere with his work but precisely the other way around: "While his case was unfolding itself, while up in the attics the Court clerks were poring over the charge papers, was he to devote his attention to the affairs of the Bank?" In Chapter IX the priest had to remind K. of the trial, and could do so without really upsetting him. They were able to discuss the court and its proceedings calmly and objectively, and, so far as K. was concerned, even indifferently at the beginning. But

in Chapter VII the trial overshadows everything: "the thought of his
case never left him now." The man who in Chapter IX was still willing
and able to work and who was perfectly aware of the need to fight
against the trial is here convinced of the need to fight *for* the trial. All
the energy that he had previously mustered for his work is now devoted to the trial, which has literally cast a spell over him, has pushed
aside everything else, all pleasures, all normal ambitions. The decisions he now reaches, "the decisions which might prove valuable,"
have nothing to do with forcing himself to work, as was still the case
in Chapter IX; they involve, for example, the question of whether to
keep or to dismiss his lawyer; they have value only in connection with
the trial. And though such decisions are the sole result of his wasted
working hours, they give him satisfaction: "the Court would encounter
for once an accused man who knew how to stick up for his rights."

Only once in this long chapter—by far the longest in the novel,
sixty-four pages, with a direct continuation in Chapter VIII—does he
momentarily remember that especially at this time he "should be devoting his mind entirely to work"; and only once does he pause briefly
over the fact that should he continue to abandon his work so completely (he is about to rush off to see Titorelli, the painter, leaving
three more clients to the Deputy Manager) "his prestige in the Bank
would suffer irreparable injury." Such thoughts have no power over
him: "almost elated," he pursues the course he knows will ruin him
at the bank. The prestige which he here sacrifices so consciously was,
we remember, intact in Chapter IX, and K. was still fighting to retain
it.[2] Furthermore, in Chapter IX K. only imagines as a fearful possibility what in Chapter VII actually happens. "In his mind [in Chapter
IX] he saw the Deputy Manager, who had always spied upon him,
prowling every now and then into his office, sitting down at his desk,
running through his papers, receiving clients who had become almost
old friends of K.'s in the course of many years, and turning them against
him . . . ." In Chapter VII the Deputy Manager actually does come
into K.'s office, he does run through K.'s papers—searches "through his
files as if they belonged to him" and even carries a huge package of
documents off to his own office—and he does, with not so much as a
murmur of complaint from K., take for himself four of K.'s clients.
Yet as K. leaves the bank immediately after this defeat, which would
once have been insufferable, he is "almost elated at the thought
of being able to devote himself almost entirely to his case for a
while . . . ."[3]

It seems clear enough on the basis of the evidence already presented—Kafka's references to weather and to the seasons and his handling of the conflict between work and trial within K.'s mind—that Chapter IX must precede Chapter VII. And if we examine the highly important conversation between K. and the priest which forms the last half of Chapter IX, we find that it, too, suggests the accuracy of the new arrangement. It is, to begin with at least, oddly vague and mild if we are to imagine it as coming after the long, even tedious, complicated characterizations of the court and of the possible judgments that flow from Huld (the advocate), Block (the commercial traveler) and Titorelli (the painter) in Chapters VII and VIII. The mildness of the priest's warning—"Do you know that your case is going badly?"—and K.'s reply—"I have that idea myself"—would perhaps seem more appropriate if they preceded instead of followed the far more pessimistic remarks (by a variety of characters, including a bank attendant, K.'s uncle, and Leni) to be found in the earlier chapters. The priest appears, furthermore, to know nothing about the ways in which K. has, in Chapters VII and VIII, conducted his defense. He says, "You cast about too much for outside help . . . especially from women." Now it is true that K. has sought for help from Fräulein Bürstner in Chapter I and the wife of the Law-Court Attendant in Chapter III and that he has found help without asking for it from Leni in Chapter VI, all of which would give the priest's remark real force if Chapter IX followed immediately after VI. But in Chapters VII and VIII, and in the fragment "The House," we learn about the discussions between K. and the advocate and about his attempts to obtain help from Block and Titorelli. It is in these chapters that we find the greatest detail and the deepest penetration; it is from these gentlemen that K. obtains the insight into the court, into its functions and procedures, that he has until then sought in vain. Yet in all of Chapter IX no mention is made, by the priest or by anyone else, of Huld, Block, or Titorelli. Is not such a silence difficult to explain unless Chapter IX does in fact precede Chapters VII and VIII?

This limited knowledge on the part of the priest has its counterpart in K.—in the conception he has here of the Court, which, he says, "consists almost entirely of petticoat-hunters. Let the Examining Magistrate see a woman in the distance and he almost knocks down his desk and the defendant in his eagerness to get at her." It is a conception based entirely upon his experiences in Chapters II and III. He shows here neither fear nor respect; his remarks reveal only scorn and indignation, an almost haughty indifference, which is of course familiar to us from that part of the novel which precedes Chapter VII. But in Chapter VII there arises a genuine longing on K.'s part to "study" the court, and this longing is stimulated by K.'s relationship with the experienced Block in Chapter VIII. Titorelli, in Chapter VII, notices it at once: "You want to find out something about the court . . . ." But there is not the slightest intimation of it anywhere in Chapter IX.

The priest makes a good impression upon K., and at one point K. says to him, "You are very good to me . . . . But you are an exception among those who belong to the Court. I have more trust in you than in any of the others, though I know many of them." By the end of Chapter VI the final pronoun would refer to the guards, the bailiff, the examining magistrate, the student, the attendant, the usher, the young lady, the advocate, the chief clerk, and several subordinate officials. But if Chapter IX follows Chapters VII and VIII, the pronoun must also refer to Titorelli. He, too, must be one of the "others" in whom K. has little trust. This does not, I think, seem likely, for K. learns a great deal from Titorelli; yet the possibility raises a most important matter: the real significance of the painter.

K. first meets Titorelli on a winter forenoon in Chapter VII; and after a long talk K. leaves, promising to return soon. " 'But you must keep your word,' said the painter . . . , 'or else I'll have to come to the Bank myself to make inquiries.' " And his next-to-last words are "till our next meeting." By the time of the fragment "The House" there have apparently been many meetings: K. and the painter have become close, almost intimate friends. This fragment, if nothing else, demonstrates that the Titorelli relationship was not conceived to end with Chapter VII; it seems, on the contrary, specifically designed (with "Journey to His Mother") to fill out the really large gap between Chapters VII–VIII (winter) and Chapter X (late spring or early summer). Here—and here in particular—the incompleteness of the novel makes itself felt in a most regrettable manner. There are of course a number of people who give K. information as he investigates the court and tries to clarify his case and discover the nature of his guilt; but the individual whose central position is most strongly emphasized is Titorelli. None other gives K. as deep an insight into the mysteries or makes him as familiar with the functions and the apparatus involved as does the painter.

The priest, to be sure, warns him against mistaken judgments; yet he affords him no better insight, not even through the parable "In the Eyes of the Law." Whatever may be the meaning of this legend, K. does not understand it, refers to it as something completely unknown to him, as he does with the other explanations of the priest, which are completely unsatisfactory and constantly digress from the point at issue. Can they, in fact, really be called "explanations"? Are they not rather a somewhat cowardly way of evading the subject? Perhaps significant in this connection is a passage which Kafka deleted from the novel: "It occurred to him that he had now talked about and criticized a legend; he didn't even know the work from which this legend came, and just as unfamiliar to him were the explanations. He had been drawn into a train of thought that was completely unfamiliar to him. Was this clergyman like all the others after all? Did he wish to discuss his affair only in hints, perhaps deceive him thereby, and remain silent at the end?" Whatever the answer to such a question, the interview with the priest leaves K. in the cold, perhaps more so than he has ever been before, especially after the priest's meaningless last words—"The Court makes no claims upon you. It receives you when you come and it relinquishes you when you go"—which provide the whole rhetorically arranged chapter with a most insipid finale and form an almost brusque contrast with what in the old arrangement is the immediately follow-ing execution.

K.'s need for instruction, for an understanding of the mysterious authorities is satisfied no better either by the lawyer, who purposely deceives him by giving him a partially false picture of the court and of his true situation, or by the helpless Block, who does, however, demon-strate in his own person what happens to those who are accused and not sentenced: they become dogs, weakened and worn out by years of torture, robbed of all their human dignity, cringing in doglike, de-basing humility, ready for any act of servility.

Between Block, the victim, and the lawyer stands the painter, the true warner. It is from his lips that K. learns everything: the inexor-ability of the court [4] and the exact nature of the various possibilities open to the accused. It follows that K. must see in Titorelli the only one who does not, "like all the others," dismiss him with vague hints but, instead, gives him the insight he craves.[5] In Chapter IX, with the priest, an occasional monumental sentence betokens a general and valid insight; in Chapter VII, with Titorelli, such insights follow each other in rapid succession to form an impressive total: "Never in any case can the Court be dislodged . . . . everything belongs to the Court. . . . A single executioner could do all that is needed." And there are many more. Titorelli knows that there are only two real alternatives to being sentenced—"ostensible acquittal and indefinite postponement"—and he leads K. to understand that while they do "save the accused from coming up for sentence," they also "prevent an actual acquittal." At which observation, Titorelli says, "You have grasped the kernel of the matter." The kernel, the heart! In other words, here is the concisely phrased significance of the painter's long, excessively long, speech (perhaps it is also Kafka's final philosophy, the only lesson to be found in his writings, a lesson of defeat): there is absolutely no way out, there is no hope. Of the one alternative, Titorelli says, "The second acquittal is followed by the third arrest, the third acquittal by the fourth arrest, and so on. That is implied in the very idea of ostensible acquittal." And of the other alternative K., in the next chapter, meets a concrete example: Block, who has experienced, over five and a half years, all that the painter describes as a possibility; his trial has gone on and on, and nothing points to a possible solution, to a possible end. This is what we recall when we are watching K.'s death, for he too recalls it. He approaches death calmly, almost joyfully, for he refuses to bear what Block has suffered. His pride intervenes: "am I to show now that not even a whole year's struggling with my case has taught me anything? Am I to leave this world as a man who shies away from all conclusions? Are people to say of me after I am gone that at the beginning of my case I wanted it to finish, and at the end of it wanted it to begin again? I don't want that to be said." He has, in effect, made the decision that Titorelli defined for him by describing the various possibilities.

We have reached our goal. The structure of *The Trial* is represented by the following new arrangement of chapters and fragments (Arabic numerals for the new numbering, Roman numerals for the old):

The District Attorney (fragment)

1 (I)	7 (IX)
2 (IV)	8 (VII)
3 (II)	9 (VIII)
4 (III)	Struggle with the Deputy Manager (fragment)
5 (V)	The House (fragment)
To Elsa (fragment)	Journey to His Mother (fragment)
6 (VI)	10 (X)

It remains only to extract from our presentation a few conclusions, already mentioned briefly in passing.

In opposition to the commonly accepted opinion that Kafka consciously aimed for chaos and confusion as elements productive of magical effects, the chronology we have discovered in the text seems to show that he in no way wished to create a chaos, a magical jumble. On the contrary, it seems to show that he envisaged a well-planned, orderly structure, determined by a compact time schedule, whose evolution is marked outwardly, so to speak, by birthdays, while the logical succession of the seasons guarantees a natural development in the factual and emotional course of the events. The whole is marked by directness, by an almost schematic rigidity. It is in the same direct manner that Kafka wished to plan and shape the core of his story, the battle between work and court, between intellectual and emotional health and sickness, between the sense of reality and fever-ridden fancies.

By moving Chapter IX to a position just before Chapter VII and by inserting the fragment "The House" after Chapter VIII, we move Titorelli, a subordinate figure in the old arrangement of the chapters, out of the shadows and throw a new light upon him. He becomes a figure of outstanding significance, a bridge, so to speak, to the second half of the novel, a half which has either been largely lost or—and this seems more probable—was never written; that half which corresponds to the gap in the time schedule (from December to the death in late spring or early summer) which is suggested rather than filled by the three fragments "The House," "The Struggle with the Deputy Manager," and "Journey to His Mother."

One becomes almost certain that it was especially the relationship between K. and Titorelli that was to be expanded in the various stages of the mysterious trial which, as Max Brod remarks in the first epilogue, were still to be described. The insight into this relationship and thus into the significance of the figure of the painter which we gain from Chapter VII and from "The House" opens the door to new possibilities; yet just here the novel is most fragmentary. Nevertheless, in Titorelli there appears in *The Trial* too that figure which is seldom missing in a Kafka story, the initiate or the group of initiates (see, for example, "The Great Wall of China," "A Hunger-Artist," "Josephine").

It is probably also the incompleted state of the novel which may have been the real reason that induced the author to forbid publication. Kafka—who published all his completed stories, who personally read the proofs of the stories in *A Hunger-Artist* even in his sick bed, who was not indifferent to fame and success—demanded that the manuscript be destroyed because he did not wish the public to see an incomplete work, a work that simply had not jelled yet.

This leads to the further consideration that we may perhaps never succeed in unraveling the secret, the deeper significance of the novel, precisely because of the incomplete and unsatisfactory development of the figure of Titorelli, which after all is only sketched in, and which might have represented, in the battle against destruction, the last and most important form of assistance: art, the written word, literature. As is plain from countless pieces of evidence, this was Kafka's main preoccupation, the content and support of his life.

Shall we therefore renounce every attempt to interpret the novel, to "translate" it, as Fr. Beissner ironically says of the interpretations that have been given? Not quite. To be sure, we shall not venture an interpretation in the most daring sense of the word. Attempts to detect the meaning even of short and therefore more easily comprehensible structures like the stories in *A Hunger-Artist* have failed. Thus the following suggestion for a possible interpretation of *The Trial* is meant only as a hypothesis.

It may be that *The Trial* is a grandly conceived psychological and autobiographical novel, a symbolic depiction of that emotional-intellectual disease, neurasthenia, which one day came upon Kafka for reasons which cannot be entered upon here (natural disposition, inheritance, relations with his father, etc.). This would then be the novel of the neurasthenic Franz Kafka who writes in his diary for May 2, 1913: "I, who wish to cure my neurasthenia through work," and who precisely in the year 1913, to which we may perhaps date the first beginnings of *The Trial*, scatters similar remarks throughout his diaries. It was especially from the comparison between Chapter IX and Chapter VII (IX now preceding VII) that we obtained the impression that the process here being described is noticeably similar to this disease with its stealthy approach and its ever more penetrating effects. It seems possible to recognize the characteristics of a hypochondriac in a hundred places, in tiny traits, in typical actions, in a growing obsession with a given notion, an *idée fixe*. It may be appropriate to signal some of these hints, always with reference to K.: the tendency to refer everything to himself or to consider it as referring to himself (the laughing or smiling of strangers), the immediate sensing of a real or only imaginary insult (Frau Grubach, the Deputy Manager); the inclination to attach undue importance to unimportant events (the behavior of Kaminer, of the uncle); the discrepancy, of which he grows progressively more strongly and painfully aware, between his will to be normal, his desire for an active life, his own abilities and potentialities, on the one hand, and the failure, on the other, of his will and his vitality as a result of his torturous wavering between deed and dream; and the ever-increasing activity of his feverish imagination. These are exactly the details which are noticeable as well in the development which takes place from Chapter IX to Chapter VII, and which are perhaps most clearly brought out in the fragment "The House."

If this suggestion about the meaning of *The Trial* is correct, then we have gained a new insight and provided new proof that Kafka—like every true poet, in my opinion—can be comprehended and illuminated through the spiritual and the biographical; that the individual cannot be separated from the author in the case of Kafka any more than is possible in the case of Kleist or of Rilke. As a result, the fundamental importance of the diaries and other documents (letters to Milena, the letter to his father, various fragments, etc.) receives new stress. And the search for the basic reason for his work may reach its goal in the possibility that Kafka, the man who knew himself and killed himself, who constantly bears witness in the diaries to his self-destructive work, wished to use *The Trial* to get his experiences out of his system.

NOTES

1. Brod says: "Upon re-examination of the manuscript it seems quite possible that Kafka intended the episode now marked Chapter V as Chapter II." This will not hold, however, for the simple reason that in Chapter V the two chastised guards, Franz and Willem, who performed the arrest in Chapter I, refer to an incident which occurred in Chapter II: "Sir! We're to be flogged because you complained about us to the Examining Magistrate." In Chapter II, Joseph K. had indeed complained to the Magistrate: "The room next to mine was requisitioned by two coarse warders. . . . These warders . . . were degenerate ruffians . . . ." Obviously, the comment of the guards (in Chapter V) cannot precede the action (in Chapter II) upon which they are commenting.

2. In Chapter IX he is aware that "now . . . all his energies were needed to retain his prestige at the Bank"; and he accordingly exerts himself the more, with apparent success.

3. André Gide and J. L. Barrault, who, in adapting the novel to the

stage, paid no attention to the time schedule, nevertheless realized that something was wrong. Accordingly, they inserted a short scene which ties in with the situation in IX, belongs factually to both IX and VII, but is spiritually aligned exclusively to VII. The Deputy Manager energetically but vainly attempts to replace K. in his role as companion of the Italian. This is pure invention; in IX there is no trace of any such intention. In VII, on the other hand, there is both a replacement and an acquiescence therein. The adapters have thus had the right instinct: only in this way could they achieve the required, natural intensification.

4. "Never in any case can the Court be dislodged from [its conviction that the accused is guilty]. If I were to paint all the Judges in a row on one canvas and you were to plead your case before it, you would have more hope of success than before the actual Court." These are the painter's words. Do they not sound like a death sentence?

5. It is only in Titorelli that he can see a possibility of escape (and this in spite of the painter's harsh remarks); this is the unequivocal sense of the fragment "The House": "Here, if anywhere, the breakthrough was possible . . . Titorelli . . . knew what K. was after . . . K. knew that he [Titorelli] was ready to grant his wish . . . ." Placing Chapter IX before Chapter VII suggests an interesting possibility in this connection: Titorelli may be the personification of the doorman in the legend "In the Eyes of the Law"—that is, the concrete representation of what is in the legend a mythical abstraction. In view of Kafka's liking for anagrams and word-plays in connection with personal names, one might see a similar game here: Titorelli-Titurel. At any rate it is worth mentioning that Titurel, the first king of the Grail, ancestor of the race of the guardians of the Grail, is the sage and initiate par excellence, from whom the younger generation seeks advice. Unfortunately I have not succeeded in discovering the etymological significance of the name "Titurel." I take the opportunity to thank my friend D. Cola Minis, of Rotterdam, for his efforts in this matter.

René Dauvin

The Trial: Its Meaning*

The Trial is so mysterious, so vague, that many interpretations
are possible. As we stand on the threshold of Kafka's work, we feel
uneasy, disoriented. The very form and structure of the novel amaze
us, for it escapes all classification and transports us into an atmosphere
of hallucination and strange disquiet. There seems to be no apparent
continuity in this world. Did Kafka, then, abandon himself to the
meanderings of dreams? I do not think so. We must take Joseph K. to
be the alter ego of Kafka. The author of *The Trial* and his hero are
both obsessed by strange visions which haunt their sleep. How can
one rid himself of these anguished specters that inhabit the most
diverse layers of the subconscious and which are ready to rise to the
surface the instant awareness of reality flags? Psychoanalysis tells us
that this can be done by an effort of the consciousness which brings
these specters out into the light. And that is precisely what Kafka does.
Literary composition was for him a sort of catharsis. That is why *The
Trial* is a plunge into the night, a long nightmare which takes us through
the stifling atmosphere of the darkest regions of Kafka's ego.

Joseph K. is arrested one morning after getting up. This is the hour,
according to Kafka's *Diary,* when "healthy men disperse the phantoms
of the night." But with him, "the phantoms return as the night wears
on, and in the morning they are all there, only they are not recognizable." Thus, K.'s arrest is the beginning of a nightmare or, more
exactly, of a series of nightmares. The action, therefore, takes place in

* Translated by Martin Nozick.

145

Kafka's soul, and the plot is symbolic of manifest or repressed tendencies. The characters of *The Trial,* whether they argue with K. or agree with him, are aspects of his ego. The novel is a dialogue Kafka has with himself; it is not by chance that one of the police inspectors actually bears the name "Franz." In his dreams, Kafka becomes aware of the deep antagonisms which tear his being apart. But he is not the master of his nocturnal visions. He allows himself to be guided by them, a fact that explains the alogical composition of the novel. These nightmares haunt him at night and on Sundays—in other words, during those hours when the congeries of daily toil no longer spreads a protective screen of banal tasks over the subconscious. That is why Joseph K. is summoned to court either at night or on Sundays. Furthermore, Joseph K., more aware than Kafka's other characters, knows very well that this mishap could not have happened to him at the office. "In the Bank, for instance, I am always prepared," said Joseph K., "nothing of that kind could possibly happen to me there. I have my own attendant, the general telephone and the office telephone stand before me on my desk, people keep coming in to see me, clients and clerks, and above all, my mind is always on my work and so kept on the alert." What, then, are these long, stifling corridors leading nowhere, these ghostlike judges with their phantom beards, these dark attics, if not the nocturnal universe of Kafka or Joseph K.? Now we know the climate in which the novel unfolds. The dream-key is the one that opens the door to this world. Let us now search out the keys which will provide the interpretation of the novel and will disclose to what extent the problems of life inspired Kafka.

Kafka was a strange personality who from childhood on struggled with the "difficulty of being"; for he wanted to live in an authentic fashion. But he could not express this strangeness; language is important because it is general; it is a tool created by the impersonal "we" and can only translate the forms of being which are of the least common denominator. But the regions explored by Kafka are "regions in which silence reigns." He could therefore use language only allusively. This he notes in his *Diaries* on January 12, 1911:

I haven't written down a great deal about myself these days, partly because of laziness (I now sleep so much and so soundly during the day, I have greater weight while I sleep), but also partly because of the fear of betraying my self-perception. This fear is justified, for one should permit a self-perception to be established definitively in writing only when it can be done with the greatest completeness, with all the incidental consequences, as well as with entire truthfulness. For if this does not happen—and in any event I am not capable of it—then what is written down will, in accordance with its own purpose and with the superior power of the established, replace what has been felt only vaguely in such a way that the real feeling will disappear while the worthlessness of what has been noted down will be recognized too late.

Therefore, for Kafka, there is an incommensurability between the specific and the general, and in the passage from the diary just quoted, we recognize the insurmountable difficulties Joseph K. came up against once he decided to write the story of his life. The strange individual is unhappy, for his uniqueness cannot be communicated. Besides, he must struggle against a society which seeks, by every means at its disposal, to wipe out the particularity of the man who wishes to live faithful to himself. "In school and at home they tried to erase individuality," said Kafka, and this reproach is like a knife-thrust aimed at society in general. If his particular individuality was condemned, how much more serious must have been the particularities he concealed and in which he himself recognized some small injustice: for example, when he would read of an evening instead of studying his lessons. This censure was not only directed *at* him by others; he also inflicted it on himself for having been derelict in his duty, and the results were extremely depressing. When he hid one of his particularities, he considered himself wicked or damned. As he grew older, his strangeness increased along with the number of his secrets, and because of his acute awareness, he knew that everything could not be confessed. Thus with an increase of awareness and the passage of time, the feeling of guilt grew in Kafka, and by extension, in Joseph K. There was no use in Kafka's confessing; he was so unique that his secret was thrown back at him by society in general, for among the living, he says, nobody can be free of himself. There is no escape. He must live with his secrets, like a windowless monad, for the confession that liberates is impossible. The odd individual is therefore guilty and Joseph K.'s crime is in part rooted in his oddity. Society can do nothing with people who will not fit into one of its categories and thus trouble the sleep of the many. The hermit had warned Zarathustra: "Men do not trust hermits; the sound of solitary feet through the deserted streets disturbs them." Joseph K. follows set paths only superficially. In truth, he lives on the periphery of society, misunderstood, unhappy over his absurd work at the bank while he feels vaguely within him an infinitely rich and complex world that causes him anguish.

The individual who stands apart from the rest therefore feels guilty over his apartness. Furthermore, his guilt feeling is aggravated when he wishes to reveal his singularity, for he must affirm it against the established order, against his father, against the Judaism he represents, and even against Christianity. Like the Kierkegaard who could not be led by the enfeebled hand of Christianity, Kafka could not imitate the Zionists and hold on to the fringes of the Jewish tallith which was going with the wind. Since he did not feel himself to be an heir of the meager positivism of his times, he turned against it.

Kafka rebelled against his father's Judaism. He attended the synagogue but saw in religious practice only a lifeless paltry ritualism. "It was indeed really, so far as I could see, a mere scrap, a joke, not even a joke," said the young Kafka in his "Letter to His Father." "On four days in the year you went to the synagogue . . . and patiently went through the prayers by way of formality . . . . And so I yawned and dozed through the many hours." A few things did amuse him, "as for instance, when the Ark of the Covenant was opened which always reminded me of the shooting-galleries where a cupboard would open in the same way whenever one got a bull's-eye, only with the difference that there something interesting always came out and here it was always just the same old dolls with no heads." Religious instruction required only ridiculous "memorization." When during the prayers for the dead, the young Kafka was sent away, he more or less unconsciously felt that something indecent must be happening in the synagogue.

God is dead or dying. This is the essence of a short story called "In Our Synagogue." The Word is embodied in an animal with a terrible snout that haunts the synagogue at prayer time. No one recognizes the divine Idea in this animal, so deformed and ugly has it become in men's hands. The rabbis scarcely tolerate it; the sexton wants to kill it with a sling. The God of the synagogue is dying.

The world has lost its spirituality, for man has become an abstract being without fervor. The Law sometimes issues warnings to this impoverished humanity, but such calls are never heeded. And so, one Sunday morning when he awakens, a man finds a blade lodged in the nape of his neck, the blade of the Law. He pulls it out. Not a drop of blood flows, for life in this person is dried up; and heedless of God, he is reassured and happy when he joins his friends in the familiar world of the Sunday stroll.

The divine Law is unknown and the Court has lost its key, for God is the creator and keeper of moral values. Henceforth any moral judgment becomes both true and vain, for it is true only because its truth is human and relative. That is why the Court which summons Joseph K. is made up of subordinate, corrupt judges. The Supreme Court is inaccessible. When life is not related to an absolute standard, it becomes gratuitous, absurd, and sin may be the acceptance of this unjustifiable life since the supreme judges cannot be touched. The court scene is to a certain extent an oblique but violent attack on the type of Judaism practiced in the Prague synagogue, which Kafka does not dare to name openly for, at bottom, he remains a Jew. Religion, born of man's existential anguish, was once the highest manifestation of the human spirit wondering about its destiny. But today it is so degraded, so obsolete, that it deserves to be relegated to the attics where the court sits. The sacred books have been replaced by obscene ones. The cruel zealous God of the Old Testament has become so inaccessible that Kafka never mentions His name. Only crude subordinate officials, stupid, pretentious bureaucrats represent Him and bar the path that leads to Him. One must rediscover the forgotten divinity cut off by all the misunderstandings that conceal His essence. There are too many servants in the Temple, says Kafka, too many servants paid by the community, people who live on religion and in religion but do not understand it and do not serve it in sacrifice and pain.

And so there is no salvation in Judaism. What does Kafka think of Christianity? The cathedral is empty, desperately empty and dark. It is no longer a place for meditation; it is an historical monument which Joseph K. visits. He does not bring a prayer book, but a sight-seers' guide. The priest, who seems inspired by the faith of old, does not preach from the main pulpit since for him it must represent the pulpit of deceit. He is satisfied with a small pulpit and chooses for his sermon a most unusual hour when the building is not profaned by an anonymous crowd who pay only lip service to faith. He would without doubt be stoned as a heretic if he wanted to bring religion back to its original purity, for

> In the pulpit and at the altar
> There was no longer a Moses or Aaron.
> The divine service was carried on

Like any other thing
Which, following the course of the world
Is dry and withered with age.

Kafka therefore rebels against Judaism and Christianity, both obstacles to his subjectivity. His uniqueness demands a break with the
synagogue; it also requires solitude, and like his Joseph K. he chooses
the celibate life after having broken his engagement five times. He is,
as a matter of fact, a taciturn, unsociable, unhappy person, although he
does not consider that to be a misfortune since his unhappiness is only
the "counterpart of the ideal he has set up." His fiancée is, on the other
hand, a healthy, cheerful, natural young girl who will be made unhappy by his temperament. He admits he is "diabolical although
innocent"; for, he says, what he will suffer and what she will suffer is
nothing in comparison to what they would have suffered together. To
these psychological reasons the Kafka who wrote *The Trial* in his
thirtieth year, or at Joseph K.'s age, adds a metaphysical one. "What I
have to do, I can do only alone: shed light on ultimate ends. The
Western Jew has no clear idea of this and therefore has no right to get
married."

Thus far, Kafka strikes us as a strange man who, jealous of his
originality, affirms it against collective tyranny. He rebels against his
father and against Judaism. Christianity finds no grace in his eyes, for
he regards it as a collection of petrified ideas. God is dead, or rather,
forgotten. The unique being requires solitude and condemns marriage.

But Kafka's personality is not that simple, for he is nothing of the
Promethean superman. Nietzsche, who murdered God, held up to man
a new ideal, the superman who replaced God; the eternal return replaced eternal happiness. Kafka took from "the requirements of life
only human weakness." We not only sinned, he says, when we ate of
the fruit of the tree of knowledge, but also because we have not yet
eaten of the fruit of the tree of life. Kafka is therefore a weak person
without the strength to make a complete denial, and antagonistic
tendencies coexist in his soul. He both denies and affirms without
daring to make a choice; he lives in anguish. If he is in conflict with
paternal authority, he is nonetheless "an eternal adolescent who never
ceases to desire a return to the father." If he condemns Judaism, he is
nostalgic for it. If he chooses solitude, he fears it, and while possessed
of a profound desire to live in the community, he stands on the border
line between solitude and community which is worse even than soli-

tude. Kafka's ego is torn by antinomies. No matter what he chooses, he still sins and is forced to punish himself. He is on the side of his executioners, like the Joseph K. who is overcome by pity for the inspectors who have arrested and robbed him; and he goes back to the Court although he has not been summoned. This anguish dominates his life, his sleep. He is the culprit and the judge.

What was the way out of this impasse? How could he make a choice? There was no more divine norm, for God had turned away from the earth. The Law is no longer understood, life is absurd, and Joseph K., like Camus's *The Stranger,* has the experience of total gratuitousness. His arrest he regards as a "ridiculous nothingness." He has a vague feeling of his original contingency and looks for judges to justify his existence, judges who will be essences. He does not possess the strength to stand up under his gratuitousness, to assume a solitude which frightens him. He would like to be integrated into a hierarchy. These are vain hopes; the judges he meets are subordinate, corrupt judges. How can he again find the calm security of his childhood and thus escape the vertigo which seizes man when faced by his gratuitousness? Only by creating a new Law, an absolute Law which will restore meaning to our existence. Let us see whether Joseph K., while he still lives, succeeds in creating this new Law.

Up to his thirtieth year, Joseph K. was a man like other men. He led the life of an automaton and found peace and security in the world of daily routine and work. He would stay at the office until nine; then he would take a little walk, alone or with colleagues, and round out the evening at the café, where he stayed until eleven usually at a reserved table in the company of older men. There were exceptions to this regime: the Manager of the Bank who thought highly of his work occasionally invited him to take an automobile ride or for dinner at his villa. Once a week K. visited a young lady named Elsa who was night waitress at a café and during the day entertained her visitors from her bed. One cannot imagine a more impersonal, anonymous existence. His name, reduced to a simple initial, is symbolic from the outset, Joseph K.'s life is a superficial one, like the lives of all those who, in an attempt to escape the anguish of original dereliction, take refuge in an arbitrary system of the world. They organize raw existence, laden with menace, and transform it into an intelligible, reassuring world. But this involves a precarious construction of the intellect which eliminates the mystery of the world and interprets everything from the practical point of view. Of course, in exchange, such men lead a calm existence; but they buy that tranquillity at the price of what is deepest in them, since they base their interpretation of themselves only on things. Everything that compromises the security of the average man is relegated to the subconscious and he lives unauthentically. In the end he no longer knows his own soul and thinks that it is that thin solidified crust under which a world of deep chaotic tendencies slumbers. He becomes incapable of fulfilling his own possibilities. Obsessed by the material world he wishes to master, concerned only with the practical problems, he no longer sees the totality of his soul and interprets himself only in the light of categories he has created to make his environment subserve his needs. He is, then, only a thing among things, and because of the hypertrophic development of his intellect, his true being becomes strange to him. Only the impersonal dictatorial "they" subsists. Joseph K.'s life seems to coincide with the portrait Heidegger paints of unauthentic man.

But sometimes, as in the case of the hero of *The Trial,* it happens that the reign of the "they" is upset. Joseph K.'s arrest is a call issued from another region of being. It is a parliamentary question that has surged up from the depths of the original chaos existing in man in a latent state, overladen and concealed by preoccupation. Joseph K. has fled his destiny, the responsibility he had not had the strength to shoulder. His deepest "I," which is truer to him than he is to himself, reveals itself in the form of fear and trembling. If Franz and Willem proceed to arrest Joseph K. in Fräulein Bürstner's room, and not in his own, it is not a chance occurrence. Joseph K. is being torn from his world and transplanted into a world which, in its terrifying strangeness, is his own. Joseph K. had lived in bad faith: obliged to choose between two existential possibilities, he had chosen unauthentic existence and betrayed what was deepest and most personal in him for the benefit of a superficial and reassuring way of life. He is guilty because he had not taken his total "I" into account. He therefore cannot be arrested in his own room which is part of his "environmental world." He is arrested in Fräulein Bürstner's room, for it represents a world foreign to K., and yet close to him: it is the dark, subconscious part of his "I." Joseph K. had, in effect, consented to live a "fallen life" and suddenly in anguish, personified by Franz and Willem, he becomes aware of this divorce in his being which, up to that point, had been frozen in the familiar world of everyday interpretations.

Joseph K. is guilty towards this deepest and original "I" which is no longer content to turn up in his sleep. Anxiety invades his life. His happy indifference is compromised by the sudden eruption of dark powers which summon him to their Court.

How can he escape this accusation, this anxiety? By becoming the champion of "infinite surrender" like Kierkegaard's Abraham, and living in a new world of being, a higher level of consciousness; by integrating into himself all the virtualities of his "I," the demoniac powers he fears, the terrifying aspect of the original absolute world. He would have to assume his personal destiny and understand the call that comes from the depths of the mutilated, travestied being. This hidden "I" is all-powerful; it is found behind all unforeseen acts which drag Joseph K. from the regular paths he had been passively following before his arrest.

The workmen's quarter which on Sunday is swarming with disorderly primitive life, Fräulein Bürstner, the girl who is so near and yet so remote, the sheriff's wife, the nurse Leni, simply represent the repressed demoniac forces that constitute a constant threat to everyday life, but are also the promise of a higher, regenerated, richer, sincerer life than the spiritless one led by the proxy, Joseph K.

The court, which represents the Synagogue of Prague, is also a manifestation of this vague feeling of basic guilt. Demoniac characters appear. They stand on a plane superior to normal existence. On that level, only being is of importance. It scarcely matters whether one is the proxy of a great bank or a house painter. These are attributes whose values exist only in a humanized world. But K., in spite of all warnings, remains a stranger to this world of being and assumes a deep guilt with regard to it. He does not understand the warning that was issued him. His servitude to the world of unauthenticity is too powerful for him to be able to free himself and understand, as Leni tells him, that all accused men are handsome, since their fate is of the elect, a fate enhanced by the tragic beauty of metaphysical anxiety. He protests that Franz and Willem have eaten his bread and butter, his honey, and have stolen his linen on the pretext that they would hold it in trust. But was that not an invitation to turn away from the human world of preoccupation and focus his attention on a world of real values, rooted in the most authentic aspects of man himself? It is at the price of such surrender that he might escape from a banal life and become like Abraham a "Champion of the faith." But he does not wish to escape from the hold of this average banal world; he clings to it and makes use of all human means to regain the sweet calm that had deserted him.

He tells Fräulein Bürstner all the details of his arrest. What does he really expect? To free himself from that anxiety which, once described and translated into everyday language, will, he hopes, cease being disquieting and unique. He accepts the suggestions of his uncle who, as a man of action, sees in Joseph K.'s arrest a threat to the entire family since it holds the unauthentic life up to doubt. He will therefore seek out a lawyer, a pale symbol of dogmatic human intelligence, one who is content with describing and remaining in the domain of the finite and foreseeable. The light which the lawyer sheds on the affair is as pale as the light of his candle. His world is at odds with the world of the Court; for Huld personifies abstract and general knowledge. He describes, without even questioning Joseph K., and moves in the sphere of the finite, without ever being able to suggest a solution for the problem of human destiny. Intellect is powerless; it cannot put an end to the trial which is a strictly personal affair and can be won by the accused only. Besides, the new forces that have been aroused in Joseph K. and have given birth to his anxiety are so imperious that he escapes, leaving his uncle and lawyer to dispose of him as of something inanimate, and follows Leni, the symbol of tendencies that cannot be reduced to the intellect.

He grows tired of his lawyer; since human reason cannot in any way help him, he will seek out the artist. Perhaps human art will bring back to him the peace he wants at any price. The solution suggested is of very little consolation. The painter lives in appearance and cannot obtain any definite acquittal. Only "apparent acquittal" and "unlimited delay" exist for him. The solution is only temporary. The painter is simply a merchant of illusions. He does not live in the world of being; his world is one of appearances. Thus Joseph K. cannot turn to anyone, he is always brought back to himself, for salvation resides only in him, in a courageous decision to shoulder life.

We therefore see the unfortunate Joseph K. oscillating between two worlds: he comes back to the Court although he has not been summoned, because he, like Frau Grubach, has the feeling that his happiness is somehow involved. Yet he still turns his back on the solitary life and seeks in the community a remedy for his anxiety; but the human community henceforth rejects him. Frau Grubach, as well as the two inspectors, refuses to shake his hand. He is at home neither in unauthentic society nor in the world of original contingency represented by the Court that is located in attics and sits only at night and on Sundays in a dehumanized region exempt from the workaday world and abstract categories.

Joseph K. is like the ape in "A Report to an Academy": in order to escape the darkness of his cage, the ape abdicates his simian nature and immediately learns to shake men's hands. He, too, gains security and freedom from care only at the price of a betrayal, by shouldering a destiny that is not his. But Joseph K. lives on the border of two worlds and in his confusion finds no lifebuoy he can hold on to.

Only now can we understand the numerous reasons why Joseph K. is sentenced to death. He must die because he does not seek out the Law. He finds it by chance, in the cathedral, but does not understand the deep causes of his anguish.

Besides, he is a selfish bachelor, arraigned by a society which condemns celibacy. According to Kierkegaard, is there any greater debt than owing one's life to a man? The *Talmud*, which Kafka quotes, proclaims that without children a man does not deserve to be called a human being. Even Kafka's father finds that he is rehabilitated because he is, in a sense, the living example of the Law obeyed. Did he not raise five children? No matter what direction Joseph K. takes, he finds himself in an impasse, and there is no way out for him other than death. He is such a model of a "utilitarian world" that he rebels against the world of authentic being and in his struggle has recourse to all operations of an all-too-human logic. If Joseph K. must die, Kafka, on the other hand, has a right to bachelorhood which, for him, is not a criminal exception. He has a right to live, also, for his books are an escape from the artificial world which will not liberate Joseph K. When, several moments before Joseph K.'s execution, Fräulein Bürstner is seen at the turning of a side-street, his executioners' hold relaxes on Joseph K., for he starts to follow her. But he does not understand the warning; he gives up his pursuit and the executioners tighten their hold. He had had no right to celibacy, for the goal of his life had not been the personal search for a new God who demands solitude.

Kafka therefore appears to us as having the characteristics of a melancholy Narcissus viewing himself in a double mirror: on the one hand, he faces Joseph K.; on the other, the more flattering face of the priest. Joseph K. is without doubt the image which Kafka's family and friends had of him and the image he had of himself when he doubted his mission. Besides, is not the day chosen for Joseph K.'s execution his birthday, the day when, thirty-one years earlier, he had received from his parents a name, the symbol of all the misunderstanding that had accumulated around his person? The priest is therefore probably the authentic portrait of Kafka as he saw himself, an idealized portrait of days of happy exaltation. His mission requires solitude, and celibacy is required of the Catholic priest. Since he too sought God and since the kingdom of God is not a kingdom that can be entered in company, Kafka had as much right to celibacy as did the Catholic priest, the rather mysterious priest who made of his quest for the Law the object of his meditations in the lonely cathedral.

In addition, Kafka had for a long time hesitated between celibacy and the married state, which was to him like the two-faced Janus. In fact, marriage might have been for him a way of understanding himself better; unknown tendencies of his spirit might have been revealed to him and might have restored him to a complete authentic personality. Fräulein Bürstner, from this point of view, doubtlessly personifies an unsuspected part of Joseph K.'s soul. Of course, the priest reproaches him for seeking out the help of women too much, for not depending on himself sufficiently to win his case. He tells him not to spread himself too thin; it is clear he wants to make him understand that he ought to give up women for one woman who will give him a more comprehensive awareness of his being. In so doing, the priest echoes Leni's suggestion to Joseph K. that a girl like Elsa was incapable of sacrificing herself for him, for he had come to her by chance and not because of an inner need. But marriage can be a yoke constraining free development of the personality. Kafka came to a clear decision only when he was struck down by illness and saw in that ordeal a Providential warning to the effect that he must give up his fiancée and devote himself to the quest of the new Law. Joseph K., on the other hand, is not aware of this dilemma. He is too much attached to the material world to discover the meaning of his anxiety. He is therefore guilty towards society and the Law.

Is this Law that Kafka must seek out inaccessible? On this count, we discern a certain hesitation in his thought. Sometimes it is the unknowable: "It is not," says Kafka, "because his life was short that Moses did not enter the promised land, but because it was a human life." The absolute, then, seems to him to be heterogeneous to weak, limited human life, and he humiliates himself before the grandeur of the Divine. But more often, he seems to believe in a "heaven of fixed stars" to which men may have access.

What is this Law, then? "It is," says Kafka, "that which is indestructible, and to believe is to free the indestructible in oneself, to be indestructible, or more exactly, to be." To be himself, without remorse, without anxiety, was the ideal Kafka tried in vain to achieve. He felt that his oddity was a sin, and then one day he understood that it was a crushing but inestimable privilege. To be oneself is the final message of the writer who never ceased hoping. To be oneself, to give up the impersonal life which men lead and ascribe even to their God, a vain and lifeless abstraction.

From this point of view, the cathedral scene is rich in meaning. Time seems to be in abeyance, transformed into a Platonic eternity. The years spent by man standing before the gates of the Law roll by rapidly in contrast with the duration that is so charged with events and constitutes the substance of the other chapters. We are, in effect, in the "heaven of fixed stars," which is an inner heaven, hidden in the deepest recesses of the individual soul. Shortly before he dies, man is astonished and asks his doorkeeper: "Everyone strives to attain the Law, how does it come about, then, that in all these years no one has come seeking admittance but me?" The doorkeeper bellows into the ears of the dying man: "No one but you could gain admittance through this door, since this door was intended only for you. I am now going to shut it." Somewhere in his notebooks, Kafka points out the analogy between the German words *sein* and *Dasein,* thus giving us to understand that life should not be anonymous but personal. Each man should seek out his Law and become himself, even if he has to struggle against society, its fixed ideals, its bloodless codes, its thingness. The doorkeeper himself is simply the symbolic representation of the world as obstacle in the path of the quest of our deepest, unconditional personality. It knows no Law; it turns its back on the Law and is naïve, as naïve as realistic doctrine. It is interested only in attributes, in the accidents of substance; it cross-examines man about the parish he lives in, asks a thousand banal questions, and accepts his gifts. Man asks his question only when he is about to die, when he is about to shake off the hold of the material world and become pure spirit, freed from artificiality. Joseph K. does not understand this parable. He is not sufficiently detached from the material world. The light of the Tabernacle counteracts the light of his electric lamp and prevents him from noticing the carvings on the altar. The lamp which the priest gives him to hold goes out in his hand.

But the priest tells Joseph K. that there are holes in the character of the guardian of the Law. That is why one can, in this life, have access to the world of truth and the absolute. This truth is one which must be discovered phenomenologically because it is hidden; its depths are covered over. "The magnificence of life," says Kafka, "is all around us in its entirety, but its depths are covered over, invisible."

To penetrate that region of feeling, one must be able to give up this world: like Abraham, one must sacrifice what is earthly. But Isaac was restored to Abraham and Abraham was twice joyous when he received his son for the second time. Job, too, after his ordeal, received everything twice, says Kierkegaard in his *Rehearsal*. This would also have been true of Joseph K., but he understood nothing about the mysterious nature of his anguish. He did not understand that it was no question of theft but of custody when Franz and Willem carried away his linen. He did not understand that everything earthly would be given back to him when he found his Law and built his life on solid foundations.

At the end of his life, Kafka became cheerful and optimistic. He had faith in the future and believed in an earthly paradise. We have been expelled from it, say the Scriptures, but it was not destroyed. In a way, the expulsion was a good thing, for if we had not been ejected, paradise would have had to be destroyed. The happiness that awaits us is therefore of this earth, for we shall find paradise again. The Messiah will come. Kafka is certain of that. "He will come as soon as an individualism of the most uncontrollable faith becomes possible. Towards that end, it will be necessary for the mediator in each man to come alive again." Kafka seems to reconcile the Jewish and Christian concepts of the Messiah, for the Messiah will come only one day after his arrival: that is, he will be truly among us the day his message becomes universal truth.

It was not without suffering that Kafka rose to this optimistic view of the world. He had to struggle, and his novels are an echo of the struggles that led him to the very heart of despair.

Of course, Kafka's world is almost entirely pervaded by the lugubrious light of a black sun, because he really wishes to free himself

from the world of doubt and uncertainty that prevents him from saying "Yea" to existence. It very often involves therapy. "I have a hundred thousand false, horrible feelings," he says, "the good ones make
their appearance only in rags and they are quite weak." He therefore
seems to hate his work and orders Max Brod, his literary executor, to
burn it. He fears, perhaps, that he is imposing on his readers that obsessive world which he himself identifies as contrary to the ideal. But
his friend's pious disobedience saved these books which one should
read against the current as one does the *Notebooks of Malte Laurids
Brigge*. His premature death deprived us of works which certainly
would have been the contrary of this nocturnal hallucinatory, absurd
and contradictory world. The *Diaries* evoke this reconciled world,
based on a deep individualism enlightened by the dazzling light of
indestructible Law, the secret home of any human personality worthy
of that name. Joseph K. dies because, like the son in "The Judgment,"
he is protected neither from on high nor from behind, neither by God
nor by an existence established on the deep foundations of the authentic being. His life is therefore no longer based on the absolute. Faith
is dead; men, whether Jews or Christians, had killed it. Life is set
adrift. Man is nothing more than a wreck; he must find his reason for
being in himself, at the very core of his existence which intellect has
reduced to the condition of an abstract category. He must rediscover
the meaning of life. The Court is in this respect, like many symbols in
the novel, a polyvalent symbol. It represents the fallen Synagogue and
the New Law, constructed on the depths of being. Joseph K. lives in
an anguish that does not create new values because he is not able to
discern its meaning clearly. He sinks into absolute nihilism, because
he cannot find a remedy for this anguish either in religion or the in-
offensive world of day-to-day existence. He cannot find himself, although summoned by his anguish to the Court of his deepest "I,"
which aspires to be, totally and absolutely, an ultimate instance. He
ought to kill himself. But this would give meaning to life. So he lets
himself be executed by his two executioners, and run-of-the-mill
humanity seems to heave a sigh of relief when Joseph K. dies. The
alarm is over. Life has ceased being problematic, for K.'s anxiety was
really a threat that compromised the tranquil existence of "intelligent
men, those intruders remorselessly present like a splinter in the flesh
of an illegal poacher." The same thing is true of "The Metamorphosis."
As soon as the corpse of the cockroach which was once Gregor Samsa

is thrown into the dustbin, the everyday world becomes calm again: cheerful heedlessness is restored and Gregor's sister blooms into a pretty girl with a good figure.

But the indestructible will reign one day. Kafka was firmly convinced of that; his hope was invincible. "To find happiness," he says, "I must raise the Universe to the Pure, the True and the Definitive." To achieve such an ideal of perfection, man will have to have the courage to be in his life what he is in his deepest self; he will have to surrender bad faith in favor of authentic being.

Kafka is therefore not a prophet of the absurd; his optimism is all the more unshakeable for his having risen above total despair and for having slowly developed a lucid, tenacious will. Gide's adaptation conceals this meaning of *The Trial*, for the parable of the Law has been eliminated, and we have only a long, hallucinatory series of reasons for despair. In reality Kafka's work is, I repeat, full of Messianic hope. A fervent admirer of Goethe, Kafka always hoped for a life made possible by an ideal human community that safeguarded the irrefutable rights of the individual. That is the lesson taught us by his book. It is a message we should meditate upon, especially at a time when the individual may be eliminated by collectivism. The individual, out of fear of loneliness, is only too prone to take refuge in a group and lose himself. Even if he triumphed over his existential anguish and made an effort to affirm himself towards and against all the rest, he would risk being wiped out, gagged by powerful collective entities. We can only hope that the meaning and the resonance of Kafka's work will be understood and will inspire man to lead his life with the courage it requires to be himself, for there is no real culture without respect of the human being as something unique and irreplaceable.

Max Brod

The Castle: Its Genesis [*]

"Temptation in the Village," a twelve-page sketch which Kafka
wrote in 1914 (*Diaries*, June 11), contains the germ of *The Castle*.
It describes the tragedy of a man who wishes to live in a village with
other people but is unable to become rooted in the strange place and
to find his way to the Castle which looms forebodingly over the village.
The mood of almost hopeless loneliness—and, as regards the villagers,
fateful mistrusting and misunderstanding—casts a shadow even in this
preliminary sketch; thus, in the very opening a native addresses his
wife: "Wait a little. I want to see what that man is going to do. He's
a stranger. He's hanging around here for no reason at all. Look at
him." Whereupon the hero (of the fragment) replies: "I'm looking
for the inn, that's all. Your husband has no right to speak of me that
way and perhaps give you a wrong impression of me." Later the wife
whispers to another person: "He talks so much." Further criticism of
the strange, unwanted intruder is superfluous.

Upon re-reading this suggestive fragment, I was reminded of the
connection between Kafka's basic concepts in *The Castle* and a novel
by the Czech writer Bozena Nemcova entitled *The Grandmother* (tr.
by Francis Gregor; Chicago, 1891)—an affinity not previously noted,
to my knowledge.

Bozena Nemcova lived from 1820 to 1862. *The Grandmother*, her
main work, an idyllic novel of tender simplicity, was used as a text-
book for students of the Czech language in the German secondary

[*] Translated by Gerhard H. Weiss.

161

schools of Prague. Thus Kafka as a student became acquainted with the wonderfully insinuating and at the same time naïve, candid, and wholesome story of the mountain village at the foot of the Riesengebirge. Thus I, too, read it with enthusiasm one year later.

It is remarkable that at almost the same time as Nemcova was describing in the Czech language the peasant life of northeastern Bohemia, Adalbert Stifter was depicting the time-honored customs, popular traditions, and religiosity of the peasants of southwest Bohemia, the area of the Bohemian forest. Stifter and Nemcova probably knew nothing about one another, though they were contemporaries and kindred souls in their love of forest loneliness. By means of her poetic folklore Nemcova furthered the Czech national renaissance movement. As political suspects her husband as well as her friends received harsh treatment from the Austrian authorities, against whom Stifter protested only pedagogically. Notwithstanding their differences, the affinities between those two writers cannot be overlooked: their search for a real, simple and spiritually directed existence.

Kafka especially loved the letters of Nemcova, this passionate, beautiful woman whose appearance, a few generations ago, was a sensation in the circles of Czech patriots and language reformers at Prague. Her unhappy marriage, her sensuous burning love for friends who shared her views, her tender care for her children, her exultations and depressions, her life, which, in contrast to her occasionally conventional style, was shaken by many storms, her premature death—all these were things that vibrated deeply in Kafka's understanding and compassion. He often read to me from these letters, which, as far as I know, have not yet been translated, though they belong among the great documents of struggling souls.

It seems to me that the basis of Kafka's *Castle* has features which may be traced back to the unconscious effect of that first compulsory but later enthusiastic reading of *The Grandmother* in school. That Kafka was open to such influences he repeatedly proves in his diaries, often with overemphasized conscientiousness, indeed even with a kind of pathetic feeling of guilt. One is familiar with the connection he feels obliged to point out between his novel *Amerika* and Dickens' *David Copperfield*. It is my impression that in stressing this influence he goes much too far, playfully too far. I should like to point out a much less deliberate but in its details quite evident aftereffect of the old classic Czech novel, an effect which, it would seem, Kafka himself failed to notice, though he mentions Nemcova several times in his letters to Milena.

The people in *The Grandmother* live in their village but do not have any access to the princess in the castle. In the village Czech is spoken, in the castle, German. This in itself produces alienation. Moreover, the princess lives in the castle only occasionally. Most of the time she is traveling, in distant Vienna or Italy. In one of the most moving passages of the book, the grandmother recounts an episode of her youth, the almost magical appearance of the good Emperor Joseph II among the astonished country folk. He moves past like a star from distant worlds. Like the Emperor, the princess is also a very kind person, an enlightened ruler. But between her and the peasants (and here the analogy to Kafka's *Castle* becomes obvious) there intervenes a dark horde of valets, castle officials, selfish, conceited, and hypocritical bureaucrats. In spite of herself, the princess is cut off from her people, and remains unapproachable and uninformed. Only the grandmother, the main character of the book, breaks through the spell, gains access to the princess and finally brings justice to the persecuted. This is something Kafka's hero constantly strives for but without success. In this respect Nemcova's novel belongs to an era which could rest its faith in the Man of Good Will with greater confidence than is permitted to our generation of the present crisis.

In the two works, however, there is a surprising correspondence in the details of the description of the characters who stand between the occupant of the castle and the peasants of the village. The place where the village opinion is formulated is, in both novels, the village inn. The quiet is disturbed by a young Italian courtier who pursues Christel, the innkeeper's beautiful daughter, and who makes indecent proposals to her, just as in Kafka's novel the court official makes advances to Amalia. It is most remarkable that this official also has an Italian name (the only one in the whole novel): Sortini. Much has been written about the strange antinomian Sortini episode in *The Castle*. It may perhaps be made clearer by comparing it with its complement in *The Grandmother*. In Nemcova's novel the girl also rejects the undisguised demands of the court official, and she too is afraid, justifiably, fearing the dangers inherent in the clash, and the powerful man's influence and vengeance. Her manner of telling the grandmother of the adventure contains much that is related to Kafka's novel. I quote a few words spoken by Christel: "Well, just imagine, that good-for-nothing, the Italian, came to the inn every day for a beer—this would not be bad, the village inn caters to all people—but instead of sitting behind the table like a decent fellow, he chased me. Wherever I turned, he followed me. My father made a wry face, but you know how he is; he is a good man and would not hurt a fly, and also does not want to alienate any guests, especially none from the castle."

It seems to me that this is clearly Kafka's equivocal note. As the story continues, this recurs again and again. There is, for example, Christel's remorse for what she had done with the best of intentions, as well as her concise description of the goings-on at the castle—how the officials up there have to be bribed: "That is our only hope. Since they have questioned him, they will perhaps help. But it often happens that they examine and do not help. They then state simply that it is not possible; and one has to be satisfied." Here the reader may notice that the uncanny aspects which reach such heart-rending proportions in Kafka's work are not completely alien to the simple realism of Nemcova.

The stimulation which Kafka obtained, I believe, from the reading of his youth he reshaped, of course, into a completely independent work. That the princess in Nemcova's book can be seen only rarely, while in Kafka's novel the lord of the manor cannot be seen at all, is more than a difference of degree, and this difference is, therefore, not meant to be minimized here.

Donald Pearce

The Castle: Kafka's
Divine Comedy

I⊤ is proverbially true that a time-lag usually intervenes between the appearance of a great writer and his universal acceptance. This is, in part, accidental, in part, necessary. It is accidental insofar as the audience may be more, or less, excitable; but necessary in that the really new has to modify existing culture both forwards and backwards before it can become the traditional: and this, in an absolute sense, requires time. In the case of Kafka, though his greatness is now generally admitted, it is still his uniqueness—and hence his separateness from classic literary tradition—that is chiefly admired. This is indeed unfortunate; for, through the nature of the problems handled and the artistic methods employed, scarcely a book comes to mind that is more squarely placed on the main road of European literature than *The Castle*.

To illustrate this it may suffice to compare Kafka with Dante: Dante not only because his central position in European literature as a whole makes him a "norm" against which to measure all comers, but also because the correspondence between the aims and methods of the two writers is strong enough to indicate that, as W. H. Auden pointed out, Kafka holds pretty much the same relation to the twentieth century that Dante held to the fourteenth. Both *The Divine Comedy* [1] and *The Castle* are quests; their ultimate objectives are identical—the Absolute; the way there and the conditions and difficulties thronging it alone are changed; and it is, in fact, by an examination of these very differences, and their consequences for the pilgrim, that the scope and significance of the later book can be most readily appreciated.

The problem of individual salvation in the fourteenth century was, we may take it, very different from what it is in ours. For Dante, though salvation was no simple affair and certainly demanded that you have your wits about you, it was only necessary *to believe* and the way to God was opened. One began the pilgrimage with the goal bright before him, the way, though long and arduous, clearly and distinctly defined. There were guides and charts. From Aquinas and the church fathers there had descended an integrated theology, ethic, dialectic, and physics—a coherent system which, if assimilated and applied, was the guarantor of personal salvation. Above and about one, visible to the eye of the body as to the eye of the mind, were the Ptolemaic spheres, sensible evidence of God's order, through which the pilgrim was to pass, by stations, to a literally conceived empyrean-heaven of God. Dante's universe, really quite compact and simple in comparison with Kafka's, was one in which man had both location and direction, in which, provided the will did not falter but clung to faith and doctrine, the soul naturally and inevitably gravitated, by a sort of spiritual entelechy, to God, the haven of all loves.[2] It is therefore appropriate that the main literary characteristic of *The Divine Comedy* should be precision, order, perfect system—a harmony of philosophical, theological, moral, and political truths, at all points consistently related and simultaneously valid.

Kafka, on the other hand, received no such positive system of directives from his age—that had all gone with the collapse of the medieval synthesis—but only uncertainty, born of a new awareness of the real complexity of the world's disharmony: "The disharmony of the world," he said, "seems, comfortingly enough, to be merely an arithmetical one." Though the heavenly goal was no less desirable and urgent, the possibility of attaining it had now receded, the way was uncertain, progress incalculable. Cartesian doubt, and its idiot offspring modern scientism, dropping like a guillotine on philosophy, had severed the spiritual and the physical worlds; and by 1900 had substituted caprice and entropy for order and teleology. Instead of cosmology Kafka inherited psychology—the irrational internal universe of Freud and Jung for the rational external universe of Aristotle and Ptolemy; instead of the doctrinal calm of Aquinas, there was the subtle anguish of Kierkegaard. All these influences shaped his work; so that whereas Dante's poem might be called a philosophical and theological treatise, *The Castle* is a case book in abnormal psychology; or if the former is a philosophic allegory, the latter is a modern *Psychomachia.*

In contrast to the lucidity and order of *The Divine Comedy*—by which on the level of rhetoric alone we discover that the relations between the heavenly and the earthly are intelligent, sane, and, even if not fully comprehensible by human reason, just and right—*The Castle* is a "system" of interferences and absurd contradictions, in which nothing is finally seen as certain or absolute (except to the peasantry, and to K. they are deluded), in which the very possibility of a reasoned theology is ruled out, and the seeker after salvation is left only with a faith which he is in imminent danger of losing because he is in danger of denying meaning to what (by human reason) appears impossible or absurd. Thus a rational and scriptural faith like Dante's [3] is impossible for K., and, in fact, for him to have faith at all means that he renounce any rational basis for it whatsoever, [4] and believe in an Absolute which cannot be discussed because it cannot be shown to exist. Salvation for Dante is impossible without a reasoned ethics (the lesson of the *Inferno;* the doctrine of Aquinas); for Kafka, however, the possibility of salvation begins only when the individual has "transcended the ethical" (the doctrine of Kierkegaard; see *Fear and Trembling*), which is exemplified (positively) in K.'s unethical treatment of Frieda and (negatively) in the Amalia-Sortini episode. [5]

Dante's path, in the *Inferno* and the *Purgatorio* at least, leads through a rational and conscious world in which the difficulties to be mastered are moral ones, *temptations;* his problem is thus ethical, his task virtuous conduct. He can provide his pilgrim with a guide (reason, in the person of Virgil) because the world through which he goes is entirely subject to logical necessity. [6] But Kafka's path leads into an irrational and unconscious world where the difficulties to be mastered are fortuitous, *tribulations;* his problem is thus not ethical but esthetic, his task suffering, endurance. He can provide his pilgrim with no such guide as Virgil, for the world through which he goes ("you are the problem; no scholar to be found far and wide") is entirely subject to causal (external) necessity and is therefore uncontrollable. Thus, whereas Dante can rejoice in ethical triumphs over temptations, Kafka can only patiently witness and record the continuous warfare of his different selves, the erratic traffic of unmanageable desires. Dante is drawn on his journey by a thirst for that knowledge which only the vision of God can appease. He is seeking, that is to say, to set his knowledge in such perfect order that in one intuitive flash he may see the whole world concentrated in a miraculous point of meaning which is God. Kafka, the modern man, is drawn on his journey by an equally insatiable desire, but it is for psychic integration. He is seeking, that is to say, to set his different selves in such perfect order that he, too, in one intuitive flash, may know himself concentered in a lucent unity of being which is God.[7] From one point of view, to have faith means for Dante to believe that the suprarational will not appear irrational to his perfected intelligence; from the same point of view, to have faith means for Kafka to believe that the sleeplessly arbitrary relations of conflictual "selves" can be assigned intelligent meaning and order.

Viewed for the moment psychologically, the behavior of the people in *The Castle*, and the relations between the community and the castle itself, will illustrate the peculiarity of Kafka's problem and its difference from Dante's. The relations between the village and the castle may be regarded as those between the conscious (earthly) and subconscious (heavenly) *in the ordinary and unreflective person*. The relations are harmonious because unquestioningly accepted; co-operation is complete; the whims, demands, or punishments emanating from the castle are unhesitatingly fulfilled and obeyed (normal integration). The system of communication within the castle itself (association of ideas, schematization in the unconscious) "works beautifully," as does a similar toylike system in the village (conscious thought processes in the immediate and simple enjoyment of life). Valid connection between the village and castle systems yields only "a sound of humming and singing far distant" (harmony of the psyche; the music of Ptolemy's spheres); an answer (an irruption from the unconscious), whether comical or hostile, is literally deceptive but privately significant (a symbol). In the castle work goes on incessantly (reception and correlation of impressions, etc.) under control-authorities (interests of the different selves); in the village work goes on leisurely and intermittently (consciousness is fitful) under a superintendent (the rational); official communications are "shy as young girls" ("the unconscious can only wish"); replies are old letters picked up at random (association of ideas and feelings); authorities are feared when they rise from their seats (dread of mental disorders); they can condemn but not pardon (supreme self-interest of the unconscious). This line of interpretation could be extended indefinitely.

K.'s relations with the castle, however, are those between the conscious and the unconscious (earthly and heavenly) in a reflective person, one who, discovering no traditional external Absolute turns inward and seeks by rational self-analysis to reach an Absolute within himself (the extremity of Romanticism; the "God Within" of Jung [8]). He is everywhere baffled by the irrational and seemingly spontaneous self-interest of his inner life, whose casual and preoccupied demands for complete and unquestioning obedience he defies because they appear, to reason, merely arbitrary; but precisely as these demands are questioned by him his relations with the castle become proportionately more disorderly and grotesque. He ceases, in short, to respect the necessary in himself, although this respect is the very condition of salvation considered in these terms. (Compare Dante's point of view—*Paradiso* XXXIII—that to be subject to God as determiner of the will's goal is fulfillment, not restriction of free will, or liberty). It is, of course, impossible for K. not to have relations with the castle, where the *numen* of his quest dwells; his error (his Dark Wood) is to suppose that they can be rational and on his terms. Dante had seen around this too: Virgil (reason) departs and Beatrice (revelation, intuition) arrives at the Earthly Paradise, or the threshold of the unconscious. The explicit warning of *Purgatorio* III comes to mind: "mad is he who hopes that our reason may compass that Infinitude which one Substance in Three Persons fills."

Again, from a slightly different point of view, K. might be regarded as a distinct personality type straight out of Jung (not by any means unique, but on the contrary appallingly universal in our time) deliberately drawn by Kafka to illustrate the psychic disorders that have attended the unrelenting post-Cartesian tyranny of the rational and conscious side of Western life. K. is an "extraverted-thinking-type" feverishly seeking to realize an objective for which he will repress, or eliminate if possible, anything in the self which impedes that realization. In *Purgatorio* XVIII, Dante had already reminded this type, however, that it is not in just loving God (which is natural), but in rejecting all impulses which do not harmonize with that love, that man's moral freedom vindicates itself; and so, to him, K.'s love is "defective through excess," [9] and defective also because he does harm to his neighbors,[10] i.e., his other selves. For K., however, the end alone justifies the means; he will betray anything—health, family, friends, assistants—for bettered chances with the castle; he has sympathy only with those who appear to be of service to his aims, dominated by which his deeper nature at last revolts (doubts), fanaticism ("overcompensated doubt") sets in, a haughty, almost bullying attitude toward the castle authorities develops,[11] and his sacred quest becomes a secular siege.

Frieda, in this light, may be seen as K.'s *anima*, or protesting inner attitude, the incarnation of the tendencies he has oppressed—in a word, his humanity—in the pursuit of his goal. And it is instructive to see the relations of K. and Frieda as the index of his relations with himself. He embraces her, at first, because she is Klamm's mistress (the "anima" lives with "the God within"), and because she is a member of the community (his inherent humanity). She yields and unites with him (psychic integration—K.'s only happy moment) because she would, in fact, help him to become a normal member of the community, his one chance of attaining the castle. But the obsessive exaggeration of his conscious and reasoning attitude toward what is properly sacred and mystical (Blake and Yeats saw this as the root of the tragedy of the West; the castle is "The Secret Rose"), causes a cleavage, and, in the end, produces a profound schizoid dissociation of the psyche with all its attendant woes.

The landlady may be regarded roughly as K.'s accusing conscience, and therefore closely related to the unconscious, to Frieda and to Klamm. She points out the falseness of his relations to Frieda and ferrets out his real motives; he comes to hate her and at last severs relations with her.

The assistants represent more specialized symptoms—psychic automatisms, released by the profound disorganization of the self, which have burst up from the unconscious; their behavior constitutes throughout a grotesque parody or mockery of K.'s struggles. They are almost indistinguishably alike because both K.'s attempts (a) to get into the castle and (b) to join the village community are not only one and the same, but equally grotesque and inadequate. At first the assistants seemed all right, and would have done average, even efficient, service, because K.'s plans and motives were at first ordinate and sound. They become progressively absurd as his attempts in both directions become more and more desperate. They are Frieda's old playmates inasmuch as the elements of the psyche are (presumably) harmonious in childhood; and they "have Klamm's eyes" because, as instincts, they are part of the essential soul. When K. turns them out of doors (out of alliance with the conscious life), he is really trying arbitrarily to annihilate his instincts, which can only signal the final revolt of the unconscious and its open challenge to the conscious for possession of the psyche. (In the end, they even take Frieda quite away from him.)

Both Kafka and Dante regard the "ever-womanly" as intrinsically and mysteriously essential to a state of grace and the attainment, or the vision, of the Absolute.[12] Dante's mystical progress through the final heaven of all loves is entrusted to Beatrice's care; and for Kafka, Frieda is the appropriate image of the soul's angel—the "anima" of the thinking man is feminine. Beatrice and Frieda are sisters. Both are surrogates for Revelation: consider, for example, Beatrice's eyes in which Dante sees the rainbow depths of Christian mystery, and Frieda's peephole into Klamm's sitting room. But whereas Dante undertook his quest *for* Beatrice, and thereby gained both heaven and his lady, K. undertook his for himself, tried to make a tool out of Frieda, and thereby lost all, or almost all—he was allowed a modest grave in the village environs.[13]

It was Dante's spiritual aim to rise far, in fact, infinitely, above the mere earthly, Kafka's "peasantry": in the Ptolemaic system the earth, as the central and therefore lowest point, was the sphere of the basest substances. But Kafka (see what five centuries can do) knows that only by absorption in humanity, "only as a worker in the village, removed as far as possible from the castle itself, can one hope to achieve anything in the castle"; [14] that the unquestioning, simple souls are the happy ones; that they alone are really rooted in life, unreflectingly fulfilling life's purpose of sheer living; that, in fact, there may be "no difference between the castle and the peasantry." For Dante, salvation means disappearance of the self in the vision of God; for Kafka, it means the setting up of right relations with humanity on the one hand and, *ipso facto,* with heaven on the other. To Dante, perhaps, Kafka would seem to be seeking merely the Earthly Paradise; but to Kafka perhaps Dante is seeking to become an angel. But their goals are not really different; as previously noted, only the way and the difficulties thronging it have changed. In the symbolic words of the landlady to K.: "And there's just one thing my poor head can't understand, that a girl who had the honor of being Klamm's mistress . . . should have allowed you even to lay a finger on her." Dante's way was cleared and made smooth by the "certainty" of medieval thought; Kafka's, we may say *ours*, so representative is he of our age and time, has been complicated and confused by that traumatic flux of traditional values which the nineteenth century bequeathed to the modern world.

NOTES

1. I have used the Modern Library edition (New York, 1932), the Carlyle-Wicksteed translation.

2. *Paradiso*, Canto I.

3. See *Paradiso*, Canto XXIV.

4. Cf. Tertullian, Kierkegaard, and Existentialism generally.

5. Kafka regarded this whole episode as a parody, or parable, of *Fear and Trembling*.

6. The line of development from Socrates' "sin is ignorance" to Dante's (Aquinas') "virtue is rational" is perfectly straight.

7. Cf. Origen's cry, "O thou who lovest, set my love in order!"

8. The writings of Carl Jung, and one might mention in particular that *The Modern Man in Search of His Soul* and *Psychological Types* were of scriptural importance to Kafka.

9. *Purgatorio*, Canto XVII.

10. *Ibid.*, Canto XVIII.

11. K.'s progress at this point is summed up in one of Kafka's aphorisms: "A man was surprised how easily he went the eternal way. He happened to be rushing backwards along it."

12. Cf. the last lines of Goethe's *Faust*, Part II.

13. For K. is not damned; though his tactics were wrong, his will was right; and in Goethe's words: "Who ever keeps on striving, him we may save."

14. Cf. the similar conclusions of Goethe (*Faust*, Part II) and Flaubert, who, speaking of peasants, said: "Ils sont dans le vrai." One recalls also Wordsworth's idealization of peasants, D. H. Lawrence's search for a more primitive level of existence, Gauguin's desire for the aboriginal, Rimbaud's utter repudiation of the complexity and sophistication of modern Europe. This romantic anti-intellectualist conception was swept up into the doctrines of Fascism (strength, simplicity, the soil) and provided one of its chief attractions both for "intellectuals" and for "peasants." Kafka, like Dante, never an optimist about humanity, would not have been surprised. And one remembers John Butler Yeats's "fear that the reformer will improve the Irish peasant off the face of the earth."

Homer Swander

The Castle: K.'s Village

NOTHING seems unqualifiedly true of Kafka or his work. He prevents criticism as he prevented his own development as an artist. Infected too thoroughly by his spirit, we can no more let go a sentence or an essay about him than he could let go his novels and many of his stories, not so much because there is more we should like to say but because what we have already written, however humbly and whether to praise or blame, seems too confident, speaks too absolutely; there remains always the ultimate qualification as yet unspoken and perhaps undiscovered but pressing down upon us all the same. And the difficulty is not simply that normal reluctance to speak confidently about any work of art. In some sense peculiar to Kafka, the difficulty here is central: the closer we get to the heart of his work, the more likely he is to cripple us in his own image. It is thus necessary for even the most reverent critics to shake off the infection—actually to offend the spirit of his art—in order to achieve the definitions which make explication and criticism possible. But the danger which then arises is that we shall offend too deeply, that in the freedom of such a violation we shall proceed as if the qualifications set in motion by his nervous imagination were not literally endless. This is precisely what we do, for example, when in discussing his last novel we speak of the Castle as Grace, let the village equal Society, and see K.'s struggle as a straight-out attempt to earn the former by taking root in the latter. To create such definitions is to break far too profoundly with the spirit of the novel; and to continue to accept them is to rest too easily in a conventionally allegorical world which is, by virtue of this offense against his art, more ours than Kafka's.

Yet this is very nearly where criticism of *The Castle*—especially that concerned with the village and with K.'s attitude toward it—rests today. Most responsible critics, from Marxists to Catholics, while disagreeing on other matters, continue to accept with no essential change the semiofficial interpretations of Max Brod and Thomas Mann in which the village represents "life, the soil, the community, healthy normal existence and the blessings of human and bourgeois society," and in which K. is seen as "driven on . . . by a need for the most primitive requisites of life, the need to be rooted in a home and a calling, and to become a member of a community." [1] Or, as R. O. C. Winkler has put it more absolutely, "the hero's whole efforts are directed immediately toward an attempt to establish himself in a home and a job, and to become a member of the village community—to come to terms, in fact, with society." [2]

I believe that if we are to appreciate the full uniqueness of Kafka's novel, especially in the ruthless dedication of the hero to a task beyond his strength, we must move more cautiously than this, violating less completely the peculiar limitations which Kafka's art places upon the critic. It is true, of course, that in the "Letter to His Father" Kafka himself seems at first glance to corroborate the traditional interpretation; for he writes:

Hence the world was for me divided into three parts: into one in which I, the slave, lived under laws that had been invented only for me and which I could, I did not know why, never completely comply with; then into a second world, which was infinitely remote from mine, in which you lived, concerned with government, with the issuing of orders and with annoyance about their not being obeyed; and finally into a third world where everybody else lived happily and free from orders and from having to obey.

Here we apparently find described—in terms of Kafka's own life and in terms apparently congenial to the Brod-Mann point of view—the stranger, the Castle, and the village. But two difficulties arise: the villagers in the novel do not live "happily and free from orders and from having to obey"; and such a neat juxtaposition of the letter and the novel leaves entirely out of consideration—as does the traditional interpretation—the vast world beyond the Castle and the village, the world the stranger has left behind him.

For K. is a traveler from afar. He has come of his "own accord" a "long and difficult journey" to a village high in the mountains, off the main road, separated from that road and from the rest of the world by a divide sufficient to require a bridge—a bridge over which K. passes only after a "long time gazing into the illusory emptiness above him." Nor is this place from which he comes and through which he has traveled—his home, his native land, the other nations of the world— to be forgotten. Though we never see it except in his thoughts, it begins with the first chapter to gather values of its own, to stand as a contrast to the village and as a possible threat to K.'s purpose in the Castle. It is a place to which he may, at any moment he wishes, retire from the struggle.

There is a moment in the first chapter when he is vividly reminded of it, and the passage—a comparison of the church tower at home with the tower of the Castle—is one of the most important in the novel. First: "The church tower, firm in line, soaring unfalteringly to its tapering point, topped with red tiles and broad in the roof, an earthly building—what else can men build?—but with a loftier goal than the humble dwelling-houses, and a clearer meaning than the muddle of everyday life." The suggestion here is clear. This is an entirely sympathetic if oversimplified view of the beauty, the clarity, the sanity, and thus the comfort of orthodox religion in an orthodox community. Here is religion performing with dignity the function most men desire of it; here is the serenity and the sense of direction, earthbound but lofty nevertheless, with which most men are understandably satisfied. But at the moment this pleasant image of K.'s native town fills his mind, he is carefully studying the Castle:

The tower above him here—the only one visible—the tower of a house, as was now evident, perhaps of the main building, was uniformly round, part of it graciously mantled with ivy, pierced by small windows that glittered in the sun—with a somewhat maniacal glitter—and topped by what looked like an attic, with battlements that were irregular, broken, fumbling, as if designed by the trembling or careless hand of a child, clearly outlined against the blue. It was as if a melancholy-mad tenant who ought to have been kept locked in the topmost chamber of his house had burst through the roof and lifted himself up to the gaze of the world.

The contrast is complete: the suggestion of insanity, the lack of purpose, the absence of form, the relevance of childish fears and carelessness—this is the world of spirit which, for K., has supplanted the sensible religion of those who have not crossed the bridge. As he himself knows, "if it was merely a question of enjoying the view, it was a pity to have come so far; [he] would have done better to revisit his native town . . . ." But he has come, of course, not merely to look and to admire, he has come, filled with "vague desires," to challenge and to attack the mad tenant of this mad tower which cannot even be seen, much less warred upon, from the comfortable community of ordinary men.

In the very next paragraph Kafka compels us to notice that, had he wished, he might have placed his church of the soaring tower within the village, as perhaps he would have been obliged to do were the village indeed Society or the World or a Microcosm. For, as we now learn, K. is standing just behind the village church while he recollects his native town and looks at the Castle; but on this plain building, neither firm in line nor suggestively erratic, there is no tower of any kind. It is, instead, "really only a chapel widened with barnlike additions so as to accommodate the parishioners." With this brief description—part of a sentence merely but following immediately after the descriptions of the two towers—Kafka obviously wishes to introduce a third side to his comparison; and in so doing he identifies exclusively with the world K. has rejected the lovely but probably superficial view of a clear meaning soaring above the muddle of life. Here in this village there is no contrast between the church and the houses around it; here the church—any orthodox theology—offers no clear alternative to everyday life: it is ordinary, uninteresting, unimportant, can play no part in K.'s strategy. And the threatening symbol which, from high on the hill, rises above all else is the broken and fumbling Castle tower, a tower which, as K. carefully notes after previous uncertainty, belongs not to a church but to a house.

This crucial, three-sided comparison proves, among other things, that there does exist a part of Kafka's universe which, unlike the village, is not under the tyrannical jurisdiction of the Castle. There is a world beyond the bridge in which everyone is (perhaps) living "happily and free from orders." And K. is not the only one who knows it. Frieda, in one of her most passionate speeches, at the moment of her apparently final break with K., and in an attempt to explain it, says: "If we had only gone away somewhere at once that night [their first together], we might be in peace now, always together, your hand always near enough for mine to grasp . . . ." Earlier in the novel, when confronted by K.'s seemingly monomaniacal attacks upon the

Castle and by her increasingly difficult relationship with K.'s assistants, she had clearly warned him: "I shan't be able to stand this life here. If you want to keep me with you, we'll have to go away somewhere or other, to the south of France, or to Spain." It is, in fact, his rejection of this warning that proves decisive in their relationship: from that moment he has inevitably lost her to the assistants, and the next time he sees her she has left him and returned, with the assistant Jeremiah, to live and work again at the Herrenhof. As the Mayor tells K. when the latter uses Frieda as an excuse for staying on in the village, "Frieda would follow you anywhere"; and in her mind, at least, that other world, that anywhere-but-here becomes identified with peace, companionship, a family, with all the possibilities of love. Only in the village, she believes, is their life together impossible. Thus if marriage is, as so many critics have urged us to believe, an important part of K.'s goal, his path seems clear. And his answer, which Kafka keeps carefully ambiguous in other respects, is unequivocal in its rejection of that path: " 'I can't go away,' replied K. 'I came here to stay. I'll stay here.' "

This insistent refusal involves goals and vague desires which K. himself does not understand, and he can only add to it a question—"a self-contradiction, which he made no effort to explain": "What could have enticed me to this desolate country except the wish to stay here?" It is dangerous, I should think, to try to answer such a question for him, to try to resolve the contradiction which he—and perhaps Kafka as well—did not resolve because he could not; for part of the meaning of the novel surely rests in there being no satisfactory answers to some of the most overwhelming questions. Certainly the answer here cannot lie in any belief on K.'s or Kafka's part that the village is that "third world where everybody else lived happily . . . ." It is, as K. says, a desolate country, a country of "eternally empty streets" and forbidding cottages, thoroughly unpleasant in almost every sense one can imagine. Never once does Kafka show us either village or villagers in a genuinely attractive light. Neither of the inns and none of the homes into which we go suggest the slightest richness or comfort; they are, for the most part, dirty, small, crowded, and harsh. And none of the villagers, with the possible exception of Frieda, seems to possess any worthwhile secret of life. The peasants, for example, are ugly, grotesquely curious, inarticulate, and possessed—or so it seems to K.—of no mutual understanding whatever. Very early in the novel Kafka describes them as they "stood gaping at [K.] with their open mouths, coarse lips, and literally tortured faces—their heads looked as if they had been beaten flat on top, and their features as if the pain of the beating had twisted them to the present shape." The villagers of higher rank—the two teachers, for example—are, for the most part, only in a physical sense more kindly imagined. The peasants and two or three others demand our pity, the outcast Olga, perhaps, arouses our admiration; but there is literally no one to move us to envy. Yet K. refuses to leave: he will not return to the soaring tower, the confident answers; he will not go with Frieda to a land where love and peace are (perhaps) possible; he insists, instead, that he will stay— and he apparently does stay until his death—in this most desolate and unfriendly of villages.

But this is not the whole story. It is essential to notice that such insistence does not begin at once, it develops only very slowly in company with K.'s developing realization that his struggle with the Castle will necessarily be long and involved. In the first hours of his arrival he actually speaks of returning home after his work is finished, says, too, that he is not really sure whether he will continue to live at the inn while he is surveying or move on to the Castle, and tells the schoolmaster that he will be staying in the village only "for some time." Unless he is lying (and perhaps we cannot be sure), it is clear, then, that he does not originally come to the village in search of a permanent residence, that this is, in the beginning at least, no part of his goal. Not until the fifth of the six days covered by the novel does he speak of anything like permanence—first in the blunt reply to Frieda, then to Olga ("of my own accord I have settled here"), and finally to Gerstäcker ("I've come here for good"). On the fourth day, to be sure, he mentions marriage; but for this, as he knows, he need not remain in the village. On the fourth day, too, he enumerates for the Mayor a few of the things that "keep" him in the village; but it is not until the following day, the fifth, the next-to-last day of the novel, that he admits to anyone, even to himself, that his stay may involve a lifetime.

It is a reluctant admission, shaped by his increasing awareness of how little chance there is that he will ever enter the Castle. Initially he does not much concern himself with becoming a part of the community simply because he hopes to take the Castle by direct assault, by walking straight up to it "that very [first] day" or (after that fails)

Gerstäcker and Lasemann in fact as well as in pretense. He knows that he will have to go at the job "in grim earnest," and he fears "the pressure of a discouraging environment, of a growing resignation to disappointment, the pressure of the imperceptible influences of every moment . . . ." With this characterization of village life as unrelievedly depressing and subtly dangerous, Kafka tells us that although K. is willing in his struggle with the Castle to put up with almost anything for strategic reasons he does not intend really or permanently to become a village worker but merely to adopt the necessary disguise; and it is clear that he looks forward with genuine displeasure to such a task. We are constantly to remember, furthermore, the carefully stated limitation of the strategy: as a village worker K.'s connection with the Castle will still be "merely apparent," scarcely the kind of connection for which he is struggling.

His displeasure with the task is so great that although we naturally expect his new plan to govern his every move, he actually waits but a few moments before launching another direct assault, this time vainly hoping to reach his goal on the hill by clinging to the arm of Barnabas. And throughout the rest of the novel he continues to devote most of his energy to such ventures—the seduction of Frieda, the attempt to intercept Klamm at his coach, the plan to use Mrs. Brunswick (the "girl from the Castle"), and the alliance with the family of Barnabas —all similar in the sense that if successful K. would apparently never have to "take root" in the village. In one or two of the many passages which Kafka deleted from the novel but preserved in his papers he comments more explicitly than elsewhere about this significance of the direct assaults; but—whatever the reason for his cutting such passages—the implied meaning of the action as he at last left it is precisely the same as the more forthright meaning of the deletions. Thus a frank comment on the seduction, for example, reveals perfectly the direction of K.'s thought whenever he is involved in any attempt to reach the Castle directly: "The conquest of Frieda meant making a change in his plans; here he gained a means to power that might make the whole period of work in the village unnecessary." In a similarly deleted passage Kafka suggests that such tactics are attempts to conquer Klamm "as by a *coup-de-main*"; and throughout both the novel and the deletions K. is never able to resist an opportunity to strike in this manner. Whenever there is a direct clash between working in the village and attempting a *coup-de-main* of any kind, such phrases as "necessarily" and "there was no choice" immediately appear in favor of the latter. That K. is perfectly aware of this compulsion and of the extent to which it decreases his security in the village is evident from his remark (in the novel proper) after Frieda has left him and has thus destroyed the possibility of his becoming a member of the community through marriage: "I should be happy if she was to come back to me, but I should at once begin to neglect her all over again."

It is possible, of course, that this is K.'s great mistake. Perhaps he should, after all, put life in the village ahead of everything else, or perhaps he should listen to Frieda and return to the other side of the bridge. In the long speech following immediately after this recognition of his compulsion, he himself has a moment of doubt: perhaps he has "striven too intensely, too noisily, too childishly, with too little experience . . . . by crying, by scratching, by tugging . . . ." But, he adds, he does not really "know whether it is like that"; and while there is too little evidence in the few remaining pages for us to know whether the momentary doubt would, in a completed novel, have affected his actions, it is hardly possible to believe that he would ever have come to hesitate before even the smallest hope of a *coup-de-main*. Whether he should hesitate, should listen to his doubt—what might, in other words, bring him success—is something we cannot know; for this is not the kind of novel in which the reader ends by possessing more wisdom than the hero.

We can, however, notice what the hero himself seems to learn from his experiences. What, for example, is his developing attitude toward the job as school janitor which does in fact become his? When the post is first offered he flatly rejects it, though it would have fallen in perfectly with his short-lived plan to become a village worker; and he at last accepts it only at Frieda's insistence when, if they are to have a place to live, there seems no alternative. Then, on the first day of work, his most significant reason for taking the brunt of the unpleasantness is to spare Frieda: "she had ambitions and he had none, she was sensitive and he was not, she only thought of the petty discomforts of the moment, while he was thinking of Barnabas and the future." The suggestion here is of course not that K. has literally no ambition but that he has none of an orthodox nature involving the job and everyday life, and that he can put up with any temporary discomforts because his only ambition is with the Castle and thus his only concern with Barnabas and with all that Barnabas, as Castle messenger, might at any moment come to mean. Of much greater significance, however, is the fact that even when K. does begin, at last, to place some importance in the janitorship, Kafka carefully maintains the initial distinction—there continues to be, that is, a profound qualitative difference between a position in the village and a connection with the Castle. This is clearest in a passage immediately after K.'s long talk with Hans Brunswick, a talk in which plans are made which may result in a meeting with Hans's mother, the "girl from the Castle." One of the central facts of K.'s existence—the absolute necessity to neglect job, home, marriage, everything connected with village life, in the interests of a greater goal—here becomes most explicit:

. . . the post was more important in K.'s eyes now than before. The conversation with Hans had raised new hopes in him, improbable, he admitted, completely groundless even, but all the same not to be put out of his mind; they almost superseded Barnabas himself. If he gave himself up to them—and there was no choice—then he must husband all his strength, trouble about nothing else—food, shelter, the village authorities, no, not even Frieda—and in reality the whole thing turned only on Frieda, for everything else [that is, food, shelter, etc.] gave him anxiety only in relation to her. For this reason he must try to keep this post, which gave Frieda a certain degree of security, and he must not complain if for this end he was made to endure more at the teacher's hands than he would have had to endure in the ordinary course. All that sort of thing could be put up with, it belonged to the ordinary continual petty annoyances of life, it was nothing compared with what K. was striving for, and he had not come here simply to lead an honored and comfortable life.

At this point, then—midway through the next-to-last day of the novel—K. wishes to keep the post as janitor simply to give Frieda that degree of security which will allow him to ignore her as he devotes all his strength to meeting and using the girl from the Castle. Nothing in the village—not even what is most valuable there, "not even Frieda"—must be allowed to obstruct even the most improbable of direct assaults upon the Castle.

The development of K.'s attitude toward marriage, an action which is of course crucial to his becoming a member of the community, is equally instructive. Here, in contrast to the janitorship, the evaluation begins high—K. for a while believes that merely announcing his intention to marry will make possible a face-to-face meeting with Klamm. In his conversation with Gardena, the landlady of the Bridge Inn, K. himself leaves no doubt that his motivation in the marriage proposal is his knowledge that Frieda was formerly Klamm's mistress and his belief that this makes necessary an interview between the old lover and the new—an interview which can be arranged if not by K. himself then surely by Frieda for him.

You see I haven't yet spoken with a real official. That seems to be more difficult to manage than I had thought. But now I'm under the obligation of speaking to him as a private person, and that, in my opinion, is much easier to bring about. As an official I can only speak to him in his office in the Castle, which may be inaccessible, or—and that's questionable, too —in the Herrenhof. But as a private person I can speak to him anywhere, in a house, in the street, wherever I happen to meet him.

But the illusion—and it is an illusion—does not last. Although he does not immediately believe Frieda and Gardena when they tell him that what he expects is "simply impossible," he soon accepts the fact that Frieda cannot help him toward his goal: "That I want to reach Klamm you know, that you can't help me to do it and that accordingly I must do it by my own efforts you know too . . . ." The truth actually seems to be very close when Gardena says that Frieda, as K.'s wife, would at last come to be, so far as the struggle with the Castle is concerned, "a possession that [had] proved to be worthless." Whether this is true or not, K.'s own understanding of Frieda's powerlessness leaves little room for us to misinterpret the motivation behind his neglecting his home in the village even at the risk of losing it.

   This is not to say, of course, that he ever ceases to value either marriage or a position in the community. But with the exception of his first, soon-forgotten reaction to Klamm's letter and his first, naïve idea about marriage opening a door to Klamm, he never places the same kind of value upon them as he does upon any direct connection with the Castle. His final evaluation both of the janitorship and of marriage appears late on the fifth day in a defense of Frieda to Olga. It is the second and last time that the novel deals explicitly with any kind of village citizenship:

. . . any prospects I may have—dark as they are, they still exist—I owe entirely to Frieda . . . . how much more complicated the game is now

that I have, so to speak, a larger circumference—which means something,
it may not be much—yet I have already a home, a position, and real work
to do, I have a fiancée who takes her share of my professional duties when
I have other business, I'm going to marry her and become a member of
the community, and besides my official connection I have also a personal
connection with Klamm, though as yet I haven't been able to make use
of it. That's surely quite a lot?

Those nervously insistent interjections—"dark as they are, they still
exist" and "which means something, it may not be much"—and perhaps the concluding question as well, in its tone of uneasy restraint,
suggest that K. is here fashioning hope out of his progress in the
village only because he is so painfully aware of his failures with the
Castle. The soldier who cannot win a battle begins half-heartedly to
comfort himself with an elaborate process of digging-in. Yet he knows
so well how little such a process is worth compared to victory in the
field that he simply cannot devote his main attention to it—which is to
say that at this very moment K. is engaged in another attempt to profit
from Barnabas' persistently intriguing connection with the Castle and
is thus characteristically neglecting the job, home, and fiancée that
he professes to value. The precise reason he professes to value them
is important. He does not say that they take him any closer to the
Castle or to Klamm, that they point the way, or that they establish
some relationship. They simply make the game "more complicated,"
provide K. with "a larger circumference." And there is no hint either
here or elsewhere that these phrases are intended to mean anything
more than a larger field of battle in which to maneuver against an
enemy who, in a series of effortless victories, has proved more difficult and more remote than could previously have been guessed. That
the complications could be multiplied and the circumference increased to such a degree that they might suddenly and literally meta-
morphose into victory, and that this socially achieved victory would
be synonymous with personal grace, is an idea which occurs only to
K.'s critics, never to K. himself.

It is important to notice that this one time in the novel when K.
specifically announces that he intends to become a "member of the
community," the home to which he refers is a public schoolroom,
the position is a janitorship, and the "real work" is the menial sweeping
and cleaning required by two arrogant teachers. Both this passage and
K.'s response to Klamm's first letter make it clear that he does not

equate community membership with the position of Land Surveyor—any petty job will serve—yet Land Surveyor is what he genuinely wants to be, something more, obviously, than a plain citizen. He wants, furthermore, not merely to be appointed but, much more significantly, to be allowed to work. His remarks and his ceaseless striving at a time (early in the novel) when he believes Klamm has officially recognized him reveal that any appointment without actual surveying duties is meaningless to him, is merely one of those "unimportant matters" in which his wishes have been all too easily met. But for the Castle to go further than this (it has not, as K. soon discovers, gone even this far) and to let him actually work is unthinkable. For a land surveyor is one who, quite literally, defines areas which have never previously been defined; and any such activity would of course amount to a serious attack upon the Castle. Distances and directions in the village are always vague and shifting, roads seem to lead up the hill and then—"as if deliberately"—to turn aside. And this is but the necessary protection of the Castle. The implications, literal and symbolic, of a fully explored, carefully surveyed village-Castle area are limitless and devastating. At the very least, the roads would lead somewhere, the Castle would be inaccessible no longer. Being Land Surveyor, then, necessarily involves much more than simply settling down in a village understood to represent Society. It involves an ambition of fantastic proportions quite out of keeping with the life of an ordinary villager and of inestimable danger to the powers in the Castle.

If Brod were correct in saying that a home, job, and village citizenship are "simply the right life, the right way (Tao)," [3] then K., the stranger, would presumably show some passionately active desire to be a stranger no longer. He would, at the very least, envy the villagers. His struggle would seem to him the fight of a lone man to become one among many, not a fight that can only be waged—or, incredibly, won—alone. Yet we remember that K. became a stranger by choice, that he came to this village from his native town—and now remains here—of his "own accord." And we find that almost never in the entire novel does K. feel drawn toward any individual unless he believes that that individual can, specifically and directly, help him to get into the Castle or to confront Klamm. He is never drawn toward anyone simply because he likes him, because he wants to emulate him, because he envies his position in life, or because he genuinely wants to become a part of his group or family circle. K.'s attitude is precisely expressed in his pleasure at the silence of Barnabas as the two of them begin what K. believes is a walk to the Castle: "for if they went on in silence, then Barnabas, too, must feel that their excursion together was the sole reason for their association." K. desires such a limitation upon their relationship even though Barnabas is at this time by far the most attractive person he has yet encountered in the village. Furthermore, when they arrive at Barnabas' home instead of the Castle, and K. thus discovers that the silence was meaningful to him alone, his fearful anger is very great: "The other people in the village, who turned him away or were afraid of him, seemed much less dangerous, for all that they did was to throw him back on his own resources, helping him to concentrate his powers, but such ostensible helpers as these, who on the strength of a petty masquerade brought him into their homes instead of into the Castle, deflected him from his goal, whether intentionally or not, and only helped to destroy him." It is a similar fear, though without the anger, that he experiences after his exhaustion has made him nearly ill: "When he felt himself well enough to leave his bed, they [Frieda and the assistants] all ran to serve him. He was not yet strong enough to ward off their services, and noted that that brought him into a state of dependence on them which might have evil consequences, but he could not help it." And Kafka adds, "Nor was it really unpleasant . . . ." K.'s fear, in other words, is not misanthropic. He does not desire independence because he hates to be served or loved but because he believes that only as an independent man, free of others and in control of himself, can he hope to carry on the struggle against the Castle.

There are, though very rarely, other brief moments of weakness or near-despair when he finds human company desirable in part at least for its own sake—first in the deserted road after he has tried to walk to the Castle, again in the wild storm after his depressing argument with Momus and Gardena. Once he wants very badly "to see human faces"—simply to be with, not as usual to make use of, other people—but this occurs immediately after the most terrifying moment of the novel. K. has failed in his attempt to intercept Klamm at the latter's coach and is standing in the cold, dark, deserted courtyard of the Herrenhof, looking toward the rooms of the gentlemen from the Castle:

. . . it seemed to K. as if at last those people had broken off all relations with him, and as if now in reality he were freer than he had ever been, and at liberty to wait here in this place, usually forbidden to him, as long as he desired, and had won a freedom such as hardly anybody else had ever succeeded in winning, and as if nobody could dare to touch him or drive him away, or even speak to him; but—this conviction was at least equally strong—as if at the same time there was nothing more senseless, nothing more hopeless, than this freedom, this waiting, this inviolability.

Here is a man who in striving for the progress of his own soul has ruthlessly freed himself from all but strategically useful human ties. The conditions of battle, as he understood them, were that he fight alone, and he has done so. But suddenly he senses, for a terrifying moment, that the forces he had hoped to reach by such a sacrifice have put themselves irrevocably beyond him and that he stands totally alone in the universe. He has fought his way to a place "usually forbidden to him," on the far outskirts of a village which is itself far beyond the community of ordinary men. In this place his liberation from others is absolute—nobody would dare even speak to him— and he can find nothing to substitute for the rejected human relationship: the incomprehensible powers in the Castle refuse even to enslave him. Thus in this moment of despairing insight he suddenly sees himself a completely free man—dependent upon no one, responsible for no one, subservient to no one, with no ties in any direction whether human or divine—and therefore a senselessly and hopelessly free man. This is a freedom for which he had not bargained, which he had never so much as imagined, the terror of which he could not have guessed; and it is little wonder that "he was shivering and wanted to see human faces . . . ." It is a measure of his determination to reach the Castle that he does not let such an experience permanently dissuade him. What if his momentary insight were correct? What if, after all he has sacrificed, there were nothing for him in the Castle, no relationship possible with those forces which, by attacking, he serves so fiercely? With such a possibility revealed to him, a man less determined than K. would have hurried to Frieda and fled with her to a hope of peace and love across the bridge.

But the idea of flight does not occur to K. That he will fight on alone is clear, and Kafka at once places him in a situation which requires him to reveal perhaps more openly than anywhere else the extent of his ambition and the extent to which his isolation is voluntary. When

he leaves the courtyard and goes back inside the Herrenhof, he meets
Gardena and Momus, the latter for the first time. If he were ever
going to envy or emulate anyone, this would be the man; for Momus
does magnificently better than simply live in the village. He is
nothing less than Klamm's village secretary—and, though "most . . .
secretaries work only for one gentleman," he is Vallabene's secretary
as well. His almost overwhelming importance first appears in the
reaction of Gardena and Pepi (the substitute barmaid) when Momus
introduces himself to K.: "seriousness descended on the room; though
the landlady and Pepi knew quite well who the gentleman was, yet
they seemed staggered by the utterance of his name and rank."
Gardena then spends the next few moments trying valiantly but un-
successfully to impress this importance upon K.:

Precisely to K., it seemed, who was not considered worthy even to be seen
in passing by Klamm, these people had described in detail the services
of a man out of Klamm's circle with the unconcealed intention of evoking
K.'s recognition and admiration. And yet K. had no proper appreciation
of it; he, who with all his powers strove to get a glimpse of Klamm, valued
very little, for example, the post of a Momus who was permitted to live
in Klamm's eye; for it was not Klamm's environment in itself that seemed
to him worth striving for, but rather that he, K., he only and no one else,
should attain to Klamm, and should attain to him not to rest with him, but
to go on beyond him, farther yet, into the Castle.

The development in the second sentence from the specific "example"
of Momus to the broad generalization about Klamm's environment
suggests that Kafka emphasized so intently the staggering importance
of Momus' position for just one reason: so that the novel could move
powerfully and dramatically toward a sharper definition, necessarily
cast mainly in negative terms, of K.'s vague goal. We now know, for
example, that if K. does not value the position of a Momus, he surely
cannot value any other position in the village; that if his goal is "not
Klamm's environment," it surely cannot be, what is much less than
that, the village environment; and that if he has no desire ever "to
rest with" Klamm, he surely cannot wish to rest merely with the
common villagers. Furthermore, if he desires that "he, K., he only
and no one else," should get into the Castle, his goal can scarcely be
marital or social in any meaningful sense. And if he will attain to
Klamm "not to rest . . . but to go beyond," then even his most hopeful
vision cannot include peace and security, in the village or anywhere

else. He insists here as elsewhere that his is a lonely struggle, that he will not let his destiny be linked with any other. He knows, too, that it is a struggle with no conceivable end. It is so endless, in fact, that Klamm and even the Castle serve as symbols of his goal only in an oddly limited sense, only, that is, because they are imaginable. What is genuinely important is precisely what is not imaginable: the deep, unknown interior far beyond Klamm and, of course, farther still beyond the village. Neither K. nor Kafka knows what lies deep inside the Castle, or how to go there. For us, then, to believe that a secure life in the village is somehow synonymous with this interior or even that such a life constitutes the way to reach the interior is to kill outright the fundamental mystery of the novel. As it is in the nature of K.'s struggle that there can be no way to judge what might bring success, so it is in the nature of his profoundly religious goal that it can be neither known nor imagined.

Of the village, however, we can be somewhat more certain, especially if we do not forget that Kafka's geography, in *The Castle* as elsewhere, is essentially spiritual. It is characteristic of him to represent movements or explorations of the spirit by long journeys—to America, to the Penal Colony, or, in "The Judgment," to Russia. Early in *The Castle* he characteristically describes the sexual act as "wandering into a strange country"; and, more significantly for the meaning of the village, he writes in his "Letter to His Father": "Sometimes I imagine the map of the world spread out flat and you stretched out diagonally across it. And what I feel then is that only those territories come into question for my life that either are not covered by you or are not within your reach. And, in keeping with the conception that I have of your magnitude, these are not many and not very comforting territories, and above all marriage is not among them." But, it would be possible to argue, the village is among them, is precisely one of these uncomfortable, even "desolate" territories—a territory of harsh spiritual experience amounting for Kafka both to an escape and a dedication, an escape from the ways and the meanings of the orthodox community, over all of which lies the gigantic form of his father, and a dedication to a vaguely defined, complex, and utterly impossible spiritual progress. Certainly K.'s journey, in the very precise terms of the novel, is a renunciation of home, of the orthodox community of men, for the purpose of carrying on a relentless, designedly lonely battle against powers of deep religious significance who can be

challenged only from the village—which is to say, I should think, only
from the spiritual posture symbolically defined by the village and by
K.'s attitude toward it. In this symbolic sense, the village is that grim,
almost impossible area of the spirit precariously inhabited by a man
who ruthlessly and of his own accord has made himself a stranger in
the community of men so that he might, in a fierce concentration of
all his powers, force a word, a gesture—some sign of genuine recognition—out of the "illusory emptiness above him." He is a man who has
consciously rejected a world in which may lie the possibility of normal
happiness; and when his fiancée begs him to return to it, he flatly
refuses. He has no friends because he has renounced friendship, no
community because he has renounced communion, and at last no
fiancée because he has renounced love. He has determined, beyond all
measure, to preserve the isolated integrity of his soul against human
invasion so as to reserve all his energies, emotional and intellectual
as well as physical, for the one great enemy in the Castle. In what
the definitive edition calls "another version of the opening paragraphs,"
he announces, with a more conscious sense of heroics than K. came
to have but with perfect accuracy so far as his actions in the novel are
concerned: "I have a difficult task ahead of me and have dedicated
my whole life to it. I do it joyfully and ask for nobody's pity. But because it is all I have—the task, I mean—I ruthlessly suppress everything that might disturb me in carrying it out. I tell you, I can be
mad in my ruthlessness." Only from such a life, he thinks, only from a
life composed of such renunciation and such ruthlessness, do roads
run to the Castle.

And he is fanatically seeking Castle roads—demanding spiritual
satisfaction from powers he can neither find nor understand but which
he will not deny; and his entry into the village, this desolate territory
of the spirit, represents the challenge he addresses to them. Remembering, as from a picture-postcard of great beauty but of no lasting significance, a peaceful territory in which the answers are unfaltering,
the goals lofty and clear, he comes—with deeper insight than those
who remain at peace—as "the attacker" prepared to use any sub-
terfuge and any weapon against a grotesque divinity symbolized by
an irregular, broken, fumbling, melancholy-mad Castle tower. Having
seen the superficiality of saneness and clarity, having guessed, perhaps
sadly, the greater truth of this absurd and ambiguous Castle, he must
strive against it; but for what he is not quite sure: for knowledge,

perhaps, some fierce progress of the soul, a saving relationship with universal powers however mad. He cannot even be sure that he should wish for victory: "a bell began to ring merrily up there, a bell that for at least a second made his heart palpitate, for its tone was menacing, too, as if it threatened him with the fulfillment of his vague desire." Having suppressed so much of life to achieve the austerity represented by his presence in the village, he would like to wage his battle in some clear, open fashion: he would like simply to confront Klamm or to walk straight up to the Castle, to plunge directly into the godhead, carrying on his struggle from there (for there is no hint of eventual peace). But the Castle has no respect even for purity of renunciation and dedication. There is here no saving dichotomy of spiritual and mundane, and he is forced always back into the "muddle" and the "petty annoyances" of "everyday life," never receiving even the minimum satisfaction of knowing that he is opposed.

It is this lack even of the recognition which opposition would signify that makes him an alien in the only sense that matters. The Castle officials let him "go anywhere he liked—of course only within the village—and this pampered and enervated him, ruled out all possibility of conflict, and transposed him to an unofficial, totally unrecognized, troubled, and alien existence." This is the specific, immediate source of his crucial alienation, an alienation which can be defined most simply as an inability to establish any relationship with those "distant and invisible masters" inside the walls of the Castle. It is this alienation that he is, throughout the novel, striving to overcome. And his quite different estrangement from the human community is a calculated rejection of ties that might, in the midst of such a struggle, prove a burden, a limitation of essential freedom. The village as such—the closed doors, the unfriendly people—is not Society into which he, the alien, is trying to enter; it is, instead, in some very complicated sense, the way Society must appear to one who, in the service of an ultimately transcendental and desperately personal goal, refuses to be social except when forced or when a limited fellowship seems strategically useful. He does not achieve such an outlook, such an arid quality of mind and spirit for its own sake; and his determination to maintain it grows only out of his inability to go beyond into that mysteriously necessary relationship with invisible masters. Security in the village is thus in no sense his goal. It provides a point of siege merely, a grim foothold from which to wage his war. His only goal is the Castle; and his only desire reaches far beyond the walls into the deep interior, into that unimaginable territory of the spirit which signifies some strange metaphysical—not social—integration: an integration which, so far as he can know, contains no promise of peace or love or grace.

NOTES

1. Thomas Mann, "Homage," *The Castle* (New York, 1954), p. xiv; Max Brod, "Additional Note," *The Castle* (New York, 1946), p. 330.

2. R. O. C. Winkler, "The Three Novels," *The Kafka Problem*, ed. Angel Flores (New York, 1946), p. 194. Harry Slochower, *No Voice Is Wholly Lost* (New York, 1945), p. 114, writes of "The Communal Castle." Walter J. Ong, "Kafka's Castle in the West," *Thought*, XXII (Sept., 1947), p. 460, says "that whatever goes for [the village] goes for everything." Charles Neider, "The Cabalists," *Kafka Problem*, p. 429, agrees with Brod "that K.'s efforts to become a member of the village community represent a search for grace, for belonging," and says (p. 435) that "the village acts as a microcosm . . . ." W. H. Auden, "K.'s Quest," *Kafka Problem*, p. 50, believes "the hero of *The Castle* wants to be allowed to settle down in the village." Nathan A. Scott, *Rehearsals of Discomposure* (New York, 1952), p. 50, says, "The Village is, of course, existence, the world. . . ." Herbert Tauber, *Franz Kafka: An Interpretation of his Works*, tr. by G. Humphreys Roberts and Roger Senhouse (New Haven, 1948), p. 133, believes that "for K. the village is worldly reality, into which it is a question of being co-ordinated somehow or other," and adds (p. 138) that "the village is a symbol of human life . . . ." Other examples are plentiful; but these will perhaps suggest the wide variety of critics who, in their understanding of K.'s relationship with the village, do not differ basically from Brod and Mann.

3. Max Brod, *The Castle* (1946), p. 330.

Part Three

DIARIES & LETTERS

Maurice Blanchot

The Diaries: The Exigency of the Work of Art[*]

IN MANY ways, Kafka was until 1912 like any young man in whom is awakening the desire to write, who recognizes his vocation there, and who also recognizes there certain exigencies but has no proof that he will be equal to them. If, until 1912, he did not devote himself to literature, he offered this excuse: "I can take nothing on myself as long as I have not achieved a sustained work that satisfies me completely." [1] This achievement, this proof, came to him during the night of September 22, 1912, the night he wrote "The Judgment" at one sitting, and which brought him decisively close to the point at which it seemed that "everything can be said, . . . for everything, for the strangest fancies, there waits a great fire in which they perish and rise up again." Shortly afterward he was confirmed in this by giving a reading of this short story for his friends: "There were tears in my eyes. The indubitability of the story was confirmed." (This need to read to his friends, often to his sisters, even to his father, what he had just written also belongs to the middle region. He never quite gave it up. It is not literary vanity—although he condemned it himself—but a need to crowd physically upon his work, to let himself be raised, drawn up by it, by making it spread out in the vocal space which his great gifts as a reader allowed him to create.)

From then on Kafka knew he could write. But this knowledge was

[*] Translated by Lyall H. Powers.

not knowledge, and this power not his own. With rare exceptions, he never found in what he wrote the proof that he was really writing. It was at most a prelude, an approach-work or mission of reconnaissance. Of "The Metamorphosis" he says (January 19, 1914): "I . . . find it bad. Perhaps I am really lost," or later, "Great antipathy to 'Metamorphosis.' Unreadable ending. Imperfect almost to its very marrow. It would have turned out much better if I had not been interrupted at the time by the business trip."

This last remark alludes to the conflict which Kafka encountered, and in which he was shattered. He had a profession and a family. He belonged to the world and had to belong to it. The world gives us time but controls it. The *Diaries* are, at least until 1915, shot through with remarks of despair where the notion of suicide recurs, for he lacked time: time, physical force, solitude, and silence. Certainly external circumstances were unfavorable: he had to work evenings or at night, his sleep was fretful, and he was exhausted by worry; but it would be vain to suppose that the conflict could have been removed by "organizing things better." Later, when illness brought him leisure, the conflict remained and became worse and of a different nature. There are no favorable circumstances. Even if one gives "all his time" to the exigencies of the work, "all" is still not enough; for it is not a matter of devoting one's time to working or of spending one's time writing, but rather of passing into another time where there is no more work, of reaching that point where time is removed, where one enters the fascination and solitude of the absence of time. When one has all the time in the world he has none at all, and the "friendly" external circumstances have reached the unfriendly point where circumstances cease to exist.

Kafka is unable, or unwilling, to write "in snatches," in the intervals of separate moments. This is what he discovered on the night of September 22 when, having written at a stretch, he grasped in all its fulness the unlimited impetus that moved him to write: "Only *in this way* can writing be done, only with such coherence, with such a complete opening out of the body and the soul." And later (December 8, 1914): "Again I realized that everything written down bit by bit rather than all at once in the course of the larger part (or even the whole) of one night is inferior, and that the circumstances of my life condemn me to this inferiority." We have here the initial explanation of all the abandoned tales whose impressive debris is revealed to us in the *Diaries* as they are presently available. Very often, the "story" extends no further than a few lines, at times it will quickly achieve coherence and density and yet stop at the bottom of a page, at others it continues for several pages, expanding and asserting its authority— and yet stops. There are many reasons for this, but primarily Kafka does not find in *his* time the extension which permits the story to develop as it would according to all directions; the story is never simply a fragment followed by another fragment; "how, starting with fragments, can I found a story capable of getting off the ground?" Thus, the story, not having been mastered, not having created the proper space in which the need to write is to be at once repressed and expressed, falls apart, wanders, steals into the dark night whence it came and there sadly holds prisoner him who was unable to bring it into the light of day.

Kafka needed more time, but he also needed less of the world. The world was first his family, whose constraint he bore with difficulty, never being able to free himself from it. It was next his fiancée and his fundamental desire to observe the law which requires man to ful- fill his destiny in the world, have a family, children, and take his place in the community. Here the conflict assumes a new aspect, enters a con- tradiction which Kafka's religious position makes especially strong. When, on the subject of his engagement with F. B.—once broken but resumed—he examined, tirelessly and with ever increasing tension, "all that is for or against our marriage," he always came up against this exigency: "My sole aspiration and my sole vocation . . . is literature. . . . What I accomplished was only the result of being alone. . . . Then I'll never be alone again. . . . Not that, not that!" During his engagement at Berlin: "Was tied hand and foot like a criminal. Had they sat me down in a corner bound in real chains, placed policemen in front of me . . . , it could not have been worse. And that was my engagement; everybody made an effort to bring me to life, and when they couldn't, to put up with me as I was." Shortly afterwards, the en- gagement was broken but the aspiration remained, the desire for a "normal" life, a desire made heartbreaking by the torment of having wounded someone near to him. The story of his engagement has been compared—Kafka thought of it himself—to that of Kierkegaard's. But the conflict was different. Kierkegaard was able to give up Regina, he could renounce the ethical stage; access to the religious stage was not thus compromised, but rather made possible. But if Kafka forsook the earthly happiness of a normal life, he forsook also the steadiness of a just life, placed himself outside the law, deprived himself and, to a certain extent, deprived the law, of the basis and the foundation he needed to exist. This is the eternal problem of Abraham. What is demanded of Abraham is to sacrifice not his son alone, but God Himself: the son is the future of God on earth, for it is time which is really the Promised Land, the true, the only dwelling place of the chosen people and of God in His people. Now Abraham must, in sacrificing his son, sacrifice time, and time sacrificed will surely not be returned to him in the eternity of the hereafter: the hereafter is nothing but the future, the future of God in time. The hereafter is Isaac.

For Kafka the trial is rendered more burdensome by all that makes it lighter for him (what would Abraham's test be if, having no son, he were yet required to sacrifice that son? we could not take that seriously, we could only laugh; this laughter is the form of Kafka's sorrow). The problem is also such that it eludes us and eludes in its indecisiveness him who tries to solve it. The confusion is great, for Kafka seemed to identify with the exigency of the work of art that which could bear the name of his salvation. If writing condemned him to solitude, made his existence that of a celibate, without love, without bonds, if however writing seemed to him—at least frequently and for some time—the sole activity which could justify him, it was because, at all events, solitude was a threat to him within and without, it was because the community was nothing more than a phantom and because the law which still speaks through it (the community) is not even the forgotten law but the feigned forgetting of the law. Writing becomes once more, then, in the midst of distress and weakness, which are inseparable from this impulse, a possibility of fulfillment, a path without a goal perhaps comparable to that goal without a path which is the only one that must be reached. When he was not writing, Kafka was not simply alone, "as alone as Franz Kafka," as he said to G. Janouch, but in a sterile, cold solitude, a petrifying coldness that he called stunned dullness and that seems to have been the great threat that he dreaded. Even Brod, careful as he was to make of Kafka a man free of anomalies, recognizes that he acted at times like one absent or dead. So very much like Hölderlin in that both of them employed the same terms of self-criticism; Hölderlin: "I am numb, I am made of stone," and Kafka (July 28, 1914): "*I am more and more unable to think, to observe, to determine the truth of things, to remember, to speak, to share an experience; I am turning to stone* . . . . If I can't take refuge in some work, I am lost."

"If I can't take refuge in some work . . . ." But why could this work save him? It seems that Kafka recognized precisely in this terrible state of self-dissolution in which he was lost for others and for himself, the center of gravity of the exigency of writing. At the point where he felt utterly destroyed is born the profundity which replaces destruction with the possibility of the greatest creation. A marvellous reversal, a hope always equal to the greatest despair, and it is easy to understand how from this experience he derived a motivating confidence which he would not willingly call into question. Work then became, especially in the early years, something of a means of psychological (not yet "spiritual") salvation, an effort towards a creation "that might be linked word for word to his life, a creation which he drew to himself so that it might draw him away from himself"; this he expressed in the most naïve and most forceful way in these terms (December 8, 1911): "I have now, and have had since this afternoon, a great yearning to write all my anxiety entirely out of me, write it into the depths of the paper just as it comes out of the depths of me, or write it down in such a way that I could draw what I had written into me completely." [2] However somber he might become, this hope never completely failed, and we always find, throughout all periods of his *Diaries,* entries of this kind (November 27, 1913): "The firmness, however, which the most insignificant writings bring about in me is beyond doubt and wonderful. The comprehensive view I had of everything on my walk yesterday!" At such moments writing is not an appeal, the expectation of grace or a dim prophetic fulfillment, but something simpler, more immediately urgent: the hope of not sinking, or more exactly of sinking faster than himself and thus recovering himself at the last minute. A duty more urgent, then, than any other, one which led him to write, on July 31, 1914, these remarkable words: "I have no time. General mobilization. K. and P. have been called up. Now I receive the reward for living alone. But it is hardly a reward; living alone ends only with punishment. Still, as a consequence, I am little affected by all the misery and am firmer in my resolve than ever. . . . But I will write in spite of everything, absolutely; it is my struggle for self-preservation."

However, it was the upheaval of war, but even more, the crisis brought about by his engagement, the movement and the deepening quest of writing, the difficulties encountered in it, it was his unhappy situation in general which little by little was to throw a different light on the existence of the writer in him. This change was never effected, resulted in no decision, was simply an indistinct perspective; but still there are certain indications: in 1914, for example, he was still striving passionately, desperately toward this single goal of finding a few moments to write, of getting a two-week leave which would be devoted solely to writing, of subordinating everything to this single, this supreme exigency—to write. But in 1916, if he asked for leave, it was to enlist. "The immediate duty is unconditional: to become a soldier." A project which would lead to nothing, but that didn't matter; the wish which was at its center shows how far Kafka already was from his "I will write in spite of everything," of July 31, 1914. Later he thought seriously of joining the pioneers of Zionism and going off to Palestine. He said as much to Janouch: "I dreamed of going to Palestine as a laborer or farm worker."—"You would give up everything here?"—"Everything, to find a life full of meaning in security and beauty." But since Kafka was already ill, the dream was just a dream, and we shall never know whether he could, like another Rimbaud, have given up his sole vocation for love of a wilderness where he would have found the security of a justified life,—nor if he would have found it there. Of all the attempts he made to give his life a different orientation, he himself would say they were but blighted efforts, just so many radii of light, their tips bristling about the center of the incomplete circle that was his life. In 1922 he enumerated all of his projects in which he saw only failure: piano, violin, languages, Germanic studies, anti-Zionism, Zionism, Hebrew studies, gardening, woodworking, literature, attempts at marriage, the bachelor life, and he adds (January 23, 1922): "If I sometimes prolonged the radius a little farther than usual, in the case of my law studies, say, or engagements, everything was made worse rather than better just because of this little extra distance."

It would be foolish to single out from passing remarks the absolute affirmations they contain; and although he himself forgets it here, we cannot forget that he never stopped writing, that he wrote right to the end. But the fact remains that, between the young man who said to the one whom he considered as his future father-in-law: "I am nothing but literature, I cannot and will not be anything else," and the mature man who, ten years later, put literature on the same level as his little stabs at gardening, there is a great internal difference, even if externally the writing force remains the same or even seems to us to be more rigorous and precise toward the end, being the force to which we owe *The Castle*.

Whence comes this difference? To answer that would be to master the inner life of a man infinitely reserved, secretive even with his friends, and, moreover, rather inaccessible to himself. No one can pretend to reduce to a certain number of precise statements something which for Kafka himself could not achieve the transparency of a tangible utterance. And we should need, furthermore, a community of intentions, which is not possible. At least we shall doubtless commit no external errors in saying that, although his confidence in the powers of art often remained great, his confidence in his own powers, put to an ever greater test, also enlightened him about this test, about its exigency; enlightened him above all about what he himself demanded of art: no longer to give his person reality and coherence, not, that is to say, to save him from insanity but to save him from perdition; and when Kafka foresaw that, banished from this real world, he was perhaps already a citizen of another world in which he had to struggle not only for himself but for that other world, then writing appeared to him simply a means of struggling, at times deceptive, at times miraculous, that he could lose without losing everything.

Compare these two notes. The first is for January, 1912:

It is easy to recognize a concentration in me of all my forces on writing. When it became clear in my organism that writing was the most productive direction for my being to take, everything rushed in that direction and left empty all those abilities which were directed toward the joys of sex, eating, drinking, philosophical reflection and above all music. I atrophied in all these directions. This was necessary because the totality of my strengths was so slight that only collectively could they even halfway serve the purpose of my writing. . . . the compensation for all this is as clear as day. My development is now complete and, so far as I can see, there is nothing left to sacrifice; I need only throw my work in the office out of this complex in order to begin my real life in which, with the progress of my work, my face will finally be able to age in a natural way.

The lightness of the irony should not mislead us, of course, but the lightness, the jauntiness are nevertheless real and illuminate, by contrast, the tension of this other note, the meaning of which is apparently the same (dated August 6, 1914):

What will be my fate as a writer is very simple. My talent for portraying my dreamlike inner life has thrust all other matters into the background; my life has dwindled dreadfully, nor will it cease to dwindle. Nothing else will ever satisfy me. But the strength I can muster for that portrayal is not to be counted upon: perhaps it has already vanished forever, perhaps it will come back to me again, although the circumstances of my life don't favor its return. Thus I waver, continually fly to the summit of the mountain, but then fall back in a moment. Others waver too, but in lower regions, with greater strength; if they are in danger of falling, they are caught up by the kinsman who walks beside them for that very purpose. But I waver on the heights; it is not death, alas, but the eternal torments of dying.

Three movements cross here: an affirmation, "nothing else [but literature] will ever satisfy me,"—doubt of himself, linked with the inexorably uncertain essence of his gifts which "is not to be counted upon"—the feeling that this uncertainty (the fact that writing is never a power over which one has free disposal) belongs to whatever is extreme in the work of art, this central, mortal exigency which "is not death, alas," which is but death held at a distance, "the eternal torments of dying."

We may say that these three movements comprise, in their vicissitudes, the test which exhausted in Kafka his fidelity to "his sole vocation," which, coinciding with his religious preoccupations, led him to read in this unique exigency something further, another exigency which tended to subordinate it, or at least to transform it. The more Kafka wrote, the less sure he was of writing. At times he tried to reassure himself by thinking that "once you have received the knowledge of writing, it can never more fail or founder, but also, most rarely, something wells up which exceeds all measure." A weak consolation: the more he wrote, the closer he came to that extreme point toward which the work of art tends as toward its origin, but which he who senses it can only regard as the empty depths of the infinite. "I can't write any more. I've come up against the last boundary, before which I shall in all likelihood again sit down for years, and then in all likelihood begin another story all over again that will again remain unfinished. This fate pursues me" (November 30, 1914).

It seems that in 1915–16, futile as it may be to try to date a movement that eludes time, a change of perspective took place. Kafka took up again with his former fiancée. This relationship which led to a new engagement in 1917 then ended immediately afterward in the illness which revealed itself at that time, and plunged him into torments which he could not overcome. He discovered with increasing anxiety that he could not live alone and yet could not live with others. The guilt of his situation, of his existence, given over to what he called bureaucratic vices, meanness, indecision, and scheming, gripped and obsessed him. He had at all costs to escape this bureaucracy, and for that he could no longer count on literature, for that work was eluding him, for that work had its share in the imposture of irresponsibility, since the work demands solitude but is also annihilated by it—whence his decision: "To become a soldier." At the same time allusions to the Old Testament appear in the *Diaries,* and these cries of a doomed man are to be heard: "Receive me into your arms, they are the depths, receive me into the depths; if you refuse me now, then later." "Take me, take me, web of folly and pain." "Have mercy on me, I am sinful in every nook and cranny of my being. . . . Don't thrust me in among the lost."

Certain of his writings were once translated into French with the word "God" added. It does not belong there. The word "God" almost never appears in the *Diaries,* and never significantly.[3] That does not mean that these invocations in their uncertainty have no religious direction, but that one must preserve in them the force of that uncertainty and not deprive Kafka of the spirit of reserve which he always showed in regard to what was most important to him. These words of distress are dated July, 1916, and correspond to a visit he spent at Marienbad with F. B. A year later, however, he was again engaged; a month after that he was again spitting blood; in September he left Prague, but the illness was still moderate and was not to become threatening until (apparently) 1922. In 1917 he wrote the "Aphorisms," the only one of his writings in which spiritual affirmation (in a general form, not concerned with him in particular) escapes from the trial of a negative transcendence.

For the years that follow, the *Diaries* are almost completely lacking. Not a word in 1918. A few lines in 1919 when he was engaged for a few months to a young woman of whom we know almost nothing. In 1920 he met Milena Jesenska, a young Czech woman, sensitive, intelligent, capable of great freedom of mind and passion, to whom a fierce emotion attached him for two years—at first full of hope and happiness, but later given over to distress. The *Diaries* resume their importance in 1921 and especially in 1922 when the difficulties of this friendship, while his illness was growing worse, brought him to such a degree of tension that his mind seemed to oscillate between madness and the decision of salvation. At this point we must insert two long quotations. The first is dated January 28, 1922:

A little dizzy, tired from the tobogganing; weapons still exist for me, however seldom I may employ them; it is so hard for me to lay hold of them because I am ignorant of the joys of their use, never learned how when I was a child. It is not only "Father's fault" that I never learned their use, but also my wanting to disturb the "peace," to upset the balance, and for this reason I could not allow a new person to be born elsewhere while I was bending every effort to bury him here. Of course, in this too there is a question of "fault," for why did I want to quit the world? Because "he" would not let me live in it, in his world. Though indeed I should not judge the matter so precisely, for I am now a citizen of this other world, whose relationship to the ordinary one is the relationship of the wilderness to cultivated land (I have been forty years wandering from Canaan); I look back at it like a foreigner, though in this other world as well—it is the paternal heritage I carry with me—I am the most insignificant and timid of all creatures and am able to keep alive thanks only to the special nature of its arrangements; in this world it is possible even for the humblest to be raised to the heights as if with lightning speed, though they can also be crushed forever as if by the weight of the seas. Should I not be thankful despite everything? Was it certain that I should find my way to this world? Could not "banishment" from one side, coming together with rejection from this, have crushed me at the border? Is not Father's power such that nothing (not I, certainly) could have resisted his decree? It is indeed a kind of Wandering in the Wilderness in reverse that I am undergoing: I think that I am continually skirting the wilderness and am full of childish hopes (particularly as regards women) that "perhaps I shall keep in Canaan after all"—when all the while I have been decades in the wilderness and these hopes are merely mirages born of despair, especially at those times when I am the wretchedest of creatures in the desert too, and Canaan is perforce my only Promised Land, for no third place exists for mankind.

The second text is dated the following day:

Suffered some attacks on the road through the snow in the evening. There are conflicting thoughts always in my head, something like this: My situation in this world would seem to be a dreadful one, alone here in Spindelmühle, on a forsaken road, moreover, where one keeps slipping in the snow in the dark, a senseless road, moreover, without an earthly goal (to the bridge? Why there? Besides, I didn't even go that far); I too forsaken in this place (I cannot place a human, personal value on the help the doctor gives me, I haven't earned it; at bottom the fee is my only relationship to him), incapable of striking up a friendship with anyone, incapable of tolerating a friendship, at bottom full of endless astonishment when I see a group of people cheerfully assembled together (here in the hotel, indeed, there is little that is cheerful; I won't go so far as to say that I am the cause of this, in my character, perhaps, as "the man with the too-great shadow," though my shadow in this world *is* too great—with fresh astonishment I observe the capacity for resistance some people have, who, "in spite of everything," want to live under this shadow, directly under it; but there is much more than this to be said on the matter), or especially when I see parents with their children; forsaken, moreover, not only here but in general, even in Prague, my "home," and what is more, forsaken not by people (that would not be the worst thing, I could run after them as long as I was alive), but rather by myself vis-à-vis people, by my strength vis-à-vis people; I am fond of lovers but I cannot love, I am too far away, am banished, have—since I am human after all and my roots want nourishment—my proxies "down" (or up) there too, sorry, unsatisfactory comedians who can satisfy me (though indeed they don't satisfy me at all and it is for this reason that I am so forsaken) only because I get my principal nourishment from other roots in other climes, these roots too are sorry ones, but nevertheless better able to sustain life.

This brings me to the conflict in my thoughts. If things were only as they seem to be on the road in the snow, it would be dreadful; I should be lost, lost not in the sense of a dreadful future menacing me but in the sense of a present execution. But I live elsewhere; it is only that the attraction of the human world is so immense, in an instant it can make one forget everything. Yet the attraction of my world too is strong; those who love me love me because I am "forsaken"—not, I feel sure, on the principle of a Weissian vacuum, but because they sense that in happy moments I enjoy on another plane the freedom of movement completely lacking to me here.

To comment on these pages seems superfluous. What should be observed, however, is how, at that date, the privation of the world is inverted to a positive experience,[4] that of another world of which he is already a citizen where he is of course only the smallest and the most uneasy, but where he also experiences overwhelming elevations, where he enjoys a freedom whose value is sensed and whose prestige is acknowledged by men. Still, not to change the meaning of such images as these, one must not read them from the common

Christian point of view (according to which there is this world and then the world of the hereafter, the only one which has value, reality, and glory), but always from the point of view of "Abraham"; for, in every respect for Kafka, to be excluded from the world means to be excluded from Canaan, to wander in the wilderness; and it is this situation which makes his struggle pathetic and his hope despairing, as though, cast out of the world into the error of infinite wandering, he had to struggle ceaselessly to make of that outside another world, and of that error the principle and origin of a new freedom. It is a struggle unproductive, uncertain, in which what he must conquer is his own loss, the truth of the exile and the return to the very bosom of the dispersal. It is a struggle which will be compared with profound Jewish speculations, when, especially after the Spanish exodus, religious minds try to overcome exile by pushing it to its ultimate.[5] Kafka clearly refers to "all such writings" (his own) as to a "new secret doctrine, a Kabbalah" which, "if Zionism had not intervened, . . . might easily have developed" (January 16, 1922). And we can better understand why he was at the same time Zionist and anti-Zionist. Zionism is the cure for exile, the affirmation that the earthly life is possible, that the Jewish people has as a dwelling place not only a book, the Bible, but the earth, and no longer dispersal throughout time. Kafka profoundly desired this reconciliation, desired it even if he was excluded from it; for the grandeur of that just conscience has always been to hope for others more than for himself and not to take his personal misfortune as the measure of general unhappiness. "All that is magnificent, except for me, and rightly so." But he did not belong to that truth, and that is why he had to be anti-Zionist for himself, lest he be condemned to immediate execution and to the despair of absolute impiety. It was to the other shore that he already belonged, and his migration did not consist of going toward Canaan, but of going toward the wilderness, the truth of the wilderness, of going ever further in that direction even when, likewise unfortunate in that other world and still tempted by the joys of the real world ("especially as far as women were concerned": this is a clear allusion to Milena), he tried to persuade himself that he perhaps still dwelt in Canaan. If he had not been anti-Zionist for himself (in the figurative sense, of course), if there had been only *this* world, then "the situation would be dreadful," then he would be doomed immediately. But he is "elsewhere," and if the strength of the human world's attraction remained great enough to lead him back as far as its frontiers and keep him there almost shattered, no less great was the attractive force of his own world, the one in which he was free, the freedom he speaks of in trembling, an account of prophetic authority which contrasts with his usual modesty.

There can be no doubt that this other world has something to do with literary activity: the proof of this fact is that Kafka, in speaking of the "new Kabbalah," speaks of it precisely in connection with "all such writing." But the fact that the exigency of the truth of this other world henceforth surpasses in his eyes the exigency of the work of art, is not exhausted by it and but imperfectly accomplished in it, that also makes itself felt. When writing becomes "a form of prayer," the suggestion is that there are doubtless other forms, and even if, as a result of this unhappy world, there were not, writing, from this point of view, would cease to be the approach to the work of art, and become the anticipation of the single moment of grace for which Kafka realizes he is waiting and in which one no longer has to write. To Janouch's question, "So poetry leads to religion?" he replied, "I will not say that, but certainly to prayer," and contrasting literature and poetry he added, "Literature strives to place things in an agreeable light; the poet is compelled to raise them into the realm of truth, purity, and the eternal." A significant reply, for it corresponds to an entry in the *Diaries* (September 25, 1917) where Kafka asks himself what joy writing can still hold for him: "I can still have passing satisfaction from works like *A Country Doctor*, provided I can still write such things at all (very improbable). But happiness only if I can raise the world into the pure, the true, and the immutable." The "idealistic" or "spiritual" exigency here becomes categorical. To write, yes, still to write, but only to "elevate to infinite life that which is perishable and isolated, to the domain of law that which belongs to chance," as he said again to Janouch. But at once the question arises: is it possible? is he sure that writing does not belong to evil? and is not writing's consolation an illusion, a dangerous illusion that must be challenged? "Undeniably, there is a certain joy in being able calmly to write down: 'Suffocation is inconceivably horrible.' Of course it is inconceivable—that is why I have written nothing down" (December 20, 1921). And hasn't the humblest reality of this world a consistency which is lacking in the most powerful work of art? "Writing's lack of independence of the world, its dependence on the maid who tends the fire, on the cat warming itself by the stove; it is even dependent on the poor old human being warming himself by the stove. All these are independent activities ruled by their own laws; only writing is helpless, cannot live in itself, is a joke and a despair" (December 6, 1921). A grimace, the grimace of a face that recoils before the light, "a defense of nothingness, a guarantee of non-being, a breath of gaiety lent to nothingness," such is art.

However, if the confidence of his early years gives way to a yet harsher view, the fact remains that in his most difficult moments, when his very integrity seems threatened, when he is prey to the almost tangible attacks of the unknown ("how that spies upon me; on the way to the doctor's, for example, down there, constantly"), even then he continues to see in his work, not the thing which threatens him, but that which can help him, can open to him the decision of salvation: "The strange, mysterious, perhaps dangerous, perhaps saving comfort that there is in writing: it is a leap out of murderers' row; it is a seeing of what is really taking place. This occurs by a higher type of observation, a higher, not a keener type, and the higher it is and the less within reach of the 'row,' the more independent it becomes, the more obedient to its own laws of motion, the more incalculable, the more joyful, the more ascendant its course" (January 27, 1922). Here literature reveals itself as the power which frees, the force which removes the oppression of the world, that world "where everything feels choked," it is the liberating passage from "I" to "he," from the introspection which had been Kafka's torment to a loftier observation rising above mortal reality toward the other world, that of freedom.

Why this confidence? One may well ask. And we may answer with the thought that Kafka belongs to a tradition in which what is highest is expressed in a book which is writing in the highest sense of the word, the Scriptures,[6] a tradition in which ecstatic experiments were conducted by means of a combination and manipulation of letters, in which it is said that the world of letters, those of the alphabet, is the true world of blessedness.[7] To write is to conjure up spirits, it is perhaps to free them against us, but this danger is part of the liberating power.[8]

Kafka was not, however, of a "superstitious" turn of mind; there was in him a cold lucidity which prompted him to say to Brod as they left the hassidic celebrations: "Really, it was almost like an African tribe, crude superstitions."[9] We should not, then, be content with explanations, perhaps well-founded but which, to say the least, do not let us understand why Kafka, so much aware that each of his steps led him astray, should abandon himself with such faith to that essential error that is writing. There too it would not be enough to recall that since his adolescence he was extraordinarily influenced by artists like Goethe and Flaubert, whom he was often ready to place above all others because they put their art above all else. Kafka doubtless never completely separated himself internally from his conception of art, but if his passion was from the beginning so strong and for so long seemed to him to be salutary, it is because, from the beginning and through "the sin of the father," he found himself cast out of the world, condemned to a solitude for which he did not have to hold literature responsible, he owed it rather his thanks for having illumined that solitude, for having made it fruitful—an opening to another world.

It can be said for him that his conflict with the father cast into the shadows the negative side of the literary experiment. Even when he sees that his work demands he wither away, even when more seriously he sees the opposition between his work and his marriage, he in no way concludes therefrom that there is in work a mortal power, an utterance which pronounces the "banishment" and condemns one to the wilderness. He does not draw this conclusion because, from the beginning, the world was lost to him, real existence was withdrawn from him or was never given to him, and when he speaks again of his exile, of the impossibility of escaping it, he writes (January 24, 1922): "It even seems to me as if I had not come by myself but had been pushed here as a child and then chained to this spot." Art did not bring him this misfortune, did not even contribute to it but, on the contrary, illumined it and was "the awareness of misfortune," its new dimension.

Art is first of all the awareness of misfortune, not its compensation. Kafka's inflexibility, his fidelity to the exigency of the work of art, and his fidelity likewise to the exigency of misfortune saved him absolutely from that fictional paradise which is the delight of so many a weak artist whom life has disappointed. Art does not have reveries and "constructs" as its objective. But neither does it describe truth: truth is to be neither known nor described, it cannot even know itself, just as earthly salvation demands to be accomplished and not questioned or imagined. In this sense there is no place for art: rigorous monism excludes all idols. But in this same sense, if art is not justified in general, it is so at least for Kafka alone; for art, like Kafka, is linked

How can we deny that distress was his element? It was his abode and his "time." But this distress was never without hope; this hope was often only the torment of distress, not that which gives hope but which prevents one from being satisfied even with despair, which makes one "while condemned to put an end to it, condemned also to defend himself right to the end," and perhaps then engaged to transform condemnation into deliverance. The essential thing in this new perspective, that of distress, is not to turn toward Canaan. Migration has as its goal the wilderness which is now the true Promised Land. "Is it over there you are leading me?" Yes, over there. But where is this "over there"? It is never in sight, the wilderness is even less sure than the world, it is never more than the approach to the wilderness and, in this land of error, one is never "here" but always "far from here." And yet, in this region where the conditions of a real dwelling place are lacking, where one must live in incomprehensible separation, in an exclusion from which one is in some way excluded, as one is there excluded from himself; in this region which is that of error because one does nothing there but wander endlessly, there subsists a tension, the very possibility of wandering, of going to the end of error, of approaching its limits, of transforming what is an aimless traveling into the certainty of a pathless goal.

We know that the story of the surveyor offers us the most impressive image of this step. From the beginning, this hero of inflexible obstinacy is described to us as having renounced this world forever, the life in which there is wife and children. From the beginning, then, he is beyond salvation, he belongs to exile, that place where he is not only not at home but where he is outside himself—in the "outside" itself, a region absolutely void of intimacy, where beings seem absent, where everything one thinks he has hold of slips away. The tragic difficulty of the undertaking is that in that world of exclusion and radical separation all is false and inauthentic as soon as one stops there; everything fails the moment one relies upon it; but yet the basis of this absence is always given anew as an indubitable and absolute presence; and the word "absolute" is here appropriate, this word that means separate, as if separation, experienced in all its severity, could be inverted into the absolutely separate, the absolutely absolute.

We must be explicit: Kafka, his mind always just and in no way satisfied with the dilemma of all or nothing which he yet conceives with more intransigence than anyone else, makes it felt that in this step outside the true there are certain rules, contradictory and untenable, perhaps, but which still authorize a kind of possibility. The first is given in the error itself: one must err and not be negligent as is the Joseph K. of *The Trial,* who imagines that things are going to continue as before, that he is still in the world, whereas from the first sentence he is cast out of it. Joseph's mistake, undoubtedly like that for which Kafka reproached himself at the time he was writing that book, is to want to win his trial in the world itself, to which he thinks he still belongs but in which his cold, empty heart, his life as a bachelor and office-clerk, his remoteness from his family—all character traits which Kafka found in himself—already prevent him from making headway. To be sure, his insouciance gives way little by little, but that is the very result of the trial, just as the beauty which illuminates the prisoners and makes them attractive to women is the reflection of their own dissolution, of the death which advances in them like a truer light.

The trial—the banishment—is doubtless a great misfortune, it is perhaps an incomprehensible injustice or an inexorable punishment, but it is also—this is true only to a certain extent, and that is the hero's excuse, the trap in which he lets himself be caught—a gift which it is not enough to challenge by invoking in hollow speeches a higher justice, but which, on the contrary, one must try to take advantage of according to the rule which Kafka made his own: "One must limit himself to what he still possesses." The "Trial" has at least the advantage of making Kafka realize what he really is, of destroying the illusion, the deceptive consolations which, because he had a good job and some indifferent pleasures, let him believe in his own existence, in his existence as a man in the world. But for all that, the Trial is not the truth; it is on the contrary a process of error like everything which is linked to the outside, these "external" shadows into which one is cast by the force of banishment; a process in which, if a hope remains, it is for him who advances, not against the current through sterile opposition, but in the very direction of error.

The surveyor is almost entirely free of the faults of Joseph K. He does not seek to return to the place of his birth: lost is the life of Canaan, erased is the truth of *this* world; he remembers it scarcely, if at all, in brief and pathetic moments. Nor is he negligent, but always active, never stopping, almost never becoming discouraged, going on from defeat to defeat with tireless movement which recalls the cold uneasiness of restless times. Yes, he goes with inflexible obstinacy always in the direction of extreme error, disdaining the village which still has some reality but wanting the Castle which perhaps has none, breaking away from Frieda who has some living reflections on her, to turn toward Olga, Amelia's sister, the doubly excluded, the rejected, and what is more, she who voluntarily, by a terrifying decision, chose to be so. Everything therefore ought to be for the best. But it is nothing of the kind, for the surveyor repeatedly falls into the mistake which Kafka terms the most serious, that of impatience.[12] Impatience at the heart of error is the essential fault because it mistakes the very truth of error, which imposes the law of never believing that the goal is near nor that one is approaching it: one must never have done with the infinite; one must never grasp as the immediate, as the already present, the profundity of the inexhaustible absence.

Certainly that is inevitable, and such is the depressing character of a quest like that. He who is not impatient is negligent; he who gives himself over to the anxiety of error loses the insouciance which would exhaust time. Hardly arrived, without understanding anything of that test of exclusion in which he is, K. immediately sets out to reach the limit at once. He neglects the intermediaries, and that is doubtless a merit, the force of straining toward the absolute; but there emerges only the more clearly his aberration, which is to take for the limit what is only an intermediate step, a representation according to his "means."

We are surely every bit as mistaken as the surveyor is when we think he recognizes in the bureaucratic phantasmagoria the fitting symbol of a superior world. This figuration is only proportionate to impatience, the perceptible form of error, through which, for the impatient eye, the inexorable force of the wrong infinite is substituted for the absolute. K. always wants to reach the goal before he has got to it. This exigency of a premature ending is the principle of the figuration, it engenders the *image* or, if you like, the idol; and the curse which is attached to it is the curse which attaches to idolatry. Man wants unity at once; he wants it in separation itself; he pictures it for himself, and that representation, the image of unity, immediately constitutes the element of the dispersion in which he is lost more and more; for the image, as image, can never be attained, and it hides from him, moreover, the unity of which it is the image, and separates it from him by making itself inaccessible and by making unity inaccessible.

Klamm is not at all invisible: the surveyor wishes to see him and he sees him. The Castle, the supreme goal, is not at all out of sight. As an image it is constantly at his call. Naturally, looked at closely, these figures are deceptive, the Castle is only a heap of village shanties, Klamm a big ungainly man seated in front of a desk. All very commonplace and ugly. Therein also lies the surveyor's good luck; it is the truth, the deceptive honesty of these images: they are not attractive in themselves, they have nothing to justify the fascinated interest one shows in them, thus they remind one that they are not the true goal. But at the same time, in this insignificance is allowed to be forgotten the other essential truth—of knowing that all the same they are images of that goal, that they participate in its ineffable value, and that not to cling to them is already to turn away from the essential.

The situation can be summed up thus: it is impatience that makes the limit inaccessible by substituting for it the nearness of an intermediate figure. It is impatience that destroys the approach to the limit by preventing us from recognizing in the intermediate the figure of the immediate.

We must restrict ourselves here to these few indications. The bureaucratic phantasmagoria, that busy idleness which characterizes it, these double beings which are its performers, guardians, assistants, and messengers, who always travel in pairs as if to make us aware that they are but the reflections of each other and the reflection of an inaccessible whole, all this chain of metamorphoses, this methodical increase of distance which is never given as infinite but deepens indefinitely in a necessary way by the transformation of the goal into obstacles, but also of the obstacles into intermediate steps leading to the goal; all this powerful imagery does not represent the truth of the higher nor even its transcendence, represents rather the happiness and unhappiness of the figuration, of the exigency by which the man of exile is obliged to make from error a means of truth, and from what deceives him indefinitely the ultimate possibility of grasping the infinite.

To what extent did Kafka realize the analogy between this procedure and the movement by which the work of art itself tends toward its origin, that center alone in which it can be fulfilled, in the quest for which it achieves reality and which, once reached, makes it impossible? To what extent did he equate the trial of his heroes with the manner in which he himself tried, as an artist, to open a way toward the work of art and by the work of art toward something true? Did he often think of Goethe's words: "It is by postulating the impossible that the artist obtains the whole of the possible"? This evidence at least is striking: the fault that he punishes in K. is also that which the artist blames in himself. This is impatience. This it is which seeks to hasten the story to its conclusion before it has developed in all directions, has exhausted the measure of time that is in it, and has raised the indefinite to a true totality in which each inauthentic movement, each partially false image can be transformed into a steadfast certainty. An impossible task, a task which if completely accomplished would destroy the very truth toward which it tends, as the work of art founders if it touches the point which is its origin. There are many reasons why Kafka finished almost none of his "stories," which led him, after hardly beginning one of them, to lay it aside and try to pacify himself in another. That he often knew the torment of the artist exiled from his work at the moment when it asserts itself and closes up, this he admits himself. That he sometimes abandoned the story in the fear that if he did not abandon it he would not be able to return to the world, this he also admits, but he was not sure that this concern, though essential, had been the strongest in him. That he abandoned it often because every conclusion carries in itself the happiness of a definitive truth which he had no right to accept, with which his existence did not yet square, this reason seems also to have played a large role; but all these movements amount to this: Kafka, perhaps unconsciously, felt deeply that writing is surrender to the incessant and, through anguish, the anguish of impatience, the scrupulous concern for the exigency of writing, he most often refused himself that leap which alone permits completion, that happy and carefree confidence by which (momentarily) a limit is put on the illimitable.

What has been so improperly called his realism betrays the same instinctive effort to stave off his impatience. Kafka often showed that he had a ready genius capable of achieving the essential in a few strokes. But more and more he imposed on himself a meticulousness, a slowness of approach, a detailed precision (even in the description of his own dreams), without which man, exiled from reality, is soon doomed to the wildness of disorder and to the merely approximate of the imagery. The more one is lost in the outside, in the strangeness and insecurity of that loss, the more he must call on the spirit of discipline, meticulousness, and accuracy, and must be present in absence by the multiplicity of images, by their determined and modest appearance (free of fascination), and their vigorously maintained coherence. One who belongs to reality has no need for so many details which, as we know, in no way correspond to the form of a real vision. But he who belongs to the profundity of the limitless and the distant, to the misfortunes of the excessive, he is indeed condemned to the excess of measure and to the search for flawless continuity without gaps and incongruities. And condemned is exactly the word, for if patience, accuracy, and cool mastery are the indispensable qualities to keep one from getting lost when nothing remains for one to cling to, patience, accuracy, and cool mastery are also faults which, dividing the difficulties and extending them indefinitely, perhaps delay the catastrophe but certainly delay the rescue, constantly transform the infinite into the indefinite, as it is likewise measure which in the work of art prevents the limitless ever being achieved.

"Thou shalt not make unto thee any graven image, or any likeness of anything that is in heaven above, or that is in the earth beneath, or that is in the waters under the earth." Felix Weltsch, Kafka's friend, who has well described his struggle against impatience, thinks Kafka took seriously these words of the Bible. If that is so, let us try to imagine a man on whom such a fundamental commandment weighs heavily, who, on pain of death, knows himself cut off from images, and who suddenly finds himself exiled in the imaginary with no other abode or subsistence except images and the domain of images. He is then obliged to live on his death and is compelled, in his despair and to escape this despair—immediate execution—to make of his condemnation his only way of salvation. But was Kafka conscious of being this man? It is impossible to say. One sometimes has the feeling that the fundamental commandment, the more he tries to remember it (for it is in any event forgotten, for the community in which it has life is virtually destroyed), the more he tries to remember the religious sense which dwells hidden in this commandment, and that with an increasingly greater severity, by creating a void within him and about him so that the idols will not be welcome there, the more he seems ready, on the other side, to forget that this commandment ought also to apply to his art. From this results a very precarious balance. This balance, in the illegitimate solitude which is his, allows him to be faithful to an ever stricter spiritual monism while giving himself up to a certain artistic idolatry, then engages him in purifying this idolatry by all the severity of an ascesis which condemns literary realities (failure to complete his works, aversion to all publication, refusal to believe himself a writer, etc.), which, moreover, and this is more serious, would subordinate art to its spiritual condition. Art is not religion, "it does not even lead to religion," but in times of distress—like ours, this time when there are no gods, a time of absence and exile—then art is justified, which is the intimacy of that distress, which is the effort to make manifest through images the error of the imaginary and, at the boundary, the elusive, forgotten truth which lurks behind this error.

That there is at first a tendency in Kafka to replace religious exigency with literary exigency, then, especially toward the end, an inclination to replace his literary experience with his religious experience, to merge them in a rather confused way by moving from the wilderness of faith into faith in a world which is no longer the wilderness but another world in which freedom will be restored to him—this is what the notes in his *Diaries* lead us to feel. "Do I live in the other world, then? Dare I say that?" (January 30, 1922) On the page which we have quoted Kafka recalls that according to him mankind never has any other choice than this: either to seek the Promised Land through the way of Canaan, or to seek it through the way of that other world which is the wilderness, "for," he adds, "there is no third world for mankind." There is none, to be sure, but perhaps one must say more, perhaps one must say that the artist, the kind of man that Kafka also wanted to be, through concern for his art and his quest for its origin, the "poet" is the one for whom not even one single world exists, since for him there exists only the outside, the shimmering of the eternal outside.

NOTES

1. Almost all the passages quoted in the following pages are taken from the complete edition of Kafka's *Diary*, which reproduces the thirteen quarto notebooks in which, from 1910 to 1923, Kafka wrote everything that mattered to him, events from his personal life, meditation on these events, descriptions of persons and places, descriptions of his dreams, narratives begun, broken off, begun again. It is, then, not simply a "diary," in the current sense of the word, but the very workings of the experience of writing, right at its very beginning and in the essential meaning which Kafka was led to give to the word. It is with this perspective that the *Diary* is to be read and examined.

Max Brod states that he has made only a few insignificant abridgments, and there is no reason to doubt this. On the other hand, it is certain that Kafka, at many crucial moments, destroyed a great part of his notes. And after 1923, the *Diary* is completely lacking. We do not know whether the manuscript destroyed at his request by Dora Dymant included the continuation of these notebooks: it is very likely. We have to say, then, that after 1923 Kafka is unknown to us, for we know that those who knew him best considered him quite differently from what he imagined himself to be.

The *Diary* (which is completed by the travel notebooks) reveals to us almost nothing of his opinions on the great topics which might have interested him. The *Diary* tells us of Kafka at that earlier stage where there are as yet no opinions and where there is hardly a Kafka. Such is its essential value. The book by Gustav Janouch (*Conversations with Kafka*: London and New York, 1953), on the contrary, enables us to understand Kafka in the free-and-easiness of more everyday conversation when he speaks just as well of the future of the world as of the Jewish question, of Zionism, religious cere-monies, and occasionally of his books. Janouch knew Kafka in 1920, in Prague. He wrote down almost immediately the conversations he reports, and Brod has confirmed the faithfulness of this echo. But in order not to be misled about the importance of these utterances we must remember that they were spoken to a very young man of seventeen, whose youth, naïveté, and trusting spontaneity touched Kafka, but also doubtless led Kafka to tone down his thoughts so as not to make them dangerous to such a young mind. Kafka, a thoughtful friend, was often afraid of worrying his friends by uttering a truth which was desperate only to himself. This does not mean that he did not say what he thought, but that he sometimes said what he did not profoundly believe.

2. Kafka adds: "This is not an artistic yearning."

3. However, on February 10, 1922, we read this note: "Neuer Angriff von G." This must doubtless be read: "New attack by God."

4. Certain letters to Milena also allude to what there was of the unknown for him in this terrible impulse (see the studies in the *Nouvelle N.R.F.*: "Kafka et Brod" and "L'echec de Milena," Oct. and Nov., 1954).

5. On this topic reference should be made to the book by G. G. Scholem, *Les Grands Courants de la Mystique juive:* "The terrors of Exile influenced the cabalist doctrine of metempsychosis, which at that time gained an im-mense popularity by insisting on the various stages of the exile of the soul. The most formidable fate which could befall the soul, much more horrible than the torments of hell, was to be 'rejected' or 'laid bare,' a state which ex-cludes either reanimation or even admission into hell . . . . The absolute deprivation of a home was the sinister symbol of an absolute impiety, of an extreme moral and spiritual degradation. Union with God or absolute ban-ishment became the two poles between which was worked out a system that offered the Jews the possibility of being under the domination of a rule which sought to destroy the forces of Exile." And this further: "There was an ardent desire to overcome Exile by aggravating its torments, in savoring its bitter-ness in the extreme (including even the night of Shekinah itself) . . ." (p. 267). That the theme of "The Metamorphosis" (as well as the obsessing fictions of animality) is a reminiscence, an allusion to the tradition of the cabalistic metempsychosis, can well be imagined even though we are not sure that "Samsa" is a recall of "Samsara" (Kafka and Samsa are related

names, but Kafka challenges this comparison). Kafka sometimes states that he is not yet born: "Hesitation before birth. If there is a transmigration of souls then I am not yet on the bottom rung. My life is a hesitation before birth" (January 24, 1922). We must remember that in "Wedding Preparations in the Country" Raban, the hero of this youthful narrative, expresses in jest the wish to become an insect (*Käfer*) which could doze away in bed and escape the unpleasant duties of the community. The "shell" of solitude is like the image which would be brought to life in the impressive theme of "The Metamorphosis."

6. Kafka says to Janouch that "the task of the poet is a prophetic task: the exact word guides; the word which is not exact seduces; it is not by chance that the Bible is called the Scripture."

7. Thus also arises the pitiless condemnation (which touched his very self) that Kafka brings against the Jewish writers who use the German tongue.

8. "But what follows from this very fact: being a poet? This act of writing is a gift, a gift silent and mysterious. But its price? In the night, the answer bursts forth upon my eyes with a dazzling sharpness: it is the wages received from the diabolic powers which one has served. This abandon of obscure forces, this loosing of powers habitually held in leash, these impure embraces, and all the rest that still is carried on in the depths, does one still know anything about them, up above, when one writes stories, in broad daylight, in the glare of the sun? . . . Does the surface retain any trace of this? Is there perhaps yet another way of writing? As far as I am concerned, I know only this one, in the night, when anguish torments me on the verge of sleep." (Cited by Brod.)

9. But later on Kafka seems to have become increasingly more attentive to this form of devotion. Dora Dymant belonged to "an esteemed hassidic Jewish family." And Martin Buber perhaps influenced him.

10. Kafka does not avoid denouncing what is tempting, the tempting facility, in the too definite differentiation of these two worlds: "And moreover the division seems to me to be much too definite, dangerous in its definiteness, sad, and too tyrannical" (January 30, 1922).

11. We must at least quote this passage from the rough draft of a letter to his fiancée in which he specifies with the greatest lucidity his relationship with his family: "However, I am descended from my parents, am linked to them and my sisters by blood, am sensible of it neither in my everyday affairs nor, as a result of their inevitable familiarity to me, in my special concerns, but at bottom have more respect for it than I realize. Sometimes this bond of blood too is the target of my hatred; the sight of the double bed at home, the used sheets, the nightshirts carefully laid out, can exasperate me to the point of nausea, can turn me inside out; it is as if I had not been definitively born, were continually born anew into the world out of the stale life in that stale room, had constantly to seek confirmation of myself there, were indissolubly joined with all that loathsomeness, in part even if not entirely, at least it still clogs my feet which want to run, they are still stuck fast in the original shapeless pulp." (October 18, 1916)

Heinz Politzer

Letter to His Father

KAFKA wrote this letter in November, 1919, at the age of thirty-six, less than five years before his death and seven years after his *annus mirabilis*, 1912, when he had started work on *Amerika*, and written "The Metamorphosis" and "The Judgment." In these two stories he had raised a father's image to almost Godlike stature: Samsa Senior, who had an inexplicable yet obvious share in his son's sudden change into an enormous bug and throve on the latter's decline; and Bende-mann Senior who, omnipotent and omniscient, sentenced his son to death. In both narrations the father-son relationship is described with much psychoanalytical acidity, increased almost beyond endurance by the superhuman dimensions of the father figures. In the two novel fragments, *The Trial* (begun around 1914) and *The Castle* (begun before 1922), which were published posthumously, the line of paternal ascension rises so high that the father figures vanish into infinity: there is little doubt that the supreme Judge of *The Trial* and the Master of *The Castle* were meant to represent paternal and divine authority; but they never materialize, and instead there opens, in the presumable place of their appearance, the gap that causes these novels to remain fragments. Obviously, Kafka succeeded here in dissolving any image he had of his father into something impalpable, incomprehensible, ineffable. Then he left it to the reader to call this supreme being father, God, or nothing. However, the letter of 1919 seems to have been written in order to reduce this metaphysical dilemma to a family conflict, and to slip a vast amount of private information into a psychiatrist's hands. What, if not self-castigation, was the meaning of this drastic reduction? Why did Kafka, at that particular moment, embark on an undertaking that was a retrogression on the way that had led him from father towards God? Did he expect any therapeutical effect from this self-analysis? "For the last time psychology!" he cried emphatically in the *Reflections* (1917–19). Did he hope to placate the father by it? "Recently," the letter starts, "you asked me why I maintain that I am afraid of you. As usual, I didn't know how to answer you. . . ." [1a] The father's question had arisen from the routine of torment that was inherent in a relationship disturbed from the very outset. There appears no reason why Kafka should have broken this routine—and his silence—to answer a question that had been, beyond any doubt, rhetorical.

In 1919 *A Country Doctor* was published, a collection of stories that contains the essence of both *The Trial* and *The Castle*. Kafka himself stressed the importance of this book by dedicating it to his father. To be sure, he had no illusions about the effect that this act of filial devotion would have on the recipient. The letter mentions "your [the father's] welcome that has become famous among us: 'Put it on the bedside table'" (where, of course, it would be left unopened). Kafka does not refer to this insult as to an individual act of cruelty or "indolence of the heart," but as to an expected reaction, and again, a routine. He does not say that *A Country Doctor* did meet with this specific welcome; he had just been expecting a similar rebuff as inevitable. Nevertheless, he embarked once more on an enterprise the outcome of which he clearly could foresee. Thus the dedication assumes the darker aspects of a provocation. And whatever the father's actual reaction to *A Country Doctor* may have been, we can rest assured that he stuck stubbornly to the established pattern of their relationship, and acted as Franz expected.

Another partial reason that might have aggravated the family situation and touched off the letter can be seen in Kafka's "last intention to marry." Two years had passed since he had broken his second engagement with Felice Bauer, thus putting an end to a love affair that had lasted since 1912. Now he had proposed to a "Fräulein J. [W.]" in Želisy, the very place where this letter was written. Brod calls the engagement unhappy and short-lived. [1b] But Kafka had not tarried in informing his father about it. A scene ensued which was stormier than any previous one, at least according to the letter writer. At that time the idea of marriage had become for him a matter of principle rather than of love, a step, ever again attempted, but never fully taken, in the direction of good life and integration, of Flaubert's being *dans le vrai.* "To marry, to found a family, to accept all children that are born, to preserve and even guide them a little in this insecure world is, in my opinion, the utmost which a man can possibly achieve." The "acceptance" ("hinnehmen" = put up with) of children might easily serve as a key to the attitude of this strange suitor who was torn between the extremes of a natural sociability that befits a family father and the ice-cold solitude of the writer, this other "utmost" of a man's achievement. The letter revolves around these two focal points: marrying and writing. But whereas the pain and bliss of writing was an ever present reality for Kafka, marriage was, and remained, a dream wish and an imperative. Therefore the person of the beloved was, in a deeper sense, of little relevance to the writer. "Both girls [Felice Bauer and J. W.] were chosen extremely well, even if by accident." And the father is reported to have referred to J. W. during the crucial conversation as "just anybody . . . probably she had put on some fancy blouse as Prague Jewesses have a knack of doing, whereupon you, of course, immediately decided to marry her." As usual, the father, arguing in his crude and businesslike fashion, hit the son's most vulnerable spot: the self-centered indifference of his life plans. (And he was borne out by reality; this reality to which, alas, womanhood subscribes even in the charismatic presence of genius: in 1920 Kafka was to befriend Milena Jesenská, a Gentile and probably the most intellectual woman of his entourage. The relationship lasted little more than two years and ended in extreme unhappiness. Only during his last summer did he meet Dora Dymant, an Eastern European Jewess who was approximately twenty years younger than he. Dora stayed at his side until his death, although both families had opposed their marriage. Undoubtedly, the ironically euphoric happiness of this last union was due to Kafka's acceptance of his own death as something inevitable and imminent.) Taking into account that the idea of marriage had become for Kafka a touchstone of his whole existence, we may see in the engagement controversy with his father another incentive for the composition of this letter.

The letter, often described as an autobiography, is indeed Kafka's *grand testament.* In September, 1917, his tuberculosis had been diagnosed. Although he was to return to his Prague office for certain stretches of time in 1918 and 1920, he seems to have adjusted to his disease by 1919 at least insofar as it gave him the long desired opportunity of staying in the country and concentrating on his writings. In the first diary entry after the decisive consultation in 1917 he had tried to reduce his sickness to a symbol, "a symbol of the infection whose inflammation is called F. [Felice Bauer] and whose depth is its deep justification. . . ." [2] The letter to his father mentions the "superhuman effort of my desire to marry [that had caused] blood to come out of my lungs." Furthermore, art is joined to sickness when the letter shifts to the poor quarters in which he had to live for the sake of his writing: "But also my living in the Schönborn *palais*—which, however, I needed only because I thought I needed it for my writing —may have had sufficient share in it." (In spite of their palatial name these quarters were no better than his previous ones in the Alchemists' Lane near the Prague Castle which Brod once described as "the monastic cell of a real writer." [3])

On the surface, then, it is the well-known triad of love, disease, and art that forms the core of Kafka's work and of this letter. To be sure, he owed much of his initial melancholy to the climate of the *fin de siècle,* and especially the Young Vienna school. But soon he developed his thematic material, deepened it by increased introspection, and attempted to reach the realm of religion. He succeeded only in the negative: he reached this realm in his despair, in the frustration of his life's plans, and in the fragmentariness of his novels. But in his work proper he never penetrated beyond the inherent ambiguity of literary language that operates with images and symbols. Literature offered him the opportunity of uniting in the *double entendre* of poetic imagery the insights of self-observation with visions of a religious character. Being a genuine writer, he was often able to incorporate this duality in a single phrase, or in one word. His style is simple, and he found in the Muirs adequate translators; yet much of the misunderstanding that he has incurred is due to the double aspect of his very simplest sentences, that defy any literal translation. [4]

A diary entry, about two weeks after the discovery of his disease: "I would put myself in death's hands, though. Remnant of faith. Return to a father. Great day of Atonement." This statement is the epitome of Kafka's ambiguity. In German, Day of Atonement ("Versöhnungstag") indicates more than the breast-beating fervor of penitence that it assumes in Jewish liturgy: as soon as the compound word is split up into its composite parts and these are taken literally, they reveal a universal mildness of reconciliation ("Tag der Versöhnung"). Furthermore, the dative "zum Vater" can be read as meaning both the return to a specific father—the physical one—and to a universal and spiritual Father, for instance the one in heaven. The entry seems to be a typical Kafka crossroads where two ways of expression meet for the one moment that is necessary to produce an image. Disease offered him the return to his father's house as a sick child, a dream that actually came true in 1924. It also offered him a homecoming on the level of Novalis' equally ambiguous sentence: "Where do we go? Always home." [5] It is against this ambiguity that the letter to his father—as well as the rest of Kafka's later writings—must be read.

The bulk of the letter is taken up by a description of his relationship with his father. He was clear-sighted enough to realize that at the roots of the conflict lay the father's abundance of what he himself was lacking most: vitality. He registers the father's "strength, health, appetite, vocal power, eloquence, self-satisfaction, superiority in all worldly matters, endurance, presence of mind, knowledge of human nature, a certain largesse, naturally combined with all the weaknesses and failings that go with these merits, weaknesses into which your temperament and sometimes your temper drive you." This is an adult's appraisal of another adult's character; and it may give us a true likeness of Hermann Kafka, a butcher's son, who had come from the country and made good in Prague. But by a twist closely related to the one that provides the narrations with much of their eerie atmosphere, the letter makes this rather ordinary portrait transparent: it shows the impact of the father on a child that had to bear all by himself the brunt of so strong a personality. (Two older brothers had died as infants; and his oldest sister was six years younger than he.) The letter opens a terrified child's world to the reader, but it assesses this world with the considerable, though not always correct, psychological insight of a grownup.

True to the pedagogical indifference of the pre-Freudian era, the father had developed a system of double standards: at dinner time the child had to concentrate on his food while the father, a fast eater, cleaned and cut his fingernails, sharpened pencils, and poked in his ears with a toothpick, heaping disgust on disdain and turning the family circle into a kind of middle-class inferno. In the sphere of human relations the father was full of a vulgar contempt which was directed especially against his Czech servants and employees ("the paid enemies"). He mistrusted everybody, and did his best to impart his feelings to his son. He undermined the child's confidence in his environment and, by the same token, raised himself to the stature of a giant. Franz kept wondering how his father managed to preserve his own equilibrium in spite of this display of mistrust, but "perhaps it was really a sovereign's emblem." The greatest suffering, perhaps, was inflicted upon the lonely, high-strung, and overly critical child by the father's irrational self-reliance, which removed him from any systematic approach to the arbitrary heights of absolute and infinite power: "Your opinion was right, everybody else's was crazy, extravagant, *meschugge,* not normal. At the same time your self-confidence was so great that there was no need for you to be consistent at all, and yet you were always right. You often even happened to have no opinion whatever on a subject, and therefore any possible opinion on this subject had to be, without exception, wrong." (Here we hear the two Bendemanns arguing with each other in "The Judgment," or K. proving his point in vain to one of the officials in *The Castle.*) The letter bristles with epithets like "superior," "sovereign," "despotic," and "tyrannical." "In your armchair you ruled the world." Thus he attempted to deify the father. Reading the letter, one cannot escape the feeling that Kafka, like his Georg Bendemann, would have thrown himself from a bridge had his father so ordained.

The letter reports in detail two examples of the pedagogy to which Kafka had been subjected. The first incident happened when he was a very young child. He was lying awake in the middle of the night, and kept crying for water. The grown-up letter writer knows, of course, that the child did not cry because he was thirsty. "Probably I cried partly because I wanted to annoy [you], partly to entertain myself." Trying to explain himself, the grownup does not act as the child's older and mature self, he starts staring at himself with the cold and irate eyes of the father whose rest had been disturbed. He ventures into his own unconscious, seemingly to find an excuse for himself; but what he discovers there are not the commonly known psychological mechanisms, but an uncommonly great amount of guilt. He always lay in ambush for his guilt, and when he had trapped it, or, rather, had been trapped by it, he betrayed his original purpose by offering the evidence to his prosecutor instead of his attorney. This is one of the sources of Kafka's bitterly masochistic irony. The child kept crying; the father resorted to threats, and since these threats, according to pattern, only served to increase the child's forlornness and lament, he took the child out of his bed and carried him into the open air. On a balcony, he left him standing in his nightshirt, exposed to complete solitude, surrounded by darkness. "For years I was tormented by the thought that the huge man, my father, the last resort and supreme judge,[6] could come, almost without any reason, in the middle of the night, and carry me from my bed to the balcony, and that therefore I was but a nonentity in his eyes." In this "therefore" originate both Kafka's trauma and Kafka's vision: it turns the clumsy expedient of a pedagogically ignorant father into a verdict of metaphysical depth. (However, he had prepared this verdict by indicting himself through a blatant misreading of his own motives.) This nocturnal experience, this nightmare come true, was a foreboding of the universal night to which Kafka's heroes are exposed, the night that terminates *The Trial* and enwraps *The Castle:* they face the darkness as helplessly and as beset by terror as the child once faced the night on the Prague balcony. It is the same anchoring of a metaphysical image in a traumatic childhood experience as the one expressed by Rilke's Christ on the Mount of Olives:

> Die Sich-Verlierenden lässt alles los,
> und sie sind preisgegeben von den Vätern
> und ausgeschlossen aus der Mütter Schoss.[7]

Rilke's image is of extreme beauty as long as it is considered within the confines of literature; extended into the sphere of religious thinking it comes dangerously near to sacrilege. Similarly, Kafka's equation

$$\text{father} = \text{Father} = \text{God}$$

is a daring literary venture; but its limits coincide with the limits of literary expression; carried beyond them, it proves no other point than that made by Freud in *The Future of an Illusion,* i.e., the final secularization of religion.

The second episode occurred during Kafka's adolescence, around his sixteenth year. He was taking a walk with his parents when he suddenly started reproaching them that they had left him uninstructed in "those interesting things." He went on, boasting of great dangers which he had approached. (He did not say "experienced," for he could not lie even when he was bragging.) Again the letter writer looks for a psychological motivation of the boy's aggression: he had broached

the subject because it gave him pleasure,[8] and also because he wanted
to take revenge on his parents, "somehow for something." The father
parried the provocation by cutting him short. He said something to the
effect that he could counsel him how to carry on "these things" without incurring any danger. The curt answer is understandable in view
of the father's temperament, his predominantly practical approach,
and the general taboo imposed on all things sexual by the European
middle class. And yet it disturbed Kafka to such an extent that he
could link this scene with the other, when, twenty years later, the
father protested against his engagement with J. W. The actual meaning
of that never forgotten walk with his parents lies in the fact that then,
possibly for the first time, the Oedipus situation had become manifest
to him. "The thought that you might have given, before your marriage,
similar advice to yourself, was completely inconceivable to me. Thus
there was almost no residue of earthly filth on you. And it was just you
who, with a few frank words, threw me down into this filth as if it had
been my destination." However, the letter writer saw this situation also
as an archetypal, almost a mythical one. The meaning of what the
father had said was, as he very well knew, "unscrupulous in a very
modern way." But behind this façade he sensed "a primeval quality,"
namely the sexual jealousy of a tribal chief or a primitive god. Here
he was able to express what he had allowed himself only to intimate in
"The Judgment": that the son's basic guilt consisted in his desire to
take a wife, to found a family, and to dispossess the father. Likewise
the love scenes in *The Trial* and *The Castle* are more than neurotic
detours from the heroes' path: they are very direct transgressions of
the paternal law of the tribunal and the castle's master. (The main
attraction the girls have for the hero stems from the fact that they
seem to be possessed by and familiar with the law.)

Thus the letter gives the blueprint of the underground foundation
upon which Kafka erected his work. That it is a literary rather than a
personal document becomes clear when we observe Kafka using the
biographical data of his life to comment upon his writings and his
writings to comment upon his life. In a sublime play of mystification
and ironical self-quotation he deliberately removed the border line
between "truth" and "fiction." At one point he calls the family situation
"that terrible *trial* that is pending between you and ourselves." Or,
more distinctly and more mysteriously, he discusses the "infinite sense
of guilt" which his father had instilled in him, and continues: "With

this infinity in mind I once wrote about somebody, quite correctly: 'He is afraid that the shame of it will outlive him.'" Here he quotes the last sentence of *The Trial*, which at that time was an unpublished manuscript that Kafka had threatened to destroy. At another point the letter gives an astonishingly accurate cosmography of his books by describing the ordeal of Kafka's childhood: through the father's authority "the world was for me divided into three parts: one, where I lived as a slave, subject to laws that had been invented exclusively with me in mind and with which, I don't know why, I never could comply. Then a second world, infinitely remote from mine, where you lived, occupied with ruling, giving orders, and with the annoyance caused by these orders not being obeyed; and finally a third world where the rest of the people lived happily and free from both orders and obedience." This third world is the one whence the explorer comes to the *Penal Colony* and which sends, in glorious indifference, the "unending stream of traffic" over the bridge from which the son jumps to his death in "The Judgment." This world encompasses Kafka's struggle as the reflection of a hope which he knew existed, but did not exist for him. Biographically speaking, it was the world of the Czech Gentiles that surrounded the Prague ghetto, the world of the peasants, proletarians, and lower middle-class people who had been born into traditional patterns of community life and community belief which they accepted without further question. (This picture is, of course, highly relative: Kafka knew from firsthand experience that the Czechs were a politically and economically suppressed people before 1918.) It also is the world of Eastern European Jews with whom Kafka had tried to blend so fervently and so fruitlessly (and who had been subjected to pogroms and large-scale persecutions throughout their history). Kafka was not blind to the predicament of the inhabitants of this third world. In his novels he saw them living in an intermediary region where they have come to terms with authority, like the courtroom attendants in *The Trial* and the peasants in *The Castle*. They follow a queer logic of their own, but they follow a logic, whereas in Kafka's own fight the law of logic has been suspended, or superseded by the martial law of the paradox. The hope he envisaged for them consisted largely in their nonparticipation in his conflict. And yet, their very existence at the periphery of his strife-infested world provided him with a certain objectivity. Even in his deadliest moments he was able to look at himself from the outside and to measure his sufferings by the standards of reality, however distorted this reality might have been in his eyes. This double vision led him, as often as not, to the composition of a (seemingly objective) commentary on his books, such as this letter.

In many respects the letter is an attempt at commenting upon Kafka's visions in terms of his psychological experiences. In this attempt he goes so far as to give positive clues to the origin of "The Metamorphosis," where, in the first sentence, Gregor Samsa finds himself changed into a "gigantic insect." It must have been a great temptation for Kafka, the teller of self-destructive parables, to visualize himself in the image of an insect: in his early novel fragment *Wedding Preparations in the Country,* Raban, the hero, fancies himself lying in bed, changed into a bug, in order to avoid the disagreeable obligations of society. But the image remained dormant until, in 1911, a Yiddish theatrical group came to Prague. One of the members, an actor by the name of Löwy, fascinated Kafka by his vitality as well as by the firm roots he had in the life of the group. He began to identify himself with Löwy who, incidentally, carried his mother's maiden name. The letter records how the father compared the actor, "without knowing him, in a terrible manner, which I have already forgotten [*sic*], with vermin." The father's invective had fallen on fertile and well-prepared ground. But it needed the shock of self-cognition to crystallize a literary image around a daydream and an insult. This shock is reflected by the shock technique of the beginning of "The Metamorphosis" which is so closely related to the first paragraph of *The Trial.* To a certain extent Kafka is indebted here to Gogol's *Nose,* where Kovalev wakes up to discover that, miraculously enough, he had been deprived of his most cherished possession, his nose. But if, as Vladimir Nabokov has pointed out, his nose had a particularly and grotesquely personal meaning for Gogol,[9] then Samsa's metamorphosis served even more as a portentous symbol for Kafka.[10] The Yiddish actor whom his father had called vermin, represented for him something he had been longing for all along, and something he would never be able to attain: the artist integrated in life, in community life. (See the grim parody of this longing in Kafka's "Josephine the Singer, or the Mouse Folk.") He himself had been offended in Löwy, his own weakness had been discovered and punished by his father's word. In the hour of his defamation Löwy became Kafka, as Kafka became Samsa (even the names are phonetic parallels), who in turn became what the father had called Löwy: an insect. So spellbound was the writer by the abuse that it did not occur to him to specify the kind of vermin into which Gregor had been changed,[11] surely an oversight in view of the magic realism which Kafka used as a style. It is the father whose curse had transformed the son into vermin, the father who thus assumed a god-like power similar to that wielded by Bendemann Senior in "The Judgment." Hence Samsa Senior's sudden second prime that coincides with Gregor's decline. Simultaneously the father only pronounces a verdict that the son had accepted long before. Toward the end of the letter Kafka has his father sum up the situation in an imaginary speech: "You have indeed got it into your head that you want to live on me altogether. I admit that we fight each other; but there are two kinds of fights: the chivalrous fight, where two independent opponents test their strength against each other; each is left to himself, loses for himself, wins for himself; and the fight of the vermin, which not only bite, but which top the biting by sucking blood to preserve their lives. They are the real professional soldiers, and that is what you are." By means of his invective the father completed a magic triangle, whose apex was occupied by himself, whereas the basis was determined by the son's guilt feelings and his wishful self-identification with the actor. By that time, however, the real Löwy had lost all importance. It was the genesis of one of Kafka's images.

Franz Kafka was as little a mental case as he was a pioneer of political or religious thinking (Max Brod).[12] He was a writer in his own right, a litterateur if there ever was one. He was infatuated by word images, by their cadence and their ambivalence; and since he was a border case in the literal meaning of the word, given to analytical thinking as well as to vision, a psychologist as well as a mystic, neither of them completely, but able to combine both in his imagery, ambiguity became the very element of his language. By his images he was able to straddle the two realms of his experience: the pseudo-mythical underworld of his childhood where the father held sway, and the pseudoreligious universe of his poetic vision where God reigned in perfect inaccessibility. By its ingrained *double entendre* Kafka's imagery could embrace both the abysm below and the abysm above (which he sometimes, erroneously, called heaven). But as soon as his imagery is interpreted as a vehicle of messages—psychological, theological, moral, or otherwise—the unity of his style is broken asunder, its ambiguity is spoiled, and the only wisdom to be gained is the insight that the incompatible is incompatible.

Thus, if Kafka's father image is different from the one the father-baiting expressionists used to paint, his vision of the Divine is likewise a long way off from any pictorialization of God in the manner of Michelangelo, Blake, or Goethe's "Prologue in Heaven." (That such a pictorialization was still possible in Kafka's own generation and in an atmosphere related to his, can be seen from Franz Werfel's poem "Der göttliche Portier." [13]) Kafka's failure to complete the equation, father = God, has to be understood in the terms of his personal history and situation.

Like many a European writer who became articulate between the turn of the century and the outbreak of the first world war, Kafka suffered from the self-hatred of the artist and from an exaggerated envy of the burgher. Like Thomas Mann's Tonio Kröger he questioned his own capacity down to the very recesses of vitality and sex, and like Tonio he bestowed his deepest and most secret love upon the robust and the normal, the "seductive banality" [14] of ordinary life. It was his misfortune that he found the blessings for which he yearned almost exclusively assembled in the person of his father. He was not able to project these wish dreams on any father substitute, nor to free himself from the omnipresence of his creator. Moreover, growing up in Prague as a German Jew, he had no immediate access to any hinterland. He grew up in the "triple ghetto" of Jewish traditionalism, of his family's prosperity, and of the German tongue, which was the language of his books, but not the language spoken in the streets around his father's house. "The German Jew in Czech Prague was, so to speak, an incarnation of strangeness and will-to-be-strange, was the people's enemy without a people of his own." [15] He had been born into a prison, a prison run and represented by his father; but it was his destiny that he had to search not only for freedom but also for security. He could not leave his father unless he was sure that in the freedom outside he could find a new home, a new fatherland. (Both Franz Werfel and Max Brod, German Jews in Prague and Kafka's contemporaries, succeeded in exchanging the ghetto for a new home: Brod found support in Zionism, and Werfel peace in a highly personal Catholicism.)

Kafka, however, was a radical; no compromise would satisfy him. The home he was looking for had to offer him the opportunity of a settlement not on sufferance but of right, and that in a more spiritual, more social, more human way than he had ever known. In his quest he turned to Christianity: he was an ardent reader of Pascal, but the baroque atmosphere that was so well preserved in Prague that it still permeated the books of Rilke and Werfel, seemed to have disturbed Kafka's austere visions and thought processes: "Pascal arranges everything very tidily before God makes his appearance, but there must be a deeper, uneasier skepticism than that of a man cutting himself to bits with—indeed—wonderful knives, but still with the calm of a butcher. Whence this calm? this confidence with which the knife is wielded? Is God a theatrical triumphal chariot that (granted the toil and despair of the stage hands) is hauled on the stage from afar by ropes?" [16] In other words, Pascal's religious self-analysis, the genuinely sacrificial character of the *Pensées,* appealed to Kafka, but they did not carry him far enough or, rather, they carried him too far, since they were oriented towards a divine dispensation such as Kafka had never been able to envisage. The central experience of conversion, Pascal's vision of fire, was altogether absent from Kafka's life. Much has been made of Kafka's relation to Søren Kierkegaard.[17] But his admiration for the Danish Protestant was for the longest time based on the figurative similarity of his biographical situation and Kierkegaard's. To Kafka the breaking of his engagement with Felice Bauer must have seemed like a re-enactment of Kierkegaard's break with Regina Ølsen. Still in 1916 he mentioned Kierkegaard together with Flaubert and Grillparzer (the common denominator being the love life of the three writers), remarking that they at least "knew very clearly how matters stood with them, were men of decision, did not calculate but acted. But in your case—a perpetual succession of calculations, a monstrous four years' up and down." [18] Although he started to study Kierkegaard more seriously in 1917, he was not able to reconcile the theologically clear-cut "Either-Or" position of the Protestant with his own thinking, which was primarily a thinking in images. Kierkegaard arrived at his paradoxes within the Christian frame of reference; Kafka performed his outside of any frame. "I was not, like Kierkegaard, introduced into life by the hand of Christianity, however heavily this hand might have been descending already; nor did I, like the Zionists, still catch the last corner of the prayer shawl as it flew away from the Jews. I am an end, or a beginning."

The letter to his father explains why Kafka could find hardly more

assurance in his native Judaism than he did in Christianity: Pascal and
Kierkegaard had at least opened new roads to him, even though he
knew that they would not lead him to his destination. But his road
to Judaism had been blocked beyond hope by his education. He
recalls how he had accompanied his father to the synagogue, four
times a year ("I experienced similar boredom, I believe, later on only
during my dancing lessons"). Liberal Jewish liturgy was for him an
ugly form devoid of any content ("the opening of the Ark of the
Covenant . . . always reminded me of a shooting range, where there
was also a box with a door which opened if you hit the bull's eye, except that there something interesting used to appear, and here were
always only the same old dolls with no heads"). Soon the child understood that the only reality which religion held for his father was a
social reality, "the opinions of a certain Jewish caste," against which,
as a son and later as a writer, he was in constant revolt. Since his
father's caste despised Jews from Eastern Europe, he associated with
them; first by making friends with the Yiddish theater troupe, then
by his union with Dora Dymant whose family was rooted in Eastern
Jewish religiosity. Since, in his father's hands, Jewish tradition had
become an empty shell just strong enough to bar him from the Gentile
world, he turned to Jewish tradition, studied Hebrew, and joined,
from a safe distance, Max Brod's Zionist aspirations. But far as he may
have traveled on this road to Judaism—and he went very far indeed in
view of his limited strength and his frustrated life—he only moved a
long distance *away* from his origins without ever getting nearer *to*
his aim, existential security. This he could have found only in a closed
religious system, such a one as Kierkegaard had never lost. He tried
to make up in his books for what he had missed in his life: both *The
Trial* and *The Castle* are attempts at constructing closed systems: he
built pyramids of officials and lawyers and judges and bureaucrats, the
secular hierarchy of a broken faith. But precisely because this faith was
broken, he could not translate it into the imagery of his books without
eliminating the top of these pyramids. There God would have had his
seat, if Kafka had ever succeeded in carrying the image of his father
up to a sphere not only of wrath but of mercy, a realm not only of
despair but of a "hope beyond hopelessness, the transcendence of
despair" (Thomas Mann).[19] Yet the novels have open endings, and
remained fragments.

The Oedipus situation which the letter had described so eloquently

had served Kafka as a literary symbol: beyond the father stands a
father image upon which Kafka had bestowed enough semblance with
Kafka Senior to prevent it from ever becoming God. Any therapeutical
intention that this letter might have had can easily be discarded as a
mystification. To be sure, it was written, as its last sentence indicates,
"to calm both of us down a little, and make life and death a little easier
for us." But this intention is clearly abandoned when, a few sentences
earlier, Kafka makes his father say: ". . . by your dishonesty you have
already achieved enough, for you have proved three things: firstly,
that you are innocent; secondly, that I am guilty; and thirdly, that out
of sheer magnificence you are ready not only to forgive me, but, what
is much more, and much less, even go further and prove, and try and
convince yourself, that I—contrary to the truth, to be sure—am also
innocent. . . ." Here, Kafka's self-reproaches have become aggres-
sions which he attributes to the father. On the level of reality the
father would surely have dismissed as extreme nonsense the com-
plexities he was supposed to have uttered. But even on the letter's own
level an extreme has been reached: the very idea of guilt and forgiveness upon which the letter is built is being tossed around until it
has lost any specific meaning. If it is the privilege—and the basic
dubiousness—of modern literature to question by thought and linguistic processes any accepted standards, then a passage like this is apt
to question the father-son relationship to a degree where there is
nothing left but two masks grinning at each other in utter despair: a
Kafka commentary on the alienation that governed his life.[20]

Kafka's novels are rich in commentaries whose one and only purpose
seems to consist in proving that "the incomprehensible is incomprehensible, and that we knew already." [21] They become part of the fable
which they seem to explain; they are not meant to decipher a poetic
image by translating it into the language of reason; rather do they
stress the fact that the image is untranslatable. The most obvious
commentary of this sort occurs in the cathedral scene of *The Trial*
where the prison chaplain first shows Joseph K. the mirror of his life
in the parable of the man before the law, and then proceeds to add
an elaborate exegesis. But this exegesis spins glitteringly around its
axis, and is as conducive to the discovery of ultimate truth as one of
Alexander Calder's mobiles. It does not show to Joseph K. anything but
the depth of the abysm that still, and now more than ever, separates
him from the tribunal, "and that he knew already." This letter, too,

is such a commentary. Tongue in cheek, Kafka used both the biographical material and the therapeutic intention of the letter to perform one of the strangest and most daring games a writer ever had played with the very substance of his life. By telling his life as a fable and commenting upon it in his peculiar way, he raised his conflict to the level of literature.

NOTES

1a. A translation of this letter by Ernst Kaiser and Eithne Wilkins can be found in Franz Kafka, *Dearest Father* (New York, 1954), pp. 138–96. However, I have used my own translation.

1b. Max Brod, *Franz Kafka: A Biography*, tr. by G. Humphreys Roberts (New York, 1947), p. 185, note.

2. *The Diaries of Franz Kafka, 1914–1923*, ed. by Max Brod, tr. by Martin Greenberg and Hannah Arendt (New York, 1949), p. 182.

3. *Franz Kafka: A Biography*, p. 156.

4. See Erich Fromm, *The Forgotten Language: An Introduction to the Understanding of Dreams, Fairy Tales and Myths* (New York, 1951), pp. 250 ff. Fromm bases his entire interpretation of *The Trial* on the key word "arrested": "To be arrested can mean to be taken into custody . . . and to be stopped in one's growth and development . . . ." However, the German "verhaftet" has the *double entendre* of "taken into custody" and of "entangled" ("er war seinem Ich verhaftet"). In *The Trial* K. "wird verhaftet"; in Fromm's interpretation he "ist verhaftet." In order to arrive at his interpretation, Fromm has to stretch a half-truth beyond its original meaning. He senses a metaphysical pun but evades an interpretation on the level of existence by embarking on a psychological approach.

5. *Heinrich von Ofterdingen*, II, Novalis, *Schriften*, ed. by Paul Kluckhohn (Leipzig, 1928), I, 229.

6. The German has simply "die letzte Instanz." "In letzter Instanz" means both "in the last resort" and "without further appeal." In view of *The Trial* it is worth noticing that the term is primarily a legal one.

7. Rilke, "Der Ölbaumgarten," *Sämtliche Werke* (Wiesbaden, 1955), I, 492–94.

8. The usual idiom would have been: "es machte mir Spass"; by substituting "Lust," Kafka opened, as it were, a linguistic trap door into the psychoanalytical underground.

9. Vladimir Nabokov, *Nikolai Gogol* (Norfolk, 1944), pp. 4–5.

10. The problem of narcissism in Gogol and Kafka has been treated by Robert Mühlher in his *Dichtung der Krise: Mythos und Psychologie in der Dichtung des 19. und 20. Jahrhunderts* (Vienna, 1951), pp. 438–43. See also I. F. Perry, "Kafka and Gogol," *German Life and Letters*, N.S., III (1953), 141–45.

11. German "Ungeziefer" means both the genus of vermin and one (un-

specified) insect of this kind ("ein Ungeziefer"). It seems to me, however, that Gregor was changed into a gigantic bedbug, since bedbugs are, in Central and Eastern Europe, the traditional plague of traveling salesmen like Samsa. It stands to reason that the unhappy son had to be transformed into what he dreaded and detested most.

12. Most pointedly in Max Brod, *Franz Kafkas Glauben und Lehre: Kafka und Tolstoi* (Winterthur, 1948), and in *Franz Kafka als wegweisende Gestalt* (St. Gallen, n.d.).

13. Franz Werfel, *Gedichte aus den Jahren 1908–1945* (Los Angeles, 1946), p. 28.

14. Thomas Mann, *Stories of Three Decades* (New York, 1936), p. 108.

15. Pavel Eisner, *Franz Kafka and Prague* (New York, 1950), pp. 36–37.

16. *Diaries*, II, 173.

17. Cf. especially Jean Wahl, "Kierkegaard and Kafka," *The Kafka Problem* (New York, 1946), pp. 266 ff.

18. *Diaries*, II, 165. Kafka continues: "The comparison with Grillparzer is valid, perhaps, but you don't think Grillparzer a proper one to imitate, do you? an unhappy example whom future generations should thank for having suffered for them." Indeed, the Austrian Grillparzer shows a greater affinity to Kafka than either Flaubert or Kierkegaard. Grillparzer, though still spellbound by Goethe's calm and harmony, heralded that "poetic nihilism" which was to find its climax in Kafka. (Cf. Werner Vordtriede, "Grillparzers Beitrag zum poetischen Nihilismus," *Trivium*, IX [1951], 102–20.)

19. Thomas Mann, *Doctor Faustus. The Life of the German Composer Adrian Leverkühn as Told by a Friend* (New York, 1948), p. 491.

20. The letter also contains the following sentences: "I would have been happy to have you as a friend, a boss, an uncle, a grandfather, even (though somewhat more reluctantly) as a father-in-law. Only as a father were you too strong for me . . . . Basically, you were a kind and soft-hearted man . . . . You have, I think, a gift for education . . . . Also you have an especially beautiful and unusual kind of quiet, content, and approving smile, which can make the recipient completely happy . . . ." In Kafka's books these mitigations of the terror inherent in authority are recaptured in scenes like the beginning of the tenth chapter of *The Castle:* there K. receives a letter from Klamm, congratulating him on the work he has done as a land surveyor. (The only semblance of work K. has performed so far was the work of a janitor.) Thus Kafka and his heroes were deprived of the certainty of condemnation, too. For Kafka even the inferno was conditional.

21. Kafka, "On Parables," *The Great Wall of China*, p. 258.

other hand, the diary veiled as part of the work. Diary entries and sketches for stories often are intertwined without visible transition. Is there anywhere a diary like Kafka's in which some of the entries exist in two or three variants? His whole work takes on the appearance of one single letter (which it is perhaps never necessary to send off) written with the purpose of disguising himself; a letter which never tends in the direction of truth.

Yet the letters reveal a feature distinct from the works of fiction. It is a linguistic distinction, not one in kind. To be sure, they are written in the same penetrating, clearly formulating idiom which we find in the works; thoughts and themes, too, are the same. But here the course of the argument is not linguistically masked. The succession within the thought structure is not intentionally telescoped. (In the diaries the "telescoping" is much stronger, since, in all likelihood, they were written with the thought of ultimate publication. For why should Kafka have destroyed many pages of them, had he not realized that the rest would some day be a semipublic document?)

When we read in one of these letters to Milena, "All the misfortune of my life—I don't wish to complain, but to make a generally instructive remark—derives, one might say, from letters or from the possibility of writing letters. People have hardly ever deceived me, but letters always—and as a matter of fact not those of other people, but my own," the linguistic succession of these sentences affords the possibility to read them differently, to "translate" them; perhaps like this: "All the misfortune of my life derives from my intention of becoming a writer (as my whole work is a letter); that is to say, one might put it that way, for what I am saying is not really the truth. I don't wish to complain; that is, that's just what I do and want to do. People have always betrayed me; not directly, but by forcing me to write to them and, by doing so, to appear to them in a light which has nothing to do with my real truth, but which I, in order to please them and to maintain myself, have nourished all my life." So we find in his diary (1917) the entry, "Yesterday's letter to Max. Lying, conceited, in the tone of a ham actor." These words certainly reveal neither anything about the letter to Brod, nor anything about Kafka's true feelings about the letter, and any Kafka criticism that naïvely "takes Kafka's word for it" starts on the wrong track. But perhaps those words do reveal something about his feelings toward Max Brod. Just as the quoted passage from the letter to Milena, written at the end of their relationship, in reality means nothing more than "Stop writing to me. I can't go on." A short time after that the correspondence comes to an end.

But these are love letters written by Kafka between 1920 (when he was 37) and 1922 to a young married woman who was translating his stories into Czech. She forced the role of passionate lover upon him. In one of the first letters he writes, "Trembling and almost unconscious I pray in the corner that you may fly out of the window as you have rushed in in your letter, I cannot after all keep a storm in my room; in these letters you must have the magnificent head of Medusa, for the snakes of terror hiss around your head and indeed around mine the snakes of fear hiss even wilder." From now on he no longer lets go this instrument of fear, but plays on it masterfully, always discovering new variations. In many a critical moment he withdraws into this fear. "It follows perhaps, that we are both married, you in Vienna, I to my Fear in Prague, and that not only you, but I too, tug in vain at our marriage." Fear, he says, is his "nature"; another time he pleads, "I consist of it and it is perhaps my best part." May he, in this case, not keep it, must he not be loved for the sake of his best part? But fear, for him, is also synonymous with being Jewish, and Milena is non-Jewish.

From all these letters hardly any factual information can be derived, simply because they consist of nothing but a self-analysis which, in one and the same instant, affirms and denies, reveals and veils. It is in this period (1921) that we find the diary entry, "This inescapable duty to observe oneself." The word "duty" here belongs not so much to the private sphere as to the public one, the sphere of him who defends himself before a committee. Such a seemingly unconditional veracity does not allow truth to emerge, not even the most subjective kind. The self-analysis, carried out step by step, does not construct truth as a whole, but, similar in this to modern natural science, atomizes it until its shape has completely dissolved. Nothing in these letters can serve the clarification of the world or even of Kafka himself.

Only as a whole, as method, as a linguistic pointer, they furnish a hint as to how Kafka probably has to be read. He had written that important letter to his father which he neither sent off nor published although he bestowed upon it some kind of official title, calling it the *Vaterbrief*. But this letter is far from being a secret private document; more than once Kafka suggests that Milena read it. When he proposes this to her for the first time he adds the warning, "And in reading try to understand all the lawyer's tricks, it's a lawyer's letter. And in doing so never forget your big Nevertheless." This warning is in itself a lawyer's trick, in which the last sentence discredits the letter so urgently recommended. This is the one point, in all these pages, where truth inadvertently breaks through and comes to the surface. For one moment Kafka forgets that Milena, after all, is just as much a tribunal for him as is his father; but to one tribunal he reveals the fact that the other person is a tribunal and that he himself is his own lawyer. With these words the linguistic structure as it is revealed in the letters and veiled in the works declares itself to be a lawyer's language: something is said which immediately is taken back by an amplifying word, whereupon the denial is retracted; but at the end Kafka is ready not to be taken too seriously with his retraction.

Again and again Milena wants Kafka to travel to Vienna so that they can meet. He fights these proposals as well as he can—and always succumbs. In prolonged arguments he demonstrates why he could not possibly come to Vienna although he has just received a telegram with specific directions. Finally he argues, "But all this is immaterial, even without the telegram I wouldn't have been able to come to Vienna, on the contrary the telegram works rather as an argument in favor of the journey. I shall certainly not come, but on the other hand should I—it won't happen—to my terrible surprise arrive in Vienna" he will be more dead than alive. Another time, faced with the same problem, he hides behind the figure of the director of his company:

Besides, I like myself so little. Here I sit in front of the Director's door, the Director is away, but I wouldn't be surprised if he were to come out and say: "I don't like you, either, that's why I'm giving you notice." "Thank you," I'd say, "I need this urgently for a trip to Vienna." "So?" he'd say, "now I like you again and I withdraw the notice." "Oh," I'd say, "now I can't take the trip." "Oh yes," he'd say, "for now again I don't like you, so I give you notice." And so it would be an endless story.

This endless story has been told and retold by Kafka. It is the real parable of his work, a peculiar transformation of the Athenian liar of Eubulides who says, "I lie." With this Sophist puzzle the endless story began which now Kafka continues. He who says "I lie" is telling a lie if by saying so he speaks the truth. But if he speaks the truth in this sentence, he is lying. The Athenian liar utters a statement which is formulated as its own denial (which is the stylistic device of the letters to Milena). As a denial of an untruth the sentence has the structure of the truth; in its quality of a theme of a denial, however, it has the structure of an untruth. It is neither true nor untrue. This is more than an idle Sophist's game, as it makes manifest the limitations of our knowledge and power of expression. The sentence, therefore, has disquieted many thinkers. Its real destructive power appears in Kafka who succumbs, not intellectually, but humanly, to this thought process and perishes under it. Every sentence by Kafka has the appendix, not always expressed: "but you must not forget, Kafka is a liar." If you take his word for it you cannot but admire his veracity at his own expense; if you refuse to believe him the truth of his mendacity is proved.

The central point of this correspondence, the only question which has to be answered again and again, the endless story, is simply this: how can we who are lovers be permanently together? All Kafka's proposals, urgent and strengthened by arguments and even reproach, to make Milena come to Prague and to enable her to divorce her husband and marry him have the form of the sentence of the Athenian liar and are their own denial: "Lonely imperfection has to be endured through every moment, imperfection shared by two does not have to be endured. Hasn't one got eyes to tear them out and a heart for the same purpose? And yet it isn't so bad, it's all an exaggeration, only the longing is true, this cannot be exaggerated." And he proceeds, "But even the truth of longing is not so much its truth, rather is it perhaps really love when I say that for me you are the most beloved; love is to me that you are the knife which I turn within myself."

Someone might argue that this stylistic device so apparent in these letters and so carefully hidden in his works appears only here, and here only because Kafka, forced into the role of lover, did not really love Milena. This would be true insofar as one admits his lack of love for Milena. But Kafka is the non-lover par excellence. The self-hater loved neither himself, nor his work, nor his family, nor the world, nor his friends, nor the women whose lover he is. Because they all help make him what he is. Kafka the non-lover is Kafka the writer; the non-lover informs his work which is the continuous and misleading justification of his lack of love. The style of these letters can be demonstrated as the method of the Athenian liar; but the method is forced upon him because he is condemned to be the advocate of himself. In this way he can avoid decisions (and decisions would be judgments) without at the same time losing the reader's sympathies. He can be a Jew, sick, a non-lover, and yet, for each of these accusations, insist on an acquittal.

One day he had found words of praise for purity. Milena was quick to hear in them some menacing accusation; but Kafka reassures her, "I'm dirty, Milena, infinitely dirty, which is why I make such a fuss about purity." And in a later letter, masterfully playing with all the possible lawyer's tricks at the same time, he says, "And as for dirt, why shouldn't I go on displaying it, my sole possession (the sole possession of all people, only I'm not quite so sure about it)? Out of modesty perhaps? Well, that would be the only justified objection." What is the poor juror (his reader) to do in the face of this clever plea in which each truth appears as untrue and each untruth as true, but which makes anything but an unconditional acquittal impossible? Another day he writes, "Yesterday I advised you not to write to me every day, this is still my opinion today and it would be very good for both of us and I suggest it once more today, and even more urgently— only, please, Milena, don't act upon it, but write me daily all the same." Kafka complains that he suffers from insomnia and suggests that this correspondence might be blamed for it; but he immediately adds the denial which cancels out the remark, ". . . sleep is the most innocent creature and a sleepless person the most guilty one." And so from page to page. Whenever he maligns or praises himself, the lawyer reaches out for the denial, neutralizes the statement, and atomizes the truth. Therefore, his terrible anti-Semitic utterances naturally cannot be taken at their face value, but solely as preventive measures. He dislikes being a Jew, but does not want to be disliked by others on account of it. When he speaks about "the subterranean, dark, low, ugly corridors" of one of his stories one does not hear a real commentary on his work but the disarming presentation in the jury-court. Toward the end of their relationship Kafka answers Milena's pompous (and touchingly ignorant) exclamation, "I am the rock on which he was shattered," with the self-accusation which is neither true nor meant as truth, "Only I am at fault, it consists in too little truth on my side, still far too little truth, still mostly lies, lies from fear of myself and from fear of people." Once more he refers to Milena's exclamation and adds, in the method of the Athenian liar: ". . . it's as incorrect as, for instance, to conceive the opposite possibility."

So one sees Kafka's work as the gigantic, ever-repeated attempt of one single lawyer to discredit the judge. Judge, policeman, the Law, judgment, trial, lawyer and all their variants are the basic symbols of his work. Opposite them stands the seemingly innocent-guilty defendant; but the defendant is in reality the lawyer bribed by himself. Always the judge is unreasonable and destructive; the law with its superhuman demands crushes the probably innocent one; the judgment is a cruel sentence; the trial is conducted without proof of guilt and the lawyer remains invisible. He has disguised himself as the victim and, through his presentation of the case, directs the affair in such a manner that from everything only an acquittal can follow on the grounds of sympathy and pity. The person whom Kafka addresses (reader, friend, beloved) can appear to him in only two guises: either as enemy—then he is the judge and must be discredited ("Your letter begins like that of a judge," he writes in one of the first letters); or as a friend. In this case he sits on the juror's bench and must be won by the Athenian liar's method. Kafka is the man who does not want to be judged. Every means to avoid or disqualify the judgment becomes permissible.

Sometimes the lawyer becomes so sure of his skill that he openly shows his hand or, at least, seems to do so (and these occasions must be the real climaxes of the advocatory game of life): "For I too, even though I may sometimes look like a bribed advocate of my 'fear,' probably agree with it deep down in myself, indeed it is part of me and perhaps the best part." The special lawyer's trick of this confession consists in the linguistic turn ("even though") which constructs a contrast which in reality does not exist. For all he says is: I defend my fear because I like it. The logical jump, moreover, is covered up by the well-placed "probably."

But there is one extraordinary difficulty for this interpretation of Kafka. It consists in those sentences in which Kafka himself seems to anticipate and agree to all that has been said here. In his diary he copies a passage from a letter to his fiancée (1917):

If I closely examine what is my ultimate aim, it turns out that I am not really striving to be good and to fulfil the demands of a Supreme Judgment, but rather very much to the contrary: I strive to know the whole human and animal community, to recognize their basic predilections, desires, moral ideals, to reduce these to simple rules and as quickly as possible trim my behavior to these rules in order that I may find favor in the whole world's eyes; and, indeed, (this is the inconsistency) so much favor that in the end I could openly act out the meanness within me without alienating the universal love in which I am held—the only sinner who won't be roasted. To sum up, then, my sole concern is the human tribunal, and this, moreover, I wish to deceive, though without practicing any actual deception.

Now here a character witness seems to speak and to admit everything. But Kafka himself is the witness; the lawyer masked as witness. It is also well to remember that this letter to his fiancée was "probably the last," as the diary states, and was most likely meant to end their engagement. He might for once prefer the judgment to his engagement. But no confession of Kafka, not even this one, can be valid as confirmation about anything concerning himself. All interpretations which quote Kafka as a witness for himself must be false from the start as they confuse the lawyer with the witness. That is why most Kafka criticism is so very misleading. In the letter quoted various tricks are employed. There is, to be sure, the reckless pleasure of playing with fire: "How far can I go without losing the law suit?" (And perhaps this time I almost want to lose it.) But at the decisive moment he turns everything to his advantage showing "the demands" of the judge to be unreasonably severe. He constructs two different judges, the Supreme Judgment and the eyes of the world; a divine judge and a human one who, one suspects, to him are really one and the same. By thus dividing the Judge into two judicial beings Kafka achieves, without seeming to do so, that the one judge discredits the other, each canceling the other out. The juror will be appalled by the superhuman demands of the divine judge and angry at the worldly judge who might, after so much striving and disarming admission, still find the defendant guilty. The very "inconsistency," the confession that he only pretends to be good in order that he be exonerated in spite of all the meanness within him, will, with its disarming pathos, win him sympathy. The last clause, "though without practicing any actual deception," is the final denial of the previous confession.

In this state of being which does not recognize the judge there is no room for the world. Nothing can exist which is not of immediate concern for the defense, and the space of the whole world shrinks to the proportion of a village tribunal. There probably is no other correspondence into which the world has entered so little. There are no remarks about the times, the cultural atmosphere, intellectual groups, or poetry and literature. There is hardly any mention of great names of representative men. When well-known names are occasionally mentioned, their bearers appear strangely changed, as though their names were mere anagrams for Kafka, Joseph K., or Gregor Samsa. At one point, for instance, a kinship with Dostoevsky is felt; but not with the writer, but with him who, according to an anecdote, accused himself of being "base." Werfel and Heine are mentioned, not as poets, but the one as the typical fat man (Kafka saw himself as the thin man par excellence) and the other as the Jew who had not told his wife about being Jewish. Casanova appears not as the great lover, but as prisoner in the lead chambers. Charles-Louis Philippe's *Marie Donadieu* which Milena had recommended displeases Kafka, because "there's so little else in the book but despair." Once Georg Kaiser comes to visit him, but Kafka sees in him only a "half-madman."

On one occasion, however, he does recommend and send a book, Grillparzer's *Poor Fiddler,* in which Grillparzer, the self-hater, portrays himself under the guise of a half-crazed fiddler who relentlessly strives for the greatest purity of his art without realizing that he only produces the most execrable screechings on his violin. Kafka ambiguously recommends the book, ". . . not because it has a great significance for me—though it had it once years ago. But I'm sending it to you because it's so Viennese, so unmusical, because it makes one weep . . . ." (Kafka had once called himself "completely unmusical.") In a later letter he denies his previous denial: "Everything you say about *The Poor Fiddler* is correct. When I said it didn't mean anything to me, I said it only out of caution; for I was not sure how you would get along with it, also because I'm ashamed of the story as though I had written it myself." But this statement, too, will be denied. Kafka continues what began as a defense of the tale:

. . . and actually it starts wrong, it has a number of inaccuracies, ridiculous and dilettantish features, affectations that make one blush (one notices this especially when reading it out loud, I could show you the passages); and this kind of music practice is really a miserably ridiculous invention, sufficient to provoke the girl to throw—in extreme anger, in which the whole world will share, I above all—everything she has in her shop at the story until the story, which deserves nothing better, perishes thus from its own elements.

But Milena had praised the story. Therefore, a final statement reverses the judgment: "It must be admitted, though, that there is no more beautiful fate for a story than for it to disappear, and in this way." In Grillparzer, then, and in one of the two works of his (the other being his drama *Sappho*) in which he existentially analyzes himself as the victim of his art, as a tragically ludicrous perpetrator of a supreme crime against life, Kafka recognizes his kin, disguising this recognition with that contempt he feels for himself, but does not want others to feel for him.

The editor of these letters, Willy Haas, has a strange revelation to make: certain passages had to be deleted out of respect for living persons; and they should, Haas advises, never be published, even at some later date. He left out these passages not to protect intimate utterances from the eyes of the curious (which would call for neither apology nor comment), but because Kafka's remarks about his intimate friends and fellow writers were so "phantastic and mistaken." Haas believes that Kafka "evidently did not clearly recognize the cause of his hatred for certain persons; the result is," Haas continues, "that we find, in these Letters, literary portraits or rather caricatures which have nothing to do with reality . . . ." We need not doubt the truth of Haas's statements, especially as we could have arrived at it almost by necessity from our previous investigations. The simple reality, the only reality which we readers are able to verify, that is to say that which, in a popular sense, is true cannot be recognized by the analyst of himself. He must blind himself to it, as he is the lawyer pleading to save his neck. This part of reality is, according to Haas, presented with "profound inaccuracy." It therefore would be dangerously wrong to approach Kafka's works as one approaches other literary works, like Goethe's *Faust,* in which the very nature of man and the world is explained in uncapricious symbols. Most questions about a direct experience of the real world cannot be asked of Kafka without receiving "phantastic and mistaken" answers. One has to read him as though his writings were the real trial records of one who, in tragic fear of being judged, broke down under the impact of truth. Only by the lawyer for the opposite party can his writings be deciphered, but never by him who starts out making Kafka's point of view his own. And all even the opposing lawyer can do is to reveal the desperately endless story which ensues from the denying statement: "Kafka lies."

Only now it becomes quite apparent that when Max Brod published Kafka's manuscripts against his friend's explicit wish he did precisely what Kafka the writer wanted him to do. As his own lawyer Kafka had declared himself a non-writer. With this provision he has assured his acquittal even beyond the grave.

Part Four

BIBLIOGRAPHIES

AND INDEX

Bibliographical Index

OF THE WORKS AVAILABLE

IN ENGLISH

This Index contains the title of every novel, short story, and other prose work Kafka wrote. The English title is followed by the original German title. For the novels, diaries and short-story collections the name of the English translator and publisher and the date of the English publication are given. Individual stories and sketches are located by volume and page; for those published in magazines, anthologies, or odd volumes, the name of the English translator and other information is added.

The Key of Abbreviations is as follows:

D 1910–13–*The Diaries of Franz Kafka 1910–1913*. Edited by Max Brod. Translated by Joseph Kresh. New York: Schocken Books, Inc., 1948.

D 1914–23–*The Diaries of Franz Kafka 1914–1923*. Edited by Max Brod. Translated by Martin Greenberg, with the co-operation of Hannah Arendt. New York: Schocken Books, Inc., 1949.

DF–*Dearest Father, Stories and Other Writings*. Translated by Ernst Kaiser and Eithne Wilkins. New York: Schocken Books, Inc., 1954.

GW–*The Great Wall of China. Stories and Reflections*. Translated by Willa and Edwin Muir. New York: Schocken Books, Inc., 1946.

P–*Parables*. In German and English. Translated by Willa and Edwin Muir, and Clement Greenberg. New York: Schocken Books, Inc., 1947.

PC–*The Penal Colony. Stories and Short Pieces*. Translated by Willa and Edwin Muir. New York: Schocken Books, Inc., 1948.

Angel Flores

Biography and Criticism:

A BIBLIOGRAPHY

The compiler wishes to thank Jörgen Born, Florence Goldberg, Klaus Wagenbach, and Marianne Zerner for helpful assistance.

Aarnes, Asbjørn S. "Franz Kafka," *Vinduet* (Oslo), May, 1950, No. 4, pp. 293–98.

Abenius, Margit. "Franz Kafka," *Bonniers Litterära Magasin* (Stockholm), April, 1938, p. 260; "Mansklig gemenskap är nyckeln till 'troende skeptikern' Kafka," *Dagens Nyheter* (Stockholm), May 12, 1949; "Men ändå frihet," *Bonniers Litterära Magasin* (Stockholm), Oct., 1945, p. 704.

Ackermann, Paul Kurt. *A Descriptive Bibliography of Franz Kafka,* Columbia Univ., M.A. thesis, 1947; "A History of Critical Works on Franz Kafka," *German Quarterly*, March, 1950, pp. 104–13.

Adeane, Louis. "The Hero Myth in Kafka's Writing," *Focus One* (London), 1945, pp. 48–56.

Adorno, Theodor W. "Aufzeichnungen zu Kafka," *Neue Rundschau*, Jahrg. 64, July–Sept., 1953, Heft 3, pp. 325–53.

Albrecht, Erich A. "Zur Entstehungsgeschichte von Kafkas Landarzt," *Monatshefte* (Univ. of Wisconsin), April–May, 1954, Vol. 46, No. 4, pp. 207–12.

Allen, Walter. "A Note on Franz Kafka," *Focus One* (London), 1945, pp. 30–33.

Anceschi, Luciano. Rev. of Oscar Navarro's *Kafka, la crisi della fede, Rassegna d'Italia*, July–Aug., 1949, pp. 823–29, rep. in *Poetica Americana*, Pisa: Nistri-Lischi, 1954, pp. 111–22.

Anders, Günther. "Franz Kafka: pro und contra," *Neue Rundschau*, Jahrg. 58, Spring, 1947, Heft 6, pp. 119–57; "Franz Kafka, Ritual without Religion," *Commentary* (New York), Dec., 1949, Vol. 8, pp. 560–69; *Kafka, Pro und Contra*, Munich: C. H. Beck, 1951.

Anders, Günther, and Max Brod. "Franz Kafka: pro und contra," *Neue Schweizer Rundschau* (Zurich), May, 1952, Vol. 20, pp. 43–50.

Angelloz, J.-F. "Le Journal Quotidien de Kafka et les Cahiers de Malte Laurids Brigge," *Mercure de France*, Feb., 1952, Vol. 314, No. 1062, pp. 340–42.

Angus, Douglas. "Kafka's 'Metamorphosis' and 'The Beauty and the Beast' Tale," *Journal of English and Germanic Philology*, Jan., 1954, Vol. 53, No. 1, pp. 69–71.

Aranguren, José Luis. "Franz Kafka," *Arbor* (Madrid), 1951, Vol. 20, No. 71, pp. 222–33.

Arendt, Hannah. "The Jews as Pariah: A Hidden Tradition," *Jewish Social Studies* (New York), April, 1944, Vol. 6, pp. 99–122; "Franz Kafka: A Revaluation," *Partisan Review*, Fall, 1944, Vol. 11, pp. 412–22; *Sechs Essays*, Heidelberg: L. Schneider, 1948.

Arnheim, Rudolf. "Franz Kafka," *Schaubühne oder Weltbühne*, Jan.–June, 1931, Vol. 27, pp. 959–61.

Auden, W. H. "The Wandering Jew," *New Republic*, Feb. 10, 1941, pp. 185–86; "Kafka's Quest," in A. Flores (ed.), *The Kafka Problem*, pp. 47–52.

Ayala, Francisco. Rev. of Gándara's *Kafka*, *Sur* (Buenos Aires), June, 1944, pp. 84–86.

Bach, Hans. "Franz Kafkas Leben," *Der Morgen* (Berlin), Dec., 1937, Vol. 13, pp. 390–93.

Balascheff, Pierre. "Contemporary Figures: Franz Kafka," *Colosseum* (London), April–June, 1939, Vol. 5, pp. 139–42.

Baldanza, Stephen. Rev. of *Amerika*, *The Commonweal*, Dec. 20, 1940, p. 234.

Basil, Otto. "Umriss von Franz Kafka," *Wort und Tat*, Jahrg. 1, Sept., 1946, No. 2, pp. 98–104.

Bataille, Georges. "Franz Kafka devant la critique communiste," *Critique* (Paris), Oct., 1950, Vol. 6, pp. 22–36.

Baudy, Nicolas. "Entretiens avec Dora Dymant," *Evidences* (Paris), Feb., 1950, No. 8, pp. 21–25.

Baum, Oskar. "Franz Kafka," *Der Jude*, 1924, Vol. 8, p. 8; "Erinnerungen an Franz Kafka," *Literarische Welt*, Jahrg. 2, 1926, p. 3; "Die Wunder einer unscheinbaren Hölle," *Berliner Börsen Courier*, 1927, No. 75; "Erinnerungen an Franz Kafka," *Witiko*, 1929, Vol. 2, No. 3, pp. 126–28;

Obituary, *Prager Presse*, 1924, Nos. 155, 168; "Der junge Franz Kafka," *Die Wahrheit*, Dec., 1936, p. 8; "Das Leben Franz Kafkas" (Rev. of Brod's *Franz Kafka, eine Biographie*), *Das Wort*, Feb., 1938, pp. 128–30; Rev. of Brod's *Franz Kafka, eine Biographie, Die Wahrheit*, Dec. 20, 1937; "Franz Kafka zum 10. Todestag," *Internationale Literatur*, Oct., 1936, pp. 156–58; "Franz Kafka," *Literarische Welt*, Jahrg. 4, June 29, 1928, No. 46, p. 3; "Recollections," in A. Flores (ed.), *The Kafka Problem*, pp. 25–31.

Beckmann, Heinz. "Kurzschluss um Kafkas Prozess," *Rheinischer Merkur*, Jahrg. 5, 1950, No. 29, p. 6; "Franz Kafkas Gruftwächter," *Rheinischer Merkur*, Jahrg. 5, 1950, No. 47, p. 8.

Beissner, Friedrich. *Der Erzähler Franz Kafka*, Stuttgart: W. Kohlhammer, 1952.

Belgion, Montgomery. "The Measure of Kafka," *The Criterion*, Oct., 1938, pp. 13–28.

Benco, Silvio. "Franz Kafka," *Il Convegno* (Milan), 1928, Vol. IX, p. 381; *Il Convegno* (Milan), Aug. 25, 1928, pp. 369–70.

Benjamin, Walter. "Franz Kafka, eine Würdignung," *Jüdische Rundschau* (Berlin), Dec. 21, 1934, Vol. 39, p. 8, and Dec. 28, 1934, p. 6; *Gesammelte Schriften*, 2 vols., Frankfurt: Suhrkamp, 1955.

Bense, Max. *Die Theorie Kafkas*, Cologne-Berlin: Kiepenheuer & Witsch, 1952.

Berence, Fred. "Prague de Kafka," *Evidences* (Paris), Dec., 1953, 5th Year, No. 36, pp. 42–45.

Berendsohn, Walter. "Kafka och Strindberg," *Dagens Nyheter* (Stockholm), Nov. 28, 1951.

Bergel, Lienhard. "An Elderly Bachelor," and "The Barrow," in A. Flores (ed.), *The Kafka Problem*, pp. 172–78, 199–206.

Bithell, Jethro. *Modern German Literature*, London: Methuen, 1939, pp. 406–11.

Blanchot, Maurice. "La lecture de Kafka," *L'Arche* (Paris), Nov., 1945, No. 11, pp. 107–16, rep. in *La Part du feu*, Paris: Gallimard, 1949 (4th ed.), pp. 9–19; "Kafka et la littérature," *La Part du feu*, pp. 20–34; "Kafka et l'exigence de l'oeuvre," *Critique* (Paris), March, 1952, Vol. 8, pp. 195–221, and in *L'Espace Littéraire*, Paris: Gallimard, 1955, pp. 52–81.

Blei, Franz. *Zeitgenössische Bildnisse*, Amsterdam: Allert de Lange, 1940.

Blumenberg, Hans. Rev. of "Letter to His Father," *Hochland*, Jahrg. 45, Feb., 1953, pp. 282–84.

Boden, Gérard. *Franz Kafka: Aspects de son oeuvre*, Algiers: Librairie Chaix, 1947.

Borges, Jorge Luis. Preface to *La Metamorfosis*, Buenos Aires: Losada, 1938, pp. 7–11; *Otras inquisiciones*, Buenos Aires: Sur, 1952, pp. 126–28.

Bosquet, Alain. Rev. of *Letters to Milena, Combat* (Paris), Jan. 15, 1953.

Braak, Menno ter. "Decadent zonder decadentie," *Verzamelde werken* IV, Rotterdam: Nijgh en van Ditmar, 1936, pp. 99–111; "Franz Kafka en Max Brod," pp. 398–401; "De joodse geest in de literatuur," pp. 473–80.

Braybrooke, Neville. "Celestial Castles: An Approach to Saint Teresa and Franz Kafka," *Dublin Review,* 1955, Vol. 229, pp. 427–45.

Brechter, Gerhard. "Josef K. in Anwendung," *Rheinischer Merkur,* Jahrg. 6, 1951, No. 2, p. 8.

Breton, André. "Têtes d'Orage," *Minotaure* (Paris), 1937, No. 10, 3rd Series, p. 7; *Anthologie de l'humour noir,* Paris: Editions du Sagittaire, 1940, pp. 208–9; "Cabezas de Tormenta," *Sur* (Buenos Aires), May, 1937, pp. 7–10, rep. in *Grafos* (Havana), Aug., 1941.

Brod, Max. "Der Dichter Franz Kafka," *Neue Rundschau,* Jahrg. 32, Nov., 1921, Heft 11, pp. 1210–16; "Franz Kafkas Nachlass," *Weltbühne,* Jahrg. 20, July 17, 1924, No. 29, pp. 106–9; "Über Franz Kafka," *Literarische Welt,* June 4, 1926, Vol. 2, p. 1; "Franz Kafka," *Berliner Tageblatt,* 1927, No. 567; "Infantilismus Kleist und Kafka," *Literarische Welt,* July 15, 1927, Vol. 3, pp. 3–4; "Nachbemerkung zu Franz Kafkas Novellenfragment," *Witiko,* 1928, Vol. I, No. 2, p. 104; "Zu Franz Kafkas Roman *Amerika, Literarische Welt,* 1927, Vol. 3, No. 44, p. 3; "Additional Note" (to *The Castle*), New York: Knopf, 1930, pp. 329–40; "Franz Kafkas Grunderlebnis," *Schaubühne oder Weltbühne,* Jan.–June, 1931, Vol. 27, p. 696; "Homage to Kafka," *The Literary World* (New York), July, 1934, pp. 1–2; *Franz Kafka, eine Biographie,* Prague: Heinrich Mercy Sohn, 1935; Berlin: S. Fischer, 1954, 3rd ed.; French translation, Paris: Grasset, 1945; English translation, New York: Schocken, 1947; Spanish translation, Buenos Aires: Emecé, 1951; "Epilogue" (to *The Trial*), New York: Knopf, 1937, pp. 291–97; "Afterword" (to *Amerika*), New York: New Directions, 1940, pp. 298–99; "Franz Kafka und das Judentum," *Neue Schweizer Rundschau* (Zurich), 1946, Vol. 13, No. 12, pp. 745–50; "The Homeless Stranger," in A. Flores (ed.), *The Kafka Problem,* pp. 179–80; "Kierkegaard, Heidegger, Kafka," *L'Arche* (Paris), Nov., 1946, No. 21, pp. 44–54, and *Prisma,* 1947, Heft 11, pp. 17–20; *Franz Kafkas Glauben und Lehre,* Winterthur: Mondial-Verlag, Munich: Desch, 1948; "Franz Kafka Versuch einer sinnvollen Erfassung," *Hamburger Akademische Rundschau,* Jahrg. 3, 1948–49, pp. 198–206; "Kleist und Kafka," *Welt und Wort* (Munich), Feb., 1949, Heft 2, pp. 52–56; "Keine Flickarbeit," *Berliner Hefte,* 1949, Heft 11, pp. 437–39; "Franz Kafka in seinen Briefen," *Merkur,* Sept., 1950, Vol. 4, pp. 942–58; "Franz Kafkas Andelige Backgruun," *Spektrum* (Oslo), 1950, No. 2; "Zur Textgestaltung der 'Hochzeitsbereitungen auf dem Lande,'" *Neue Rundschau,* Jahrg. 62, Jan.–March, 1951, Heft 1, pp. 18–20; "Bemer-

kungen zu Kafkas *Schloss,*" *Neue Züricher Zeitung,* Oct. 20, 1951, p.
5; *Franz Kafka als wegweisende Gestalt,* St. Gallen: Tschudy, 1951;
"Ermordung einer Puppe namens Franz Kafka," *Neue Schweizer Rundschau* (Zurich), Feb., 1952, Vol. 19, Heft 10, pp. 613–25; "Kafka, pro
und contra," *Neue Schweizer Rundschau* (Zurich), May, 1952, pp.
43–50; "Neue Züge zum Bilde Franz Kafkas," *Merkur,* 1953, Vol. VII,
Heft 6, No. 64, pp. 518–30; Int. to Gustav Janouch, *Conversations with
Kafka,* London: Verschoyle, New York: F. A. Praeger, 1953; "Bemerkungen zur Lebensgeschichte Franz Kafkas," *Neue Rundschau,* Jahrg.
64, April–June, 1953, Heft 2, pp. 232–44; "Die Hoffnung auf das
Vollkommene ist nicht sinnlos," *Programmheft des Staatstheatre Braun-
schweig,* Spielzeit 1953/54, Heft 4, p. 36; "Ein arabisches Buch über
Kafka," *Aufbau-Zeitgeist* (New York), May 22, 1955.

Brück, Max von. "Das Labyrinth," *Die Wandlung* (Heidelberg), May,
1947, Vol. II, No. 4, pp. 295–309; "Versuch über Franz Kafka," *Die Gegenwart* (Freiburg im Breisgau), Jahrg. 3, April 1, 1948, Nos. 7–8, pp. 25–30.

Buber, Martin. "Ein Wort über Franz Kafka," in *Kampf um Israel,* Berlin:
Schocken, 1933, pp. 233 f.; *Two Types of Faith,* London and New York:
Macmillan, 1951, pp. 162–69.

Buchheit, G. Rev. of *The Castle, Gral,* Jahrg. 21, p. 582.

Burgum, Edwin Berry. "Kafka on Many Levels," *Virginia Quarterly Review,* Summer, 1948, Vol. 24, No. 3, pp. 464–69; "Kafka and the Bank-
ruptcy of Faith," *Accent,* Spring, 1943, pp. 153–67.

Burnham, James. "Bemerkungen über Kafka," *Amerikanische Rundschau*
(Munich), Jahrg. 3, 1947, Heft 15, pp. 44–54.

Burns, Wayne. "Kafka and Alex Comfort: The Penal Colony Revisited,"
Arizona Quarterly (Univ. of Arizona), Summer, 1952, Vol. 8, pp. 101–20.

Cáceres, J. A. *Panoramas del hombre y del estilo,* Bogotá: Ediciones Espiral
Columbia, 1949, pp. 31–35.

Camus, Albert. "Hope and Absurdity," in A. Flores (ed.), *The Kafka
Problem,* pp. 251–61; *Le Mythe de Sisyphe,* Paris: Gallimard, 1946;
The Myth of Sisyphus, New York: Knopf, 1955, pp. 124–38.

Carrive, Jean. Brief note on "The Little Woman" (Die kleine Frau), *Le
Cheval de Troie* (Paris), 1948, No. 6, pp. 808–9.

Carrouges, Michel. *Franz Kafka,* Paris: Labergerie, 1948 (Collection "Con-
tacts"); "La machine-celibataire selon Franz Kafka et Marcel Duchamp,"
Mercure de France, June, 1952, Vol. 315, pp. 262–81.

Caspel, J. van. "Josefine und Jeremias," *Neophilologus,* 1953, Vol. 37, No.
4, pp. 241–45.

Chastel, André. Rev. of *The Castle, Cahiers du Sud* (Marseilles), March,
1940, Vols. 26–27, pp. 193–98.

Collignon, Jean. "Kafka's Humor," *Yale French Studies*, Winter, 1955–56, No. 16, pp. 53–62.

Cook, Mary J. *The Woman Characters in the Novels of Franz Kafka*, Columbia Univ., M.A. thesis, 1947.

Crouzet, Guy. Rev. of *The Castle, Notre Temps*, Nov. 6, 1938.

Csokor, Franz Theodor, Willy Haas, Heinz Politzer, etc. "Franz Kafka Homage," *Forum*, Jan.–July–Aug., 1954, Vol. I, Nos. 7–8.

Dalmau Castañón, Wilfredo. "El caso clínico de Kafka en 'La Metamorfosis,' " *Cuadernos Hispanoamericanos* (Madrid), March, 1952, No. 27, pp. 385–88.

Daniells, Roy. "In the Labyrinth: A Note on Franz Kafka," *Manitoba Arts Review* (Senior Arts Council of the Univ. of Manitoba), Spring, 1942, Vol. 3, pp. 3–13.

Daniel-Rops. "A French Catholic Looks at Kafka," *Thought* (New York), Sept., 1948, Vol. 23, pp. 401–4; "L'Univers desesperé de Franz Kafka," *Cahiers du Sud* (Marseilles), March, 1937, Vol. 24, pp. 161–76; Rev. of *The Castle, Nouvelle Revue Française*, March, 1939, pp. 526–29; *Où passent des anges*, Paris: Plon, 1947; "The Castle of Despair," in A. Flores (ed.), *The Kafka Problem*, pp. 184–91.

Dauvin, R. " 'Le Procès' de Kafka," *Etudes Germaniques*, Jan.–March, 1948, 3e. Année, No. 1, pp. 49–63.

Demetz, Petr. "Zur Interpretation Franz Kafkas," *Plan* (Vienna), 1948, Vol. 2, No. 6, pp. 370–78; "Franz Kafka a cesky narod," in *Franz Kafka a Praha*, Prague: V. Zikes, 1947, pp. 43–53; "Franz Kafka in England," *German Life and Letters*, Oct., 1950, Vol. 4, pp. 21–30; "Kafka, Freud, Husserl: Probleme einer Generation," *Zeitschrift für Religions- und Geistes-geschichte*, 1955, VII, 1, pp. 59–60.

Derycke, Gaston. Rev. of *The Metamorphosis, Le Rouge et le Noir*, May 5, 1938.

Deutsch, Babette. Rev. of *Amerika, New York Herald Tribune Books*, Feb. 16, 1941, p. 13; Rev. of *A Franz Kafka Miscellany, New York Herald Tribune Books*, Feb. 16, 1941, p. 13.

Döblin, Alfred. "Romane von Kafka," *Literarische Welt*, 1927, Vol. 3, No. 7, p. 1.

Drenner, Don V. R. "Kafka, Warner and the Cult of Power," *Kansas Magazine*, 1952, pp. 62–64.

Dubois, P. "Franz Kafka en Milena Jesenska," *Het Vaderland*, Jan. 17, 1953.

Dumont, F. "Kafka und das Théâtre Noir," *Die Quelle*, Jahrg. 2, 1948, Heft 5, pp. 33–36.

Dupee, F. W. "The Fabulous and the Familiar," *Partisan Review*, Dec., 1937, Vol. 4, pp. 66–69.

Dymant, Dora. "Ich habe Franz Kafka geliebt," *Die Neue Zeitung*, Aug. 18, 1948, p. 1 of the *Feuilleton und Kunstbeilage*.

E., P. Rev. of Brod's *Franz Kafka, eine Biographie, Prager Presse*, March 19, 1938.

Edfelt, Johannes. "Nya Kafkabrev," *Dagens Nyheter* (Stockholm), Feb. 2, 1953.

Ehrenstein, Albert. "Franz Kafka," *Aufbau* (New York), July 2 and 9, 1943, pp. 10, 16–17.

Eisner, Pavel. *Franz Kafka and Prague*, tr. Lowry Nelson and René Wellek, New York: Arts, Inc., 1950 (Golden Griffin Books).

Ekelöf, Gunnar. "Brod och Kafka," *Bonniers Litterära Magasin* (Stockholm), Feb., 1950, p. 145.

Eloesser, Arthur. *Modern German Literature*, New York: Knopf, 1933, pp. 405–6.

Emrich, Wilhelm. "Franz Kafka," in Hermann Friedmann and Otto Mann (eds.), *Deutsche Literatur im zwanzigsten Jahrhundert*, Heidelberg: Wolfgang Verlag, 1954, pp. 230–48.

Engelstad, Carl Fredrik. "Profiler: Franz Kafka," *Morgenbladet* (Oslo), Oct. 15, 1949.

Felheim, Marvin. "The Judgment," in M. Felheim, F. B. Newman, and W. R. Steinhoff (eds.), *Study Aids for Teachers for Modern Short Stories*, New York: Oxford Univ. Press, 1951, pp. 36–39.

Flores, Angel (ed.). "Homage to Kafka," *The Literary World* (New York), July, 1934, pp. 1–4; Rev. of *The Castle, Books Abroad* (Univ. of Oklahoma), Autumn, 1941, Vol. 15, p. 480; "Franz Kafka," in Stanley J. Kunitz and Howard Haycraft (eds.), *Twentieth Century Authors*, New York: H. W. Wilson, 1942, pp. 740–41; *Franz Kafka, A Chronology and Bibliography*, Houlton, Maine: Bern Porter, 1944; *The Kafka Problem*, New York: New Directions, 1946; "The Art of Kafka," *Yale Review*, Winter, 1949, pp. 365–67; "Light on the Hideous," *New York Herald Tribune*, Aug. 10, 1947, sec. vii, p. 4.

Flores, Kate. "Biographical Note," in A. Flores (ed.), *The Kafka Problem*, pp. 1–19; "The Judgment," *Quarterly Review of Literature*, 1947, Vol. III, No. 4, pp. 382–405.

Florman, Samuel C. *American Criticism of Franz Kafka, 1930–1946*, Columbia Univ., M.A. thesis, 1947.

Fontana, Oskar Maurus. "Nya tyska böcker," *Bonniers Litterära Magasin* (Stockholm), Feb., 1938, pp. 125–35.

Fraenkl, Pavel. "Livsangst i moderne Diktning," *Hedemarkens Amtstidende* (Kongsvinger), May 5, 1951.

Fraiberg, Selma. "Kafka and the Dream," *Partisan Review*, Winter, 1956, Vol. 23, pp. 47–69.

Fraigneux, Maurice. "Kafka, suppliant," *Civitas* (Immensee), Jahrg. 6, 1951, Heft 10, pp. 598–605.

Frank, Waldo. "Homage to Kafka," *The Literary World* (New York), July, 1934, p. 2.

Friedmann, R. "An Analytical Note on the Allegory," *Focus One* (London), 1945, pp. 45–47.

Friedrich, Heinz. "Heinrich von Kleist und Franz Kafka," *Berliner Hefte*, Nov., 1949, Heft 11, pp. 440–49.

Friedrich, Hugo. "Franz Kafka," *Neue Schweizer Rundschau* (Zurich), April, 1930, Vol. 23, pp. 265–69.

Friedrich, O. C. "Der doppeldeutige Franz Kafka," *Prisma* (Munich), 1948, No. 22, pp. 8–9.

Fromm, Erich. *The Forgotten Language,* London: Gollancz, 1952, pp. 213–24.

Fuchs, Rudolf. Rev. of Brod's *Franz Kafka, eine Biographie, Internationale Literatur,* April, 1938, pp. 119–21; "Social Awareness," in A. Flores (ed.), *The Kafka Problem,* pp. 247–53.

Furst, Norbert. *Die offenen Geheimtüren Franz Kafkas,* Heidelberg: W. Rothe, 1956.

Gabel, Joseph. "Kafka romancier de l'aliénation," *Critique* (Paris), Nov., 1953, Vol. 9, pp. 949–60.

Galinsky, Hans. *Deutsches Schrifttum der Gegenwart in der englischen Kritik der Nachkriegszeit (1919–1935),* Munich: Max Hueber, 1930, pp. 265 ff.

Gándara, Carmen R. L. de. *Kafka o el pájaro y la jaula,* Buenos Aires: El Ateneo, 1944.

Gibian, George. "Dichtung und Wahrheit: Three Versions of Reality in Franz Kafka," *German Quarterly,* Jan., 1957, Vol. 30, pp. 20–31.

Giesekus, Waltraud. *Franz Kafkas Tagebücher,* Bonn Univ., dissertation, 1954.

Girard, A. "Kafka et le problème du Journal Intime," *Critique* (Paris), June, 1946, Vol. I, No. 1, pp. 23–32.

Girard, René. "Franz Kafka et ses critiques," *Symposium* (Syracuse, N.Y.), May, 1953, Vol. 7, pp. 34–44.

Glaser, Hermann. "Franz Kafkas 'Auf der Galerie,'" in *Interpretationen Moderner Prosa,* ed. by Fachgruppe Deutsch-Geschichte im Bayerischen Philologenverband, Frankfurt: Verlag Moritz Diesterweg, 1957 (new ed.), pp. 40–48.

Glaser, Martha. "Dichtung am Rande Christentums," *Zeitwende* (Munich), Feb. 15, 1952, Vol. 23, pp. 528–37.

Glicksberg, Charles I. "Nihilism in Contemporary Literature," *Nineteenth Century*, Oct., 1948, Vol. CXLIV, pp. 214–22; "Art and Disease," *Nineteenth Century*, March, 1949, Vol. CXLV, pp. 180–90.

Göthberg, Lennart. "En Framsynt," *Stockholm Tidningen*, June 7, 1945.

Goldschmidt, H. L. "Key to Kafka," *Commentary* (New York), Aug., 1949, Vol. 8, pp. 129–38.

Gómez, Carlos Alberto. "El hombre Kafka," *Sur* (Buenos Aires), March–April, 1954, No. 227, pp. 23–30.

González Paredes, Ramón. "El mundo de Franz Kafka," *Revista Nacional de Cultura* (Caracas), May–June, 1954, Vol. XVI, No. 104, pp. 75–89.

Goodman, Paul. *Kafka's Prayer*, New York: Vanguard, 1947.

Gordon, Caroline. "Notes on Hemingway and Kafka," *Sewanee Review*, Spring, 1949, Vol. 57, pp. 215–26, rep. in C. Gordon and A. Tate (eds.), *House of Fiction*, New York: Scribner, 1950.

Goth, Trudy. "Kafka nella musica di Gottfried von Einem," *La Scala* (Milan), Oct., 1953, No. 47, pp. 24–26.

Gravier, Maurice. "Strindberg et Kafka," *Etudes Germaniques*, 1953, 8e. Année, pp. 118–40.

Gray, Ronald. *Kafka's Castle*, Cambridge Univ. Press, 1956.

Greenberg, Clement. "The Jewishness of Franz Kafka," *Commentary* (New York), April, 1955, Vol. 19, pp. 320–24.

Gregory, Horace. Rev. of *The Trial*, *New York Herald Tribune Books*, Oct. 24, 1937, p. 7.

Grenzmann, Wilhelm. *Dichtung und Glaube. Probleme und Gestalten der deutschen Gegenwartsliteratur*, Bonn: Athenäum-Verlag, 1950, pp. 63–82; *Deutsche Dichtung der Gegenwart*, Frankfurt: Menck Verlag, 1953, pp. 335–40.

Groethuysen, Bernard. Int. to *Le Procès*, French translation of *The Trial*, Paris: Gallimard, 1933; "A propos de Kafka," *Nouvelle Revue Française*, April 1, 1933, pp. 588–606; "Apropos of Kafka," *Quarterly Review of Literature*, 1945, Vol. II, No. 3, pp. 237–49; "The Endless Labyrinth," in A. Flores (ed.), *The Kafka Problem*, pp. 376–90.

Grüntner, Rainer. "Beitrag zur Kafka-Deutung," *Deutscher Merkur* (Baden-Baden), Jahrg. 4, 1950, No. 3, pp. 278–87; "Kafka in der englischen und amerikanischen Kritik," *Literarische Deutschland* (Heidelberg), Jahrg. 2, 1951, No. 12, p. 6.

Gürster, Eugen. "Das Weltbild Franz Kafkas," *Hochland*, Jahrg. 44, April, 1952, pp. 326–37.

Gütling, Alois. "Erinnerungen an Franz Kafka," *Prager Nachrichten* (Gräfelfing/München), Jahrg. II, Oct. 1, 1951, No. 10, pp. 3–5.

Guignard, R. "Romanciers allemands contemporains. IX. Les Romans de Kafka," *Revue de Cours et Conferences*, Feb. 28, 1933, 34 Année, 1 Ser., No. 6, pp. 563–76.

H., L. "Die Wirklichkeit der neuen Dichtung: Meditationen über ein Thema von Kafka," *Begegnung* (Koblenz), 1949, Vol. 4, Heft 10, pp. 314–15.

H——g, O. "Gåtan Kafka," *Dagens Nyheter* (Stockholm), Dec. 30, 1949; "Den intressanta Kafka," *Dagens Nyheter* (Stockholm), Oct. 15, 1946; "Kafka," *Dagbladet* (Oslo), July 19, 1947.

Haas, Willy. "Franz Kafkas Glaube," *Das Tagebuch*, Jahrg. 10, June 15, 1929, Heft 24, p. 994; "Über Franz Kafka," *Literarische Welt*, Jahrg. 5, Aug. 30, Sept. 6 and 13, 1929, pp. 3–4, 5–6, 7; *Gestalten der Zeit*, Berlin: Gustav Kiepenheuer Verlag, 1930, pp. 172–99; "Prague in 1912," *Virginia Quarterly Review*, Summer, 1948, pp. 409–17.

Hahn, Ludwig. "Franz Kafkas 'Der Kübelreiter,'" in *Interpretationen Moderner Prosa*, ed. by Fachgruppe Deutsch-Geschichte im Bayerischen Philologenverband, Frankfurt: Verlag Moritz Diesterweg, 1957 (new ed.), pp. 49–54.

Hajek, Siegfried. "Franz Kafka: 'Der Nachbar,'" *Der Deutschunterricht* (Stuttgart), Jahrg. 7, 1955, Heft 1, pp. 5–12.

Hall, Vernon. "Kafka, Lessing and Vigny," *Comparative Literature*, Winter, 1949, Vol. I, No. 1, pp. 73–77.

Hardt, Ludwig. "Recollections," in A. Flores (ed.), *The Kafka Problem*, pp. 32–36; "Erinnerung an Kafka," *Die Fähre* (Munich), Jahrg. 2, 1947, pp. 75–78; "Brief an Peter Panter," *Weltbühne*, Jahrg. 22, April 6, 1926, No. 14, pp. 545–46; "Erinnerung an Franz Kafka," *Jüdische Rundschau* (Berlin), June 1, 1934, Vol. 39, p. 4; Rev. of Brod's *Franz Kafka, eine Biographie, Neue Weltbühne*, Jan. 28, 1938, Vol. 33, No. 5, pp. 121–23.

Hartung, Rudolf. "Die Gestalt des Vaters in der modernen Literatur," *Eckart* (Berlin), Oct.–Dec., 1953.

Hecht, M. B. "Unconscious, Yearning and Franz Kafka's Work," *Imago*, April, 1952.

Heiseler, Bernt von. "Sonnenfinsternis," *Zeitwende* (Munich), Jahrg. 23, Jan. 1, 1952, pp. 436–40; *Ahnung und Aussage*, Gütersloh: C. Bertelsmann Verlag, 1952, pp. 232–40.

Heldmann, Werner. *Literarische Form der Parabel und ihre Funktion in Kafkas Dichtung*, Münster Univ., dissertation; *Die Parabel und die parabolischen Erzählformen bei Franz Kafka*, Münster Univ., dissertation, 1953.

Hellenes, Nills. "Franz Kafka," *Dagbladets Kronikk* (Oslo), Dec. 7, 1951.

Heller, Erich. *The Disinherited Mind*, Cambridge: Bowes & Bowes, 1952, Philadelphia: Dufours, 1953, pp. 157–81; "Die Welt Kafkas," *Rundschau* (Hamburg), Jahrg. 3, 1948–49, pp. 120–24; "Die Welt Franz Kafkas," *Hamburger Akademische Rundschau*, Jahrg. III, 1948/49, Heft 2, pp. 120–42.

Hentig, Hans von. Brief rev. of *Der Prozess, Monatsschrift für Kriminalpsychologie und Strafrechtsreform* (Heidelberg), April, 1927, p. 224.

Hering, Gerhard F. "Franz Kafkas *Tagebücher*," *Merkur*, Jahrg. 2, 1948, Heft 1, No. 7, pp. 96–109; "Zur Neuausgabe von Franz Kafkas *Prozess*," *Literarische Deutschland* (Heidelberg), Jahrg. 1, 1950, No. 3, p. 4; "Franz Kafkas Tagebücher," *Deutsche Zeitung* (Stuttgart), Jahrg. 6, 1951, No. 74, p. 15.

Heselhaus, Clemens. "Franz Kafka Erzählenformen," *Deutsche Vierteljahrsschrift für Literaturwissenschaft und Geistesgeschichte*, 1952, Vol. 26, Heft 3, pp. 353–76.

Hesse, Hermann. "Franz Kafka," *Berliner Tageblatt*, 1925, No. 427, p. 3; "Franz Kafkas Nachlass," *Der Lesezirkel* (Zurich), Jahrg. 16, Jan., 1929, No. 5, pp. 61–63; Rev. of Brod's *Franz Kafka, eine Biographie, Nationalzeitung* (Basel), Dec. 5, 1937; Rev. of *The Trial, Die Neue Rundschau*, Jahrg. 42, June, 1935, pp. 664–72.

Hilsbacher, Walter. "Die Widersprüche des Daseins," *Frankfurter Hefte*, Oct., 1952, Vol. 7, pp. 797–99.

Hodin, J. P. "Erinnerungen an Franz Kafka," *Der Monat* (Munich), Jahrg. 1, June, 1949, Heft 8/9, pp. 89–96; "Interview with Dora Dymant," *Die neue Zeitung*, Aug. 18, 1948, p. 1 of the *Feuilleton und Kunstbeilage;* "Memories of Franz Kafka," *Horizon* (London), Jan., 1948, Vol. 17, No. 97, pp. 26–45; *The Dilemma of Being Modern*, London: Routledge, 1956, pp. 3–22.

Hoel, Sigurd. Int. to the Norwegian translation of *The Trial* (*Prossessen*), Oslo: Gyldendal Norsk Forlag, 1953, pp. 5–8.

Hoffmann, Frederick J. "Kafka and Mann," in *Freudianism and the Literary Mind*, Baton Rouge, La.: Louisiana State Univ. Press, 1945, pp. 181–92; "Escape from Father," in A. Flores (ed.), *The Kafka Problem*, pp. 214–46.

Hohoff, Curt. "Franz Kafka. Der verborgene Gott und der einsame Mensch," *Rheinischer Merkur*, Jahrg. 3, 1948, No. 31, pp. 5–6; "Die Botschaft des Kaisers. Franz Kafka als Dichter," *Rheinischer Merkur*, Jahrg. 6, 1951, No. 46, p. 7; *Geist und Ursprung*, Munich: Ehrenwirth, 1954; "Kafka oder Stifter?" *Christ und Welt* (Stuttgart), Jahrg. 2, 1949, No. 34, p. 7.

Holthusen, Hans Egon. *Der unbehauste Mensch*, Munich, 1952.

Hontsch, F. "Gericht und Gnade in der Dichtung Franz Kafkas," *Hochland*, Jahrg. 31, May, 1934, pp. 160–67.

Hubben, William. "Kafkas apokalyptiske budskap," *Vårt Land* (Oslo), Feb. 11, 1948; *Four Prophets of Our Destiny: Kierkegaard, Dostoevsky, Nietzsche, Kafka,* New York: Macmillan, 1952, pp. 129–44.

Hullen, Werner. "Zwischen Angst und Glauben. Die Weltschau Franz Kafkas," *Begegnung* (Koblenz), Jahrg. 6, 1951, Heft 3, pp. 93–95.

Huyghe, René. "Das Zeitalter des Absurden," *Die Quelle* (Urach, Württ.), 1947, Vol. I, No. 1, pp. 6–20.

Ihlenfeld, Kurt. "Anwärter der Gnade," *Evangelische Welt* (Bethel), Jahrg. 6, 1952, pp. 128–29.

Isemann, Bernd. "Der Roman des 20. Jahrhunderts," *Die Schöne Literatur,* Bd. 26, 1925, p. 259.

Jacob, Heinrich Eduard. "Kafka oder die Wahrhaftigkeit," *Der Feuerreiter* (Berlin), Aug.–Sept., 1924, pp. 61–66; "Truth for Truth's Sake," in A. Flores (ed.), *The Kafka Problem,* pp. 53–59.

Jänsson, Knut. "Kafkanoveller," *Dagens Nyheter* (Stockholm), Nov. 12, 1951; "Kafkas Dagböcker," *Dagens Nyheter* (Stockholm), March 29, 1953; "En stor process," *Bonniers Litterära Magasin* (Stockholm), Jan., 1946, p. 67.

Jaffe, Adrian H., and Virgil Scott. Analysis of "In the Penal Colony," *Studies in the Short Story,* New York: Dryden Press, 1949, pp. 468–71.

Jaloux, Edmond. "Franz Kafka," *Excelsior* (Paris), April 28, 1938.

Jancke, Oscar. *Kunst und Reichtum deutscher Prosa,* Munich: R. Piper & Co., 1954, pp. 425–43.

Janouch, Gustav. "Erinnerungen an Franz Kafka," *Neue Rundschau,* Jahrg. 62, Jan.–March, 1951, Heft 1, pp. 49–64; *Gespräche mit Kafka,* Frankfurt: Fischer Verlag, 1951; *Kafka m'a dit,* Paris: Calmann Levy, 1952; *Conversations with Kafka,* London: Verschoyle, New York: F. A. Praeger, 1953.

Jens, Walter. "Franz Kafka, eine vorläufige Analyse seiner Welt und seines Werkes," *Deutsche Universitäts Zeitung* (Göttingen), Jahrg. 6, Jan. 12, 1951, Heft 1, pp. 13–17.

Joachim, Heinz. "Kafka in Musik gesetzt," *Das Musikleben* (Mainz), Jahrg. 5, 1952, Heft 2, p. 54.

Joffe, Adrian. "Franz Kafka et le héros solitaire dans le roman americain contemporain," *Roman* (Paris), March, 1951, No. 2, pp. 142–49.

Johansen, Niels Kaas. "Efteraarets Gaade: Kafka," *Socialdemokraten* (Copenhagen), Sept. 20, 1945.

Jolas, Eugene. "Franz Kafka's Stories and Ascending Romanticism," *Vertical Yearbook,* New York: Gotham Book Mart, 1941, pp. 169–72.

Jonas, Klaus W. "Franz Kafka: An American Bibliography," *Bulletin of*

Bibliography (Boston), Sept.–Dec., 1952, Vol. 20, No. 9, pp. 212–16; Jan.–April, 1953, Vol. 20, No. 10, pp. 231–33.

Jor, Finn. "Det søkende Menneske," *Morgenbladets Kronikk* (Oslo), May 16, 1953.

Kahler, Erich. "Untergang und Übergang der epischen Kuntsform," *Neue Rundschau,* Jahrg. 64, Jan.–March, 1953, Heft 1, pp. 1–44.

Kaiser, Hellmuth. *Franz Kafkas Inferno, Eine psychologische Deutung seiner Strafphantasie,* Vienna: Internationaler Psychoanalytischer Verlag, 1931 (originally published in *Imago,* Feb., 1931, pp. 41–193).

Kaiser, Joachim. "Glück bei Kafka," *Frankfurter Hefte,* April, 1954, Vol. 9, pp. 300–304.

Karpfen, O. M. "Franz Kafka oder Der Durchbruch," *Die Erfüllung* (Vienna-Leipzig), 1934–35, Heft 1.

Kassner, Rudolf. "Stil und Gesicht: Swift-Gogol-Kafka," *Merkur,* Jahrg. 8, 1954, Heft 8, No. 78, pp. 737–52, 834–45.

Kauf, Robert. "Once Again—Kafka's 'Report to an Academy,'" *Modern Language Quarterly,* Dec., 1954, Vol. 15, pp. 359–66.

Kazin, Alfred. "Kafka e il dolore del secolo," *Ponte* (Florence), Oct., 1947, pp. 899–904.

Kelly, John. "Franz Kafka's *Trial* and the Theology of Crisis," *Southern Review,* Spring, 1940, pp. 748–66; "*The Trial* and the Theology of Crisis," in A. Flores (ed.), *The Kafka Problem,* pp. 151–71.

Kemp, Friedhelm. "Entwicklung eines Negativs, Zum Beginn der deutschen Ausgabe von F. Kafkas Werken," *Die Neue Zeitung,* Nov. 11, 1950, pp. 24–29.

Kemp, Robert. "Qui était Franz Kafka?" *Les Nouvelles Littéraires* (Paris), Nov. 22, 1945.

Kerkhoff, Emmy. "Franz Kafka," *Levende Talen. Tijdschrift voor Sonderbruck,* Dec., 1953, No. 172, 21 pp.

Klossowski, Pierre. "Introduction au *Journal Intime,*" *Cahiers du Sud* (Marseilles), March–April, 1945, Vol. XXII, pp. 148–60; "Kafka Nihiliste?" *Critique* (Paris), Nov., 1948, pp. 963–75.

König, Gerd. *Franz Kafkas Erzählungen und kleine Prosa,* Univ. of Tübingen, dissertation, 1954.

Kopke, Carlos Burlamaqui. *Fronteiras estranhas,* São Paulo: Liv. Martins, 1946.

Korst, Marianne Ruth. *Die Beziehung zwischen Held und Gegenwelt in Franz Kafkas Romanen,* Univ. of Marburg, dissertation, 1953.

Kraft, Werner. "Über den Tod, Zu Franz Kafkas 'Traum,'" *Der Morgen* (Berlin), Jahrg. 11, 1935, pp. 81–83; "Über Franz Kafkas 'Elf Sohne,'" *Die Schildgenossen* (Augsburg), XII, 2/3, pp. 120–32; "Kafka un. d.

Religiöse," *Die Fähre* (Munich), Jahrg. 2, 1947, pp. 13–17; (Berlin), Jahrg. 4, 1949, Heft 22/23, p. 8; "Franz Kafkas Erzählung 'Das Ehepaar,'" *Die Wandlung* (Heidelberg), Jahrg. 4, 1949, Heft 2, pp. 155–60.

Krell, Max. Rev. of *The Stoker, Die Neue Rundschau*, Jahrg. 28, Jan.–June, 1917, pp. 270–77.

Kronenberger, Louis. Rev. of *The Trial, New York Times*, Oct. 24, 1937, p. 8.

Kyler, Ingrid E. *The Pilgrimage of Franz Kafka*, Columbia Univ., M.A. thesis, 1948.

L., E. "Franz Kafka, Gibs auf!" *Trivium* (Zurich), Jahrg. 9, 1951, Heft 2, pp. 131–32.

Lancelotti, Mario A. *El universo de Franz Kafka*, Buenos Aires: Argos, 1950.

Landsberg, Paul L. "Franz Kafka," *L'Esprit*, Sept., 1938, pp. 672–84; "Kafka and 'The Metamorphosis,'" *Quarterly Review of Literature*, 1945, Vol. II, No. 3, pp. 228–36; "The Metamorphosis," in A. Flores (ed.), *The Kafka Problem*, pp. 122–33; *Problèmes du Personnalisme*, Paris: Editions du Seuil, 1952, pp. 83–98.

Landsberger, Fritz. "Franz Kafka" (Rev. of *Amerika*), *Neue Rundschau*, Jahrg. 40, Oct., 1929, pp. 574–75.

Lavrin, Janko. "Franz Kafka," *Review 43* (London), 1943, Vol. I, No. 1, pp. 8–12.

Lecomte, Marcel. "Le plus proche village," *Cahiers du Sud* (Marseilles), March–April, 1945, Vol. XXII, p. 147.

Ledgard, Rodolfo. "La realidad de Franz Kafka," *Tres* (Lima, Peru), March–June, 1941, pp. 84–91.

Léger, François. "De Job a Kafka," *Cahiers du Sud* (Marseilles), March–April, 1945, Vol. XXII, pp. 161–65.

Lehmann, John. *New Writing in Europe*, London: Pelican Books, 1940, pp. 58–59.

Lennartz, Franz. *Die Dichter unserer Zeit*, Stuttgart: Kroner, 1952, pp. 233 ff.

Lenz, Hermann. "Franz Kafka und die 'Mächte,'" *Weltstimmen* (Stuttgart), Jahrg. 18, 1949, Heft 12, pp. 1–8.

Lerner, Max. "Franz Kafka and the Human Voyage," *Saturday Review of Literature*, June 7, 1941, pp. 3–4 ff., and later in *Ideas for the Ice Age*, New York: Viking, 1941, pp. 143–51; "The Human Voyage," in A. Flores (ed.), *The Kafka Problem*, pp. 38–46.

Lewin, B. D. Rev. of the *Diaries, Psychoanalytic Quarterly*, 1949, Vol. 18, No. 1, pp. 97–98.

Li, Chu-Tsing. *Franz Kafka's Theory of Literature*, State Univ. of Iowa, M.A. thesis, 1949.

Linde, Ebbe. "Drömstilen hos Strindberg og Kafka," *Bonniers Litterära Magasin* (Stockholm), Nov., 1946, pp. 760–65.

Linke, Lilo. Rev. of *America, Life and Letters* (London), Nov., 1938, pp. 99–100.

Lion, Ferdinand. *Die Geburt der Aphrodite*, Heidelberg: W. Rothe, 1955.

Litterair Paspoort, Franz Kafkanummer, Aug.–Sept., 1949.

Loeblowitz-Lennard, Henry. "Some Leitmotifs in Franz Kafka's Works Psychoanalytically Explored," *University of Kansas City Review*, Winter, 1946, Vol. 13, No. 2, pp. 115–18.

Lührsen, Hans Detlef. "Franz Kafka. Einführung und Bibliographie," *Europa-Archiv* (Frankfurt), Jahrg. 5, 1950, pp. 3527–34.

Lüth, P. E. H. "Kafka und die Zeit," *Der Bogen* (Wiesbaden), Jahrg. 2, 1947, No. 1, pp. 22–24.

Luke, F. D. "Kafka's 'Die Verwandlung,'" *Modern Language Review*, April, 1951, Vol. 46, pp. 232–45.

Lundkvist, Artur. "Gide dramatiserer Kafka," *Vi* (Stockholm), April 5, 1947.

MacAfee, Helen. Rev. of *The Trial*, *Yale Review*, Winter, 1938, p. viii.

Madden, William A. "A Myth of Mediation: Kafka's 'Metamorphosis,'" *Thought* (New York), Summer, 1951, Vol. 26, No. 101, pp. 246–66.

Magny, Claude-Edmonde. "Kafka o la objetivación de lo absurdo," *Sur* (Buenos Aires), April, 1941, pp. 15–38; "The Objective Depiction of Absurdity," *Quarterly Review of Literature*, 1945, Vol. II, No. 3, pp. 211–27; *Les sandales d'Empédocle*, Neuchâtel: Baconniere, 1945, and in A. Flores (ed.), *The Kafka Problem*, pp. 75–96.

Maier, Anna. *Franz Kafka und Robert Musil als Vertreter der ethischen Richtung des modernen Romans*, Univ. of Vienna, dissertation, 1949.

Maier, Hansgeorg. "Franz Kafka: Nachruhm und Schicksal seines Werks," *Die Zeit* (Hamburg), Jahrg. 6, 1951, No. 4, p. 4.

Maione, Italo. *Franz Kafka*, Naples: Libreria Scientifica Editrice, 1952.

Mallea, Eduardo. "Introducción al mundo de Franz Kafka," *Sur* (Buenos Aires), Dec., 1937, pp. 7–37 (included as "Alejamiento de Franz Kafka" in *El Sayal y la Púrpura*, Buenos Aires: Editorial Losada, 1941).

Mann, Klaus. "Franz Kafka," *Neue Weltbühne*, Aug. 12, 1937, Vol. 33, No. 33, pp. 1030–33; Preface to *Amerika*, Norfolk, Conn.: New Directions, 1940, pp. vii–xviii.

Mann, Thomas. "Verjüngende Bücher," *Magdeburger Zeitung*, 1926, No. 249; Brief note in "Homage to Franz Kafka," *The Literary World* (New York), July, 1934, p. 1; "Homage" (in *The Castle*), New York: Knopf, 1941 (2nd ed.), pp. v–xvi.

Marcuse, Ludwig. "Franz Kafka," *Hannoverischer Kurier*, 1928, 84/85 (Literarische Beilage).

Margeson, John. "Franz Kafka, A Critical Problem," *University of Toronto Quarterly*, Oct., 1948, Vol. 18, pp. 30–40.

Martínez Estrada, Ezequiel. "Acepción literal del mito en Kafka," *Babel* (Santiago de Chile), Año XI, 1950, Vol. 13, pp. 24–28; "Intento de señalar los bordes del 'Mundo' de Kafka," *La Nación* (Buenos Aires), May 14, 1944, Sec. II, p. 1; "Intuition," in A. Flores (ed.), *The Kafka Problem*, pp. 348–53.

Martini, Fritz. *Das Wagnis der Sprache*, Stuttgart: Klatt, 1954, pp. 287–335.

Mauer, Otto. "Kafka post festum," *Wort und Wahrheit* (Freiburg), Jahrg. 6, April, 1951, pp. 300–301; "Franz Kafka," *Wort und Wahrheit* (Freiburg), Jahrg. 2, 1948, No. 2.

Mazzuchetti, Lavinia. "Franz Kafka e il novecentismo," *Libri dei Giorno*, Jan., 1927, pp. 9–10.

Mehring, Walter. *The Lost Library*, London: Secker & Warburg, 1951.

Meidinger-Geise, Inge. "Franz Kafka und die junge Literatur," *Die Erlanger Universität*, Jahrg. 5, 1951, No. 6, pp. 1–6, and *Welt und Wort* (Tübingen), Jahrg. 7, June, 1952, Heft 6, pp. 189–94.

Mendelssohn, Peter de. "Fünf Tage Kafka. Ein Unvorgesehener. Theater und seine Gesetzmässigkeit," *Die neue Zeitung* (Munich), 1950, No. 96.

Mennemeier, F. N. "Der paradoxe Kafka," *Frankfurter Allgemeine Zeitung*, 1950, No. 11.

Meyerhoff, H. "Kafka in Amerika," *Neues Europa* (Hanover), Jahrg. 2, 1947, Heft 24, p. 32.

Micha, René. "Le fantastique kafkaien sur le plan de l'art," *L'Arche* (Paris), June, 1946, No. 16, pp. 43–50; "Une explication nouvelle de l'oeuvre de Kafka: devant le labyrinthe du château de Prague et celui des coutumes bureaucratiques," *Figaro Littéraire*, Feb. 5, 1949, 4 Année, No. 146, p. 6.

Michael, Wolfgang. "The Human Simian," *The Library Chronicle* (Philadelphia), 1952–53, Vol. 19, No. 1, pp. 35–44.

Milch, Werner. "Der deutsche Roman auf neuen Wegen," *Neue Auslese* (Munich), Jahrg. 2, Dec., 1947, Heft 12, pp. 16–19.

Molitor, Jan (Andrée van Santen). *Asmodai in Praag. Franz Kafka, zijn tidj en Werk*, 's Graveland: De Driehoek (Paria Reeks), 1950.

Monserrat, Santiago. "Franz Kafka y el oscuro presente," in *Interpretación histórica del Quijote*, Edit. Facultad de Filosofía y Humanidades, Universidad Nacional de Córdoba, Córdoba (Argentina), 1956.

Montano, L. "The Unveiling of Kafka (a Note on H. Tauber's *Franz Kafka*)," *Focus One* (London), 1945, pp. 57–59.

Montenegro, Ernesto. "El realismo mágico de Kafka," *Babel* (Santiago de Chile), Año XI, 1950, Vol. 13, pp. 50–55.

Motekat, Helmut. "Franz Kafkas 'Ein Landartz,' " *Interpretationen Moderner*

Prosa, ed. by Fachgruppe Deutsch-Geschichte im Bayerischen Philologenverband, Frankfurt: Verlag Moritz Diesterweg, 1957 (new ed.), pp. 7–27.

Mühlberger, Josef. *Hugo von Hoffmannsthal—Franz Kafka,* Esslingen: Bechtle Verlag, 1953, pp. 31–70; "Zeitungsstimmen über Kafka," *Witiko,* 1928, Vol. I, No. 4, p. 349; "Franz Kafka," *Witiko,* 1928, Vol. I, No. 2, pp. 105–8; "Sudetendeutsche Dichtung 1930," *Witiko,* 1930, Vol. III, No. 1, pp. 34–39.

Mühlher, Robert. *Dichtung der Krise,* Vienna: Verlag Herold, 1951, pp. 438–43.

Muir, Edwin. *Transition, Essays on Literature and Society,* New York: Viking, 1954, pp. 120–24; "Pornamka k Franzi Kafkovi," in *Franz Kafka a Praha,* Prague: V. Zikes, 1947, pp. 35–39; "Note on Franz Kafka," *The Bookman* (New York), Nov., 1930, pp. 235–41; "Introductory Note" (to *The Castle*), New York: Knopf, 1930, pp. v–xi; "Introductory Note" (to *The Great Wall of China*), London: Secker, 1933; "Franz Kafka," *The Bookman* (London), 1933–34, Vol. 85, pp. 139–40; "Franz Kafka," *Life and Letters* (London), June, 1934, pp. 341–51; "Franz Kafka," in *A Franz Kafka Miscellany,* New York: Twice A Year Press, 1940, pp. 55–56.

Munnich, Horst Richard. "Der Dichter Franz Kafka," *Die Wochenpost* (Stuttgart), Jahrg. 2, 1947, Heft 23, p. 5, rep. from *Der Zwiebelfisch,* Jahrg. 25, 1946, Heft 1, pp. 16–21.

Musil, Robert. Rev. of *Meditation* and *The Stoker, Die Neue Rundschau,* Jahrg. 25, July–Dec., 1914, pp. 1166–72.

Nadolny, Burkhard. "Zerrühmter Kafka," *Hier und Heute* (Frankfurt), Feb. 9, 1951, No. 5, p. 16.

Navarro, Oscar. *Kafka, la crisi della fede,* Turin: Taylor, 1949.

Neider, Charles. *The Frozen Sea,* New York: Oxford Univ. Press, 1948, sub. tit. *Kafka: His Mind and Art,* London: Routledge, Kegan Paul, 1949; "Kafka Mirrors Our Uncertainties, Frustrations, Fears," *New York Times Book Review,* Aug. 6, 1945, pp. 6, 30; "Kafka and the Cabalists," *Quarterly Review of Literature,* 1945, Vol. II, No. 3, pp. 250–62; "Two Notes on Franz Kafka," *Rocky Mountain Review,* Winter, 1946, pp. 90–95; "The Cabalists," in A. Flores (ed.), *The Kafka Problem,* pp. 398–445.

Nemeth, André. *Kafka ou le mystère juif,* Paris: Jean Vigneau, 1947.

Neumann, Heinz. "Franz Kafka," *Bücherei und Bildung* (Bremen), Jahrg. 3, 1951, pp. 263–65.

Neuse, Werner. "Franz Kafka," *Books Abroad* (Univ. of Oklahoma), Summer, 1935, Vol. 9, pp. 266–68.

Nicholson, Norman. *Man and Literature,* London: Student Christian Movement Press, 1943, pp. 162–78.

Nostiz, Oswalt von. "Das Unzerstörbare," *Rheinischer Merkur,* Jahrg. 6, 1951, No. 2, p. 7.

Oliass, Heinz Günther. "Ein grosser Dichter unseres Zeit," *Der Weg* (Berlin), Jahrg. 4, 1949, Nos. 22–23, p. 8; "Franz Kafka," *Welt und Wort* (Tübingen), 1949, pp. 52–56.

Ong, Walter J. "Kafka's Castle and the West," *Thought* (New York), Sept., 1947, Vol. 22, pp. 439–60.

Paludan, Jacob. "Franz Kafka—*Amerika,*" *Nationaltidende* (Copenhagen), Jan. 16, 1954.

Panter, Peter. "Kafkas Prozess," *Weltbühne,* Jahrg. 22, I, March 9, 1926, No. 10, pp. 383–86; "Auf dem Nachttisch," *Schaubühne oder Weltbühne,* Jan.–June, 1939, p. 337.

Paoli, Rodolfo. "Sulle 'Lettere a Milena,'" *Annali della Facolta di Lettere e Filosofia e di Magistero dell'Università di Cagliari,* 1953.

Parigi, H. "Dino Buzzati und sein Verhältnis zu Franz Kafka," *Prisma* (Munich), 1948, Heft 17, pp. 26–29.

Parry, Idris F. "Kafka and Gogol," *German Life and Letters,* Jan., 1953, Vol. 7, pp. 141–45; Rev. of *Letters to Milena, The Listener* (London), Dec. 17, 1953, Vol. 50, No. 1294, p. 1057, col. 2; Rev. of *The Castle, The London Magazine,* May, 1954, Vol. I, No. 4.

Pascal, Roy. *The German Novel,* Univ. of Toronto Press, 1956, pp. 215–57.

Paulsen, Wolfgang. "Franz Kafka," *Monatshefte* (Univ. of Wisconsin), Dec., 1937, pp. 373–88.

Pearce, Donald. "Dante and *The Castle,*" *Northern Review* (Montreal), June–July, 1947, pp. 2–8.

Petry, Walter. "Franz Kafka oder Bemerkungen zu Prinzipien der Prosa," *Die neue Bücherschau,* Jahrg. 6, F. 4, Schr. 1, pp. 14–20.

Peut, A. "Der Moralist des Nichts: Franz Kafka, ein 'Heiliger vor den Toren,'" *Sonntagsblatt* (Hamburg), Jahrg. 6, 1953, No. 25, p. 7.

Pfeiffer, Johannes. "Franz Kafka: 'Eine kleine Frau,'" in *Wege zur Erzählkunst,* Hamburg: Wittig, 1953, pp. 108–16.

Phillips, Wm. Rev. of *The Trial, The Nation* (New York), Oct. 23, 1937, p. 448.

Poggioli, Renato. "Mitologia di Kafka," *Solaria* (Florence), 1934–35, Vol. 9, p. 10; *Pietri di Paragone,* Florence: Parenti, 1939, pp. 161–73; "Kafka and Dostoyevsky," in A. Flores (ed.), *The Kafka Problem,* pp. 97–107.

Politzer, Heinz. "Nachwort" (to *Vor dem Gesetz*), Berlin: Schocken Verlag, 1934, pp. 75–80; "Franz Kafka (Versuch einer Deutung der Anekdote

'Gibs auf.' mit Abdruck der Anekdote)," *Jüdische Welt-Rundschau* (Jerusalem), Jahrg. 13, June 9, 1939, p. 5; "Franz Kafka und diese Zeit," *Der Turm* (Vienna), Jahrg. 2, 1946–47, pp. 66–69, and *Neues Europa* (Hanover), Jahrg. 2, 1947, Heft 10, pp. 28–33; "Problematik und Probleme der Kafka-Forschung," *Monatshefte*, Jahrg. 42, 1950, pp. 272–80; "Jenseits von Joyce und Kafka. Zu Hermann Brochs Die Schuldlosen," *Neue Rundschau*, Jahrg. 63, Jan.–March, 1952, Heft 1, pp. 152–59; "Recent Trends in Kafka Criticism," *Books Abroad* (Univ. of Oklahoma), Spring, 1953, Vol. 27, No. 2, pp. 379–80; "Franz Kafka's Letter to His Father," *Germanic Review*, Oct., 1953, Vol. 28, pp. 165–79; "Prague and the Origins of R. M. Rilke, F. Kafka and F. Werfel," *Modern Language Quarterly*, March, 1955, Vol. 16, No. 1.

Pongs, Hermann. "Kleist und Kafka," *Welt und Wort* (Munich), Jahrg. 7, Nov., 1952, Heft 11, pp. 379–80; *Im Umbruch der Zeit*, Göttingen: Göttinger Verlagsanstalt, 1952, pp. 67–87.

Powolny. "Hinweis auf Franz Kafka," *Die Lücke* (Heidelberg), 1948, Heft 5–6, p. 31.

Praag, S. van. "Franz Kafka," *Nieuwe Gids* (The Hague), Jahrg. 45, 1, 1930, pp. 688–98.

Pratt, Audrey E. (McKim). *Franz Kafka und sein Vater: das Verhältnis der Beiden und dessen Einwirkung auf Kafkas Werk*, McGill Univ. (Montreal), thesis, 1949.

Prigge-Kruhoeffer, Maria. "Eine andere Welt," *Die Literatur*, Oct., 1928, pp. 19–21.

Pulver, Max. *Erinnerungen an eine europäische Zeit*, Zurich: Orell Füssli Verlag, 1953, pp. 50–57.

Quintero Alvárez, Alberto. "La fatalidad en Kafka" (Rev. of *The Metamorphosis*), *Taller* (Mexico City), April, 1939, pp. 37–39.

Rahv, Philip. "The Hero as Lonely Man," *The Kenyon Review*, Winter, 1939, pp. 60–74; "Death of Ivan Ilyich and Joseph K.," *Southern Review*, Summer, 1939, pp. 174–85; Rev. of *Amerika*, *The Nation* (New York), Oct. 26, 1940, p. 396; Exegetical Notes to "Investigation of a Dog," "The Great Wall of China," and "The Giant Mole," in Franz Kafka, *The Great Wall of China*, New York: Schocken, 1946, pp. 309–15.

Raine, Kathleen. "A Note on Kafka," *Focus One* (London), 1945, pp. 44–45.

Rajan, B. "Kafka, A Comparison with Rex Warner," *Focus One* (London), 1945, pp. 7–14.

Rang, Bernhard. "Franz Kafka, Versuch eines Hinweises," *Die Schildgenossen* (Augsburg), XII, 2/3, pp. 107–19.

Reed, Eugene E. "Moral Polarity in Kafka's *Der Prozess* and *Das Schloss*,"

Monatshefte (Univ. of Wisconsin), Nov., 1954, Vol. 46, No. 6, pp. 317–24.

Reichert-Heidt, Vally. "Sühne und Befreiung: Wesen und Werk Kafkas," *Die Osterr. Furche*, 1949, No. 23.

Reichmann, Peter. "Franz Kafka and New Trends in Europe," *Canada Bookman*, June, 1939, pp. 17–19.

Reiss, H. S. "Franz Kafka," *German Life and Letters*, April, 1948, Vol. I, No. 3, pp. 186–96; "Franz Kafka's Conception of Humour," *Modern Language Review*, Oct., 1949, Vol. 44, pp. 534–42; "Zwei Erzählungen Franz Kafkas 'Der Schlag ans Hoftor' und 'Die Prüfung,'" *Trivium* (Zurich), Jahrg. 8, 1950, Heft 3, pp. 218–42; *Franz Kafka*, Heidelberg: Schneider, 1952; "Kafka's *Letters to Milena*," *German Life and Letters*, Oct., 1953, Vol. 7, pp. 44–47; "Zum stil zur Komposition in der deutschen Prosa Erzählung der Gegenwart," *Studium Generale*, Jahrg. 8, 1955, Heft 1, pp. 19–31; *Franz Kafka, eine Betrachtung seines Werkes*, Heidelberg: Verlag Lambert Schneider, 1956.

Revol, Enrique L. *Al pie de las letras*, Buenos Aires: Reunión, 1949.

Robert, Marthe. *Introduction à la lecture de Kafka*, Paris: Edition du Sagittaire, 1946; "Zu Franz Kafkas Fragment 'In Our Synagogue,'" *Merkur*, Jahrg. 2, 1948, Heft 1, No. 7, pp. 113–14; "La lecture de Kafka," *Temps Modernes* (Paris), Année 8, 1952, Nos. 84–85, pp. 646–78; "Dora Dymants Erinnerungen an Kafka," *Merkur*, Jahrg. 7, Sept., 1953, Heft 67; "Les 'Tagebücher' de Franz Kafka," *Temps Modernes* (Paris), Dec., 1951, Année 7; Int. to French ed. of *Diaries*, Paris: Grasset, 1954, pp. v–xxi; "Notes inédites de Dora Dymant," *Evidences* (Paris), Nov., 1952, 4th Year, No. 28, pp. 28–42; "Mes parents ne sont pas venus," *Evidences* (Paris), June–July, 1953, 5th Year, No. 33, pp. 7–13.

Rocco, Enrico. "Uno che risuscita: Franz Kafka," *Pegaso* (Florence), Jan., 1933, pp. 108–12.

Rochefort, Robert. *Kafka; ou, L'irréductible espoir*, Paris: R. Julliard, 1947.

Rohner, Wolfgang. *Franz Kafkas Werkgestaltung*, Freiburg Univ., dissertation, 1950.

Rommerskirch, Erich. "Prozess gegen Gott," *Geist und Leben* (Würzburg), Jahrg. 22, 1949, pp. 81–90.

Roque da Costa, Constancio. "Franz Kafka visto por um oriental," *Atlantico* (Lisbon), 1949, Ser. No. 2, pp. 89–92.

Rosenfeld, Paul. Rev. of *Amerika*, *Saturday Review of Literature*, Oct. 26, 1940, p. 18; Rev. of *A Franz Kafka Miscellany*, *Saturday Review of Literature*, Feb. 8, 1941, p. 20.

Rothman, N. L. Rev. of *The Trial*, *Saturday Review of Literature*, Oct. 30, 1937, p. 19.

Rougemont, Denis de. *Les personnes du drame,* New York: Pantheon Books, Inc., 1945, pp. 105–26.

Rubinstein, William C. "A Hunger Artist," *Monatshefte* (Univ. of Wisconsin), Jan., 1952, Vol. 44, pp. 13–19; "A Report to an Academy," *Modern Language Quarterly,* Dec., 1952, Vol. 13, pp. 372–76.

Russell, Francis. *Three Studies in Twentieth Century Obscurity,* Aldington, Ashford, Kent: The Hand and Flower Press, 1954, pp. 45–65.

Rutz, H. "Gottfried von Eonems opera naar Franz Kafkas roman," *Algemeen Handelsblad,* Feb. 7, 1953.

S., C. R. "Das Gespenst Gottes," *Basler Nachrichten,* Aug. 19, 1951; "Vom möglichen Ende der Verzweiflung," *Basler Nachrichten,* April 8, 1951; "Zwei Bände Kafka," *Basler Nachrichten,* Dec. 4, 1953.

Sackville-West, Edward. Rev. of *The Trial, The Spectator* (London), July 23, 1937, p. 152; Rev. of *America, The Spectator* (London), Oct. 7, 1938, p. 576.

Saillet, Maurice. "Franz Kafka ou la traversée de la nuit," *Cahiers du Sud* (Marseilles), Oct., 1938, Vol. 25, pp. 721–25.

Samuel, Richard, and R. Hinton Thomas. *Expressionism in German Life, Literature and the Theatre (1910–1924),* Cambridge (England): Heffer, 1939, pp. 139–44.

Sarraute, Nathalie. "De Dostoievski a Kafka," *Temps Modernes* (Paris), Oct., 1947, Année 3, No. 25, pp. 664–85.

Saurat, Denis. "Homage to Kafka," *The Literary World* (New York), July, 1934, p. 3; *Modernes,* Paris: Denoël et Steele, 1935; "A Note on *The Castle,*" in A. Flores (ed.), *The Kafka Problem,* pp. 181–83.

Savage, D. S. "Franz Kafka: Faith and Vocation," *Focus One* (London), 1945, pp. 14–26, and in A. Flores (ed.), *The Kafka Problem,* pp. 319–36.

Schab, Günther. "Kafkas dramatisierter Prozess," *Die Erzählung* (Constance), Jahrg. 4, 1950, Heft 9, p. 50.

Schaefer, Georg. "Franz Kafka," *Literarische Blätter der Kölnischen Volkzeitung,* Sept. 15, 1927, p. 439.

Schaufelberger, Fritz. "Kafkas Prosafragmente," *Trivium* (Zurich), Jahrg. 7, 1949, Heft 1, pp. 1–15.

Scherer, René. Rev. of *The Great Wall of China, Confluences,* Jan.–Feb., 1945, pp. 109–10.

Schneller, Christian. "Bekenntnis zu Franz Kafka," *Deutsche Beiträge* (Munich), Jahrg. 4, 1950, Heft 3, pp. 193–98.

Schönwiese, Ernst. "Das Werk Franz Kafkas," *Der Standpunkt,* Jan. 5, 1951.

Schoeps, Hans Joachim. "Theologische Motive in der Dichtung Franz Kafkas," *Neue Rundschau,* Jahrg. 62, Jan.–March, 1951, Heft 1, pp.

21–37; "Die geistige Gestalt Kafkas," *Die Christliche Welt,* Jahrg. 43, Aug.–Sept., 1929, Nos. 16–17, pp. 761–71; On *The Great Wall of China, Der Morgen* (Berlin), Jahrg. 6, 1930, Heft 3, pp. 219–31; "Das verlorene Gesetz. Zur religiösen Existenz Franz Kafkas," *Der Morgen* (Berlin), Jahrg. 10, 1934, pp. 71–75; *Gestalten an der Zeitenwende,* Berlin: Vortrupp Verlag, 1936; "The Tragedy of Faithlessness," in A. Flores (ed.), *The Kafka Problem,* pp. 287–97; "Aufzeichnungen aus dem Nachlass von Franz Kafka," *Die Literarische Welt* (Berlin), Jahrg. 6, 1930, No. 31, p. 3.

Schouten, J. H. "Franz Kafka," *Duitse Kroniek* (Amsterdam), 1952, No. 4, pp. 91–97.

Schrade, Wolfgang. "Frisch 'Max' und Kafka auf Berliner Bühnen," *Neue Literarische Welt,* Jahrg. 4, 1953, No. 11, p. 10.

Schwartzmann, Félix. "Fantasía y realidad en Kafka," *Babel* (Santiago de Chile), Año XI, 1950, Vol. 13, pp. 61–68.

Scott, Nathan A. *Rehearsals of Discomposure,* New York: King's Crown Press, London: Lehmann, 1952, pp. 11–65.

Seelig, Carl. "Franz Kafka," *Atlantis* (Zurich), 1949, Heft 12, pp. 16–18; "Franz Kafka," *Neue Züricher Zeitung,* April 18, 1928, No. 705.

Seidel, Bruno. "Franz Kafkas Vision des Totalitarismus. Politische Gedanken zu Kafkas Roman *Das Schloss* und George Orwell's *Utopie 1984,*" *Die Besinnung* (Nuremberg), Jahrg. 6, 1951, pp. 11–14.

Seidler, Manfred. *Strukturanalyse der Romane "Prozess" und "Schloss" von Franz Kafka,* Bonn Univ., dissertation, 1953.

Selander, Sten. "Kafka," *Svenska Dagbladet* (Stockholm), April 3, 1946.

Serrano Plaja, Arturo. "Kafka y la segunda consulta del Doctor Negro," *Sur* (Buenos Aires), March, 1949, No. 173, pp. 79–87.

Seyppel, Joachim H. "The Animal Theme and Totemism in Franz Kafka," *Literature & Psychology* (Newsletter of the Conference in Literature and Psychology, Modern Language Assoc.), Sept., 1954, Vol. IV, No. 4, pp. 49–63.

Sherwood, R. E. Rev. of *The Castle, Scribner's,* Dec., 1930, p. 21.

Siebenschein, Hugo. "Prostredi a cas. Ponamky k osbnosti a delu Franze Kafky," in *Franz Kafka a Praha,* Prague: V. Zikes, 1947, pp. 7–24.

Slochower, Harry. "Franz Kafka, Pre-Fascist Exile," in *A Franz Kafka Miscellany,* New York: Twice A Year Press, 1940, pp. 7–30.

Sokel, Walter H. "Kafka's 'Metamorphosis,' Rebellion and Punishment," *Monatshefte* (Univ. of Wisconsin), April–May, 1956, Vol. 48, pp. 203–14.

Solier, René de. "Les Voies de l'inversion," *Les Cahiers de la Pléiade* (Paris), April, 1947, No. 2, pp. 29–32.

Solumsmoen, Odd. "Franz Kafkas dagbøker," *Arbeiderbladet* (Oslo), May 23, 1953.

Spaini, Alberto. Preface to his Italian translation of *The Trial,* Turin: Frassinelli, 1933; "The Trial," in A. Flores (ed.), *The Kafka Problem*, pp. 143–50.

Spann, Meno. "Die beiden Zettel," *Monatshefte*, Nov., 1955, pp. 321–28.

Spector, R. D. "Kafka's 'The Stoker' as Short Story," *Modern Fiction* (Purdue Univ.), May, 1956, Vol. II, No. 2, pp. 80–81.

Spender, Stephen. Rev. of *The Trial, New Republic*, Oct. 27, 1937, p. 347; Rev. of *Amerika, Living Age*, Dec., 1938, Vol. 355, p. 382.

Stallman, Robert W. "The Hunger Artist," *Accent*, Winter, 1948, No. 8, pp. 117–25, rep. in R. W. West and R. W. Stallman (eds.), *Art of Modern Fiction*, New York: Rinehart, 1949, pp. 366–72, and in R. W. Stallman and R. E. Watters (eds.), *Creative Reader*, New York: Ronald, 1954.

Starke, Ottomar. "Kafka und die Illustration," *Neue Literarische Welt*, Jahrg. 4, 1953, No. 9, p. 3.

Starobinski, Jean. "Figure de Franz Kafka," Int. to *La Colonie pénitentiaire*, Paris: Egloff, 1945, pp. 8–67; "Kafka et Dostoievski," *Cahiers du Sud* (Marseilles), 37 Année, 1950, Vol. 32, No. 304, pp. 466–75; "El sueño se hace arquitecto: los interiores de Franz Kafka," *Espacio*, No. 5, pp. 6–7.

Steiner, Franz Baermann. "Aus den Notizen über Kafka," *Merkur*, Jahrg. 8, Jan., 1954, Heft 1, pp. 39–41.

Steinhoff, P. A. "Franz Kafka Dichter," *Aufbau* (Berlin), Jahrg. 3, 1947, pp. 481–87.

Stoessl, Otto. "Erzählende Literatur, behandelt unter anderem *Der Prozess*," *Zeitwende* (Munich), July, 1926, Vol. 2, pp. 94–100.

Stonier, G. W. Rev. of *The Trial, New Statesman & Nation*, July 3, 1937, p. 18; Rev. of *America, New Statesman & Nation*, Oct. 15, 1938, p. 574.

Stroman, B. "Franz Kafka's dagboeken," *Algemeen Handelsblad*, Nov. 1, 1952; "Kafka's brieven aan Milena Jesenska," *Algemeen Handelsblad*, Feb. 21, 1953.

Stromberg, Kyra. "Der Höhepunkt der Gelsenkirchener Festspiele: Kafka's *Prozess*," *Wirtschaft und Erziehung* (Wolfenbüttel), Jahrg. 5, 1950, No. 54, p. 17.

Stumpf, W. "Kafka, Persönlichkeit und geistige Gestalt," *Die Fähre* (Munich), Jahrg. 2, 1947, pp. 387–97; "Franz Kafka," *Die Fähre* (Munich), Jahrg. 3, 1948, Heft 5, pp. 281–84; "Das religiöse Problem in der Dichtung Kafkas," *Orient und Occident* (Leipzig), 1931, Heft 5, pp. 48–63; "Franz Kafka," *Die Furche* (Berlin), 1932, Heft 3; "Franz Kafkas Werdegang," *Die Schildgenossen* (Augsburg), April–May, 1935; "Franz Kafka," *Literarische Revue*, 1949, Vol. III, pp. 281–83.

Sturmann, Manfred. "Franz Kafkas Sendung," *Jüdische Rundschau* (Berlin), March 9, 1928, Vol. 33, No. 20, p. 143; "Franz Kafka und sein Roman

Amerika," *Gemeindeblatt der Israelit. Religionsgemeinde* (Dresden), Feb., 1931, Vol. 7, No. 2.

Süskind, W. E. "Franz Kafka," *Neue Merkur,* Sept., 1924, pp. 1010–14.

Susman, Margarete. "Das Hiob-Problem bei Franz Kafka," *Der Morgen* (Berlin), Jahrg. 5, 1929, Heft 1, pp. 31–49, rep. in *Gestalten und Kreise,* Stuttgart: Diana Verlag, 1943, pp. 348–66.

Sykes, Gerald. Rev. of *The Castle, The Nation* (New York), Oct. 15, 1930, p. 411.

Tauber, Herbert. "Die Aktualität Kafkas," *Weltwoche* (Zurich), Jahrg. 15, 1947, No. 695, p. 5, and *Neue Auslese* (Munich), Jahrg. 2, 1947, pp. 115–17; *Franz Kafka, An Interpretation of His Work,* Yale Univ. Press, 1948; *Franz Kafka, eine Deutung seiner Werke,* Zurich-New York: Oprecht Verlag, 1941.

Taylor, Coley. Rev. of *The Castle, New York Herald Tribune Books,* Sept. 21, 1930, p. 7.

Tedlock, E. W., Jr. "Kafka's Imitation of *David Copperfield,"* *Comparative Literature,* Winter, 1955, Vol. VII, pp. 52–62.

Thiebaut, Marcel. Rev. of *The Castle, Le Jour* (Paris), Oct. 21, 1938.

Thieberger, Friedrich. "Erinnerungen an Franz Kafka," *Eckart* (Berlin), Oct.–Dec., 1953, pp. 49–53.

Thierry, Werner. "Hvad er meningen med Kafka?" *Dansk Tidsskrift for Kultur,* 1950, I, pp. 91–96.

Thomas, R. H. "Franz Kafka and the Religious Aspect of Expressionism," *German Life and Letters,* Oct., 1937, Vol. 2, pp. 42–49.

Thompson, Ralph. Rev. of *The Trial, New York Times,* Oct. 18, 1937, p. 15.

Thurston, Jarvis A. "The Married Couple," in J. A. Thurston (ed.), *Reading Modern Short Stories,* Chicago: Scott, Foresman, and Co., 1955, pp. 371–77.

Tomlinson, K. C. Rev. of *The Castle, Nation and Athenaeum,* May 10, 1930, p. 182.

Tuominen, Mirjam. *Besk brygd betraktelser,* Helsinki: Söderström & Co., 1947.

Tuverlin, Jacques. "Les derniers travaux sur Kafka," *Allemagne d'Aujourdhui* (Paris), 1953, No. 2, pp. 181–86.

Tyler, Parker. "Kafka and the Surrealists," *Accent,* Autumn, 1945, pp. 23–27; "Kafka's and Chaplin's Amerika," *Sewanee Review,* Spring, 1950, Vol. 58, pp. 299–311; "Kafka und die Surrealisten," *Das Lot* (Berlin), 1948, Bd. 2, pp. 75–82.

Ulshöfer, Robert. "Entseelte Wirklichkeit in Franz Kafkas *Verwandlung,"* *Der Deutschunterricht* (Stuttgart), Jahrg. 7, 1955, Heft 1, pp. 27–36.

Urzidil, Johannes. "Meetings with Franz Kafka," *Menorah Journal* (New York), April–June, 1952, Vol. 40, pp. 112–16; "Begeignungen mit Franz Kafka," *Literarische Deutschland* (Heidelberg), Jahrg. 3, 1953, No. 2, p. 3; "Kafka's *Briefe an Milena*," *Neue Literarische Welt*, Jahrg. 4, March 16, 1953, No. 5, p. 6; Rev. of *Tagebücher* and of Max Bense's *Die Theorie Kafkas, Germanic Review,* Oct., 1953, Vol. 28, pp. 235–37; "Franz Kafka," *Das Kunstblatt,* Vol. 8, p. 250; "Franz Kafka, Novelist and Mystic," *Menorah Journal* (New York), Oct.–Dec., 1943, Vol. 31, pp. 273–83; "Personal Notes on Franz Kafka," *Life and Letters* (London), Sept., 1944, pp. 134–40; "Recollections," in A. Flores (ed.), *The Kafka Problem,* pp. 20–24; "Franz Kafka and Prague," *Germanic Review,* April, 1951, Vol. 26, No. 2.

Utitz, Emil. "Vzpominky na Franz Kafka," in *Franz Kafka a Praha,* Prague: V. Zikes, 1947, pp. 25–30.

Uyttersprot, Herman. *Zur Struktur Kafkas "Der Prozess,"* Brussels: Marcel Didier, 1953 (rep. from *Revue des Langues Vivantes,* 1953, Vol. 19, pp. 333–76); *Zur Struktur von Kafkas Romanen,* Brussels: Marcel Didier, 1954 (rep. from *Revue des Langues Vivantes,* 1954, Vol. 20, pp. 367–83); *Beschouwingen over Franz Kafka,* Brussels: De Vlaamse Gids, 1953.

Vasata, Rudolf. "Dickens and Kafka," *The Central European Observer* (London), Feb. 9, 1945, pp. 49–50; "*Amerika* and Charles Dickens," in A. Flores (ed.), *The Kafka Problem,* pp. 134–39.

Vennberg, Karl G. "Franz Kafka," *Forumnytt* (Stockholm), Sept., 1945, No. 5; *Kritiskt 40-tal,* Stockholm: A. Bonnier, 1948.

Verbenne, Pierre. "Franz Kafka," *Dietsche warande en Belfort,* 1938, pp. 387–90.

Vestdijk, Simon. "De kolossale schuld," *Groot Nederland,* March, 1939, pp. 243–60; "Der Prozess van Franz Kafka," in *De Poolsche Ruiter,* Bussum: F. G. Kroonder, 1946, pp. 72–82; "Het genie en zijn profeet," *Muiterij tegen het etmaal II,* 1947, pp. 236–40.

Vietta, Egon. "Franz Kafka und unsere Zeit," *Neue Schweizer Rundschau* (Zurich), Jahrg. 24, July, 1931, pp. 565–77; "The Fundamental Revolution," in A. Flores (ed.), *The Kafka Problem,* pp. 337–47.

Vivas, Eliseo. "Kafka's Distorted Mask," *Kenyon Review,* Winter, 1948, pp. 51–69, and in his *Creation and Discovery,* New York: Noonday Press, 1955, pp. 29–46.

Vogelmann, D. J. "Raigambre y desarraigo de Franz Kafka," *Heredad* (Buenos Aires), Jan.–Feb., 1946, pp. 13–22, and *Babel* (Santiago de Chile), Año XI, 1950, Vol. 13, pp. 36–41; "Datos para una clave de Kafka," *La Nación* (Buenos Aires), April 6 and 20, 1941, Sec. II, p. 3.

Volkening, Ernesto. " 'La Metamorfosis' de Kafka," *Revista de las Indias* (Bogotá), March–May, 1948, pp. 465–75.

Volkmann-Schluck, K. H. "Bewusstsein und Dasein in Kafkas *Prozess*," *Neue Rundschau*, Jahrg. 62, Jan.–March, 1951, Heft 1, pp. 38–48.

Votaw, Albert. "Kafka and Mrs. Blandish," *Horizon* (London), Sept., 1949, Vol. 20, No. 117, pp. 145–60.

Wagner, Marianne. "Franz Kafka," *Der Bücherwurm*, Jahrg. 16, Sept., Heft 10, p. 276.

Wahl, Jean. "Kierkegaard and Kafka," in A. Flores (ed.), *The Kafka Problem*, pp. 262–75; *Esquisse pour une histoire de l'existentialisme, Kafka et Kierkegaard*, Paris: Ed. Club Maintenant, 1947, Paris: Arche, 1949.

Waismann, F. "A Philosopher Looks at Kafka," *Essays in Criticism* (Oxford), April, 1953, Vol. 3, No. 2, pp. 177–90.

Walker, Augusta. "Allegory, A Light Conceit," *Partisan Review*, Fall, 1955, Vol. 22, No. 4, pp. 480–90.

Walser, Martin Johannes. *Beschreibung einer Form. Versuch über die epische Dichtung Franz Kafkas*, Univ. of Tübingen, dissertation, 1952.

Warren, Austin. "Kosmos Kafka," *Southern Review*, Autumn, 1941, pp. 350–65, and in A. Flores (ed.), *The Kafka Problem*, pp. 60–74; *Rage for Order*, Univ. of Chicago Press, 1948.

Warshow, Robert. "Kafka's Failure," *Partisan Review*, April, 1949, Vol. 16, No. 4, pp. 428–31.

Webster, Peter Dow. "Arrested Individualism or the Problem of Joseph K.," *American Imago*, Nov., 1948, Vol. 6, pp. 3–15; "Dies Irae in the Unconscious, or the Significance of Franz Kafka," *College English* (Chicago), Oct., 1950, Vol. 12, No. 1, pp. 9–15.

Weidlé, Wladimir. *Les Abeilles d'Aristée. Essai sur le destin actuel des lettres et des arts*, Paris, 1938, Chap. V, Sec. 4; *Ensayo sobre el destino actual de las letras y las artes* (Spanish translation of the above by Carlos María Reyles), Buenos Aires: Emecé, 1943, pp. 225–36; "The Negative Capability," in A. Flores (ed.), *The Kafka Problem*, pp. 354–62.

Weidner, Walther. "Goethe weniger lebensnotwendig als Kafka," *Die Besinnung* (Nuremberg), 1949, Vol. 4, Nos. 4–5, pp. 147–50.

Weiss, Ernst. "Franz Kafka, Die Tragödie Lebens," *Pariser Tageszeitung*, Oct. 29, 1937; "Bemerkungen zu den Tagebüchern und Briefen Franz Kafkas," *Mass und Wert*, Nov.–Dec., 1937, pp. 319–25; "The Diaries and Letters," in A. Flores (ed.), *The Kafka Problem*, pp. 207–13.

Weiss, T. "The Economy of Chaos," in A. Flores (ed.), *The Kafka Problem*, pp. 363–75.

Wellek, R. Rev. of Brod's *Franz Kafka, eine Biographie*, *Scrutiny*, June, 1938, pp. 88–89.

Weltsch, Felix. "Religiöser Humor bei Franz Kafka," in Max Brod, *Franz Kafkas Glauben und Lehre*, Winterthur: Mondial, Munich: Desch, 1948, pp. 155–92; "Kafkas *Briefe an Milena*," *Der Monat* (Munich), Jahrg. 5, 1953, Heft 57, pp. 311–17; "Freiheit und Schuld in Kafkas *Der Prozess*," *Jüdischer Almanach auf das Jahr 5687* (Prague), 1927, pp. 115 ff.; "Franz Kafka's Metarealismus," *Literarische Welt*, June 4, 1926, Vol. 2, pp. 4 f.

Wenzig, E. "Mysterium der ungelösten Frage," *Die Tat* (Jena), March, 1929, pp. 904 f.

Werenskiold, Nils. "Drømmen om Oklahoma," *Dagbladet* (Oslo), Aug. 13, 1949.

Werfel, Franz. "Recollections," in A. Flores (ed.), *The Kafka Problem*, p. 37.

Werner, Herbert. "Der Mensch in dieser Welt. Franz Kafka: *Der Prozess*," *Die Stimme* (Stuttgart), Jahrg. 3, 1951, No. 1, pp. 15–16; "Die Gottlosen haben keinen Frieden. Zu dem Roman von Franz Kafka: *Das Schloss*," *Die Stimme* (Stuttgart), Jahrg. 3, 1951, Heft 2, pp. 15, 389–90; "Das Geheimnis Israels und die Dichtung Franz Kafkas," *Evangelische Theologie* (Munich), Jahrg. 11, 1951–52, pp. 533–48.

Westerlinck, A. "Kafka en Milena," *Dietsche warande en Belfort*, 1953, pp. 19–24.

Wiese, Benno von. "Franz Kafka," *Vossische Zeitung*, July 29, 1928 (Unterhaltungs Blatt der Vossischen Zeitung); *Die deutsche Novelle*, Düsseldorf: August Bagel, 1956.

Wilson, Edmund. "A Dissenting Opinion on Kafka," *The New Yorker*, July 26, 1947, Vol. 23, pp. 58–64, rep. in *Classics and Commercials*, New York: Farrar, Straus & Co., 1950, pp. 383–92.

Winkler, R. O. C. "Significance of Kafka," *Scrutiny*, Dec., 1938, pp. 354–60; "The Three Novels," in A. Flores (ed.), *The Kafka Problem*, pp. 192–98.

Wolff, Kurt. "On Franz Kafka," *Twice A Year* (New York), 1942, Nos. 8–9, pp. 273–79.

Woodcock, George. *The Writer and Politics*, London: Porcupine Press, 1948, pp. 197–206; "Kafka and Rex Warner," *Focus One* (London), 1945, pp. 59–65, and in A. Flores (ed.), *The Kafka Problem*, pp. 108–16.

Zambrano, Maria. "Franz Kafka Mártir de la miseria humana," *Espuela de Plata* (Havana), Aug., 1941.

Zangerle, Ignaz. "Die Bestimmung des Dichters," *Der Brenner* (Innsbruck), 1946, No. 16, pp. 112–20.

Zimmermann, Werner. *Deutsche Prosadichtungen der Gegenwart*, Düsseldorf: Pädagogischer Verlag Schwann, 1954, pp. 159–74.

Zolle, Elemire. "Le maschere e il volto di Franz Kafka," *Letterature Moderne*, March, 1954, Vol. 5, No. 2, pp. 151–59.

Zylberberg, H. "Das tragische Ende der drei Schwestern Kafkas," *Eba*, 1946–47.

Index